OUSELEY AND HIS ANGELS

OUSELEY AND HIS ANGELS

The Life of St Michael's College, Tenbury and its Founder

by

David Bland

With a Foreword by

Dr Roy Massey MBE

Organist and Master of the Choristers of
Hereford Cathedral

First published in 2000 by

David Bland
Broadbent Cottage
Willowbrook
ETON
Berkshire
SL4 6HL

ISBN 0 9538702 0 0

Designed and produced by

The Short Run Book Company Ltd
St Stephen's House
Arthur Road
Windsor
Berkshire, SL4 1RY, UK

DEDICATION

This book is dedicated to the memory of the Reverend John Gray, Priest, Artist and Musician, who was part of the life and work of St. Michael's College and Parish Church for over forty years.

May he rest in peace

FOREWORD

BY
DR. ROY MASSEY MBE
ORGANIST AND MASTER OF THE CHORISTERS OF HEREFORD CATHEDRAL

I first became acquainted with St. Michael's Tenbury while still an undergraduate. I was researching the eighteenth-century English organ concerto for a degree dissertation and my supervisor had arranged for me to consult in the College library an early printed edition of concerti by William Felton, a former Vicar Choral of Hereford Cathedral. I remember the rattling ride in an elderly carriage from Kidderminster on the single-track railway before it fell victim to Dr Beeching's axe. I also recall the not inconsiderable tramp from Tenbury station, up the hill and over the common until the roof of the chapel hove into sight, with the promise of a welcome cup of tea on arrival. Some years later I was invited to play a recital on the chapel organ and I much enjoyed exploring the splendours of the Tenbury Father Willis, without realising anything of its provenance or appreciating the stature of the man who designed it. Later, when I became organist of Hereford Cathedral I slowly began to discover something of the work and influence of Sir Frederick Ouseley in his role as Precentor of Hereford, at a time in the nineteenth century when the worship and music of the Cathedral was being painfully resurrected after a long period of neglect. Recent research by the present Precentor, Canon Paul Iles, has revealed the considerable extent of Ouseley's influence for good in the Cathedral, even though he was a non-residentiary Canon for most of his life and therefore having to exercise his authority from a distance. In another sphere, as organs adviser to the Diocese of Hereford, I have, over the years, discovered several instruments designed by Ouseley for village churches, organs distinguished by their enterprising specifications and built to a quality which has enabled them to survive to the present day. But it was only after my election as a Fellow of St Michael's in 1975 that I really began to discover and appreciate more fully the stature and achievements of the Founder. I learned of his vision and philanthropy in founding the college, together with his single-mindedness and self-sacrifice in keeping it going, often against formidable odds. One read of his influence for good as Professor of Music at Oxford and his scholarly interest in collecting music and manuscripts, a collection which later became of immense significance to scholars. I so well remember a fascinating session in the company of the late Harold

Watkins Shaw, who showed me some of the treasures in the library, and it was interesting to learn from him of the significance of Ouseley's encouragement of gifted young musicians, many of whom went on to important cathedral appointments. Above all, I learned of his selfless vision of what cathedral music should be, a vision which has always inspired me in my work at Hereford, and I felt very proud and privileged to be numbered among the members of his Tenbury Foundation.

David Bland has chronicled the story of Frederick Ouseley and his college in some detail and in eminently readable style. He traces its early years, the time of its greatness, and the sad but probably inevitable decline in a changing world. But Ouseley's great work continues in a new guise, and the author speaks of the wonderful role of the Ouseley Trustees who, these days, have been able to support and encourage Ouseley's vision on a much wider canvas. I felt sure that Ouseley would rejoice that choral and organ music at the start of this new millennium is treasured, appreciated and encouraged in cathedrals in a manner that he could only have dreamed of. It is therefore, entirely fitting that his name should be linked in perpetuity with the valuable financial support that Trustees have given in recent years to practically every cathedral in the land. He would be sad that his beloved college had to close, but he would rejoice that his vision is alive and well, nurtured and administered in his name by faithful Trustees.

PREFACE AND ACKNOWLEDEGEMENTS

Although I had been familiar with the name of St Michael's College, Tenbury for many years, I first visited the College in the spring of 1995, before starting work at what was the 'new' College in the following September. I had been a member of church choirs throughout most of my life and had a great love of choral and organ music and I soon became conscious of the magic of St Michael's, its glorious situation, its sense of history and its musical heritage. I discovered that there was no complete record of the life of the College, from its beginnings in 1856 to its closure in 1985. In the Alderson and Colles book (published in 1943) and in Watkins Shaw's book published in 1986, only very brief details of College life are given, with much space devoted to the Music Library and the music sung in the church. The only biography of Ouseley was published in 1896 by the son of a lifelong friend and I felt that I had the opportunity to look at the whole life of the College and that of its Founder. However, my duties at the College precluded my developing an interest in Ouseley and the History of the College to any depth and it was not until I left the College in August 1997 that I was able to start what became two years of intensive research. In September 1998, I was unexpectedly asked to become Assistant Verger at Eton College Chapel and for over a year, I have successfully managed to cope with the varied demands of work in the College Chapel, as well as undertaking more research and, since April 1999, writing this book.

Although this book will cover most aspects of Ouseley's life and that of his College, I have not attempted to make a study of Ouseley as a composer. Much has already been written about this aspect of his work and I would refer those interested to some of the books listed in the bibliography, particularly those by Joyce, Bumpus, and more recently, Rainbow, Charlton, and Dibble. Some of Ouseley's choral and organ music is still performed in cathedrals and parish churches (see Appendix 3 b), but sadly, this represents a very small part of his extensive musical output.

In the November 1999 issue of *The Organists' Review*, John Scott, Organist of St Paul's Cathedral, in his capacity as newly-elected President of the Incorporated Association of Organists, wrote as follows:

> I am pleased to note that there appears to be a renewed interest in the work of our 19th Century English composers....Fond as I am of the Mendelssohn Organ Sonatas, we should not ignore the original works of Best, Smart, Ouseley, S.S. Wesley, Hollins and others who

represent a school of writing full of integrity, and whose achievements have been ignored for far too long. The list may be extended to included many other central figures such as Parry, Stanford and Harwood, and it is particularly good that the reputation of Whitlock, after a period in the wilderness, has re-emerged as an organ composer of great originality, flair and craftsmanship.

Of course John Scott's remarks particularly addressed organ music, but many of the composers he mentioned wrote very good choral music, much of which has been neglected and little used for many years.

At Hereford Cathedral, Dr Roy Massey plays a number of Henry Smart's Postludes and Marches on a regular basis and such music can make a glorious conclusion to a service. Winchester College recently paid one of their regular visits to Eton College Chapel to sing a combined Evensong with the Eton College Chapel Choir. Unusually, Winchester had chosen Henry Smart's *Magnificat and Nunc Dimittis in Bb* for the Canticles setting, and for someone like myself, who has listened to and sung many of the usual settings of the Canticles, this was like a breath of fresh air. The *Magnificat* opens with a very loud organ introduction, further enhanced with the great Eton tuba, and this combination reappears at intervals throughout the piece, ending with a magnificent Gloria. Add to the organ a combined choir of over 100 voices and you have a sound which could not be rivalled anywhere, and which was written by a nineteenth century English composer!

Perhaps we now have the opportunity to re-examine the work of some of the nineteenth century English composers such as Harwood, Ouseley, Smart, Stainer, Stanford, etc.

I can only echo the sentiments of Michael Hurd, author of a biography of Ivor Gurney, the Gloucestershire poet and composer. 'The greatest reward the biographer of a composer or poet can receive is to find that his book has acted as a stimulus to the performance, publication and understanding of his subject's work.'

David Bland
November 1999

ACKNOWLEDGEMENTS

I am deeply grateful to all the many people who have helped me in writing this book

SPECIAL THANKS are due to the following:–

- Dr Roy Massey, Organist of Hereford Cathedral, for kindly consenting to write a Foreword to this book and for checking parts of Chapter 7

CONTENTS

ST MICHAEL'S TENBURY

There side by side the Church and College stand,
A noble work, to God's own glory raised;
Here daily, by the clear-voiced, white-robed band,
Is the most holy Name in chorus praised.
Here heavenly music spreads her wings o'er all,
And sanctifies the drudgery of life,
Restraining with a sweet ennobling thrall
Young ardent spirits – arming for the strife
Of after life, by storing memory
With holy words, for ever fixed there
By the strong power of sacred harmony.
Here lingers still the Founder's selfless prayer,
That Heaven, amid these walls, young souls might bless,
And lead in paths of peace and holiness.

TERRA COTTA

(The above poem appeared in the *Church Times* of 17 May 1889, shortly after the Founder's death.)

St. Michael's College and Church nears completion, 1856

Photo courtesy of English Heritage, National Monuments Record

CHAPTER ONE

THE OUSELEY FAMILY

ORIGINS

'The Ouseley family appears to have been one of those families, well known to the historical and geographical enquirer, which, possessing gentle blood, merit and wisdom, frequently deserve, and appear to be on the point of achieving greatness, and as often by the inconstancy or unkindness of fortune, are thrown back again into their former station.'(1)

The name OUSELEY, together with a number of variant spellings, OSELEY, OWSLEY and OSLEY, has been the name of a land-owning family and can be traced back many centuries. The first form of the name (OISLE), is of Norman–French origin and can be found in the Battle Roll of companions of William the Conqueror. The family was recorded as living in the County of Shropshire for several centuries before Elizabeth I, with several branches of the family settled in different counties – Dorset, Somerset, Essex, Cheshire and Leicestershire. There are also various traditions dating back to the time of Edward I.

> The family could boast long lineage. Tradition maintained that in the thirteenth Century, it was settled in Shropshire. And there the Ouseley of that day, recently married to one Agnes, rode out to welcome King Edward I en route to Wales. Agnes was attacked by a black wolf emerging from a holly thicket, which bit off her right hand before the gallant husband was able to kill it. To this incident is ascribed the addition to the family arms (hitherto simply *Or, a chevron and chief sable)* of three holly leaves, and a grant of the crest 'a black wolf's head erased with a right hand in its mouth couped at the wrist, gules, and a ducal coronet.' The heraldic motto then became *Mors lupi, agnis vita.* (The death of the wolf (is) life to the lamb.) The word agnis being a play on the word Agnes. (2)

However, the name only appears in authentic documents listing rank, residence, etc. in the name of Thomas Oseley, of the Parish of St Winifred's in the County of Shropshire in 1486. Another branch of the family is reported to be living at the same time in the Parish of Worfield, near Bridgnorth.

Thomas Oseley can therefore be nominated as the earliest traceable ancestor of Frederick Arthur Gore Ouseley, the subject of this book.

Thomas's grandson, another Thomas, was employed in the public service and died in 1557, having received certain grants of land from the Crown for his services. His son Richard served the Court, and by greater service received greater reward, the most considerable being the Manor of Courteenhall in Northamptonshire. This land had been granted to him by Elizabeth I, and in 1571 he moved from Shropshire to Northamptonshire, died there in 1598 and was buried in the family vault at Courteenhall Church. Richard's son, John, was knighted by James I in 1603 but was killed at the Siege of Breda in 1625.

In the English Civil Wars, the Ouseley family, as might be expected, served the Royalist cause and perhaps suffered for their fidelity. The Courteenhall Estate was forfeited during the time of the Commonwealth and was settled upon the nephew of Sir Samuel Jones, a cousin of Richard Ouseley and a supporter of Cromwell. 'The Ouseleys were members of that large class of less wealthy gentry who were ruined by the Civil War. On the Restoration of Charles II to the throne of England, they could justly expect some reward for their support of the Royalist cause, but sadly, these claims could not easily be satisfied.' (3)

After the Civil War, great parts of Ireland had been forfeited to the Crown and the sons of Sir John Ouseley, Richard and Jasper, settled in Ireland. Richard was given a grant of land in October 1666 at Ballycogley Castle in the County of Wexford. He emigrated there, together with other members of his family, including his third brother, Jasper. Richard died without issue on 15 May 1669 and Ballycogley Castle then passed by marriage to the Barrington family. By now, Jasper had moved to Tralee and was succeeded by his son, also Jasper, who moved his residence to Dunmore Castle in Galway. (NB. There is a tradition that the Ouseleys were related to an ancient Irish family, the branches of which also gave to the world the Wellesleys and the Wesleys. While it is possible to see linguistic similarities between the three names, there is no direct evidence to support this alleged relationship.)

Three generations later, the Ouseleys were still settled in Ireland. Jasper's son, William had married his first wife, Elizabeth Morley and they had one son who died without issue. William's second wife was a Mary Fox. She had one son, Ralph, who later became the father of Gore Ouseley. Ralph married Elizabeth Holland of Limerick and they produced numerous offspring, of whom eight survived. (Ralph died on 18 February 1803.) Their eldest son, William, became a noted Oriental scholar and was later knighted. Ralph's second son, Gore, was born on 24 June 1770 and was the father of Frederick, the Founder of St Michael's College.

GORE OUSELEY

Little information survives about Gore's earliest years, apart from that he was expected to join some learned profession.

At that time, there was a revival of attention in the affairs of the East, and of Oriental Literature, particularly as a result of the successes of Lord Clive in India and the affairs of the East India Company and this may have attracted Ralph's attention as to careers for some of his sons. As a result, both William and Gore later became associated with high achievement in Oriental researches. (4)

Gore's father decided that Gore should travel abroad, and in 1787 at the age of 17 years, he was sent to India, where he undertook a number of commercial engagements. Even at this age, it was said of Gore that he already possessed 'a love of, and skill in classical learning, all manly exercises, courage, good sense and pleasing manners.'(5) In 1792, Gore had written to his father and brother from his bungalow at Bygorbarree, and told them that he had obtained a number of Persian versions of the Koran, and that his studies in Persian, Bengalese, Hindu, Arabic and Sanskrit were going well. He had collected Hindu, Kashmirian and Persian airs and songs, and could 'converse in Persian quite well, but in Hindu like a native.' He also told his family that he had between 60 and 70 servants, 'none of whom could speak a word of English.' (6)

After being in various parts of the East Indies, he moved to Lucknow in 1795, the capital of the Province of Oude. At the age of twenty-eight, he came to the notice of the Nabob Vizir, first as Major Commandant and later as Aide-de-Camp, after directing a party of troops besieging a fort, an exploit which inspired the Nabob Vizir with confidence in his courage. 'His manners and diplomacy, together with his extensive knowledge of Eastern languages and culture, enabled him to develop good relations between Britain and the Indian State of Oude.' (7)

His reputation reached the British authorities in India and he was well thought of by the Governor General, the Marquess Wellesley, brother of the Duke of Wellington, being highly commended and mentioned in despatches. In an extract from his despatches, he praised Gore very highly.

Sir Gore Ouseley's conduct during the time of his residence at Lucknow was most useful to the British interests and was fully approved by the Governor General. In consequence of the strong recommendation of Mr H. Wellesley (now Lord Cowley), the Governor General sanctioned the the appointment of Major Ouseley as Aide-de-Camp to the Nabob Vizir, Sadaat Ali. Sir Gore availed himself with judgement and wisdom of every opportunity to cultivate a good understanding between the State of Oude and the British powers, whose interests are in fact inseparable. At the start of the Marhalta War in 1803, he persuaded the Nabob to provide almost 4,000 horses for the 8th Royal Irish Dragoon Regiment, recently arrived in India, but unhorsed. Sir Gore's conduct at Lucknow and his intimate acquaintance with the Persian language induced Wellesley to recommend him for the post of Ambassador to the King of Persia. (8)

It was only in 1805, some seventeen years after his first arrival, that the then Major Ouseley returned to England, now aged 34 years. A year later, on 12 April 1806, he married Harriet Georgina Whitelock, the daughter of John and Mary Whitelock, at the Church of St Mary-le-Bow. The service being taken by the Reverend William Boldero. There is some evidence to show that an ancestor of Harriet Georgina was Sir Bulstrode Whitelock, a Commissioner of the Great Seal during the Commonwealth and Protectorate and a famous Ambassador to Queen Christina of Sweden. Ouseley's Library at St Michael's contained a manuscript, presumably inherited through Gore's wife, in the hand of Sir Bulstrode. There was also a large family Bible and Prayer Book depicting the coat of arms of King Charles II, which had belonged to Harriet's father. In 1919, this Bible and Prayer Book were bought by Her Majesty Queen Mary and are now in the Royal Library at Windsor Castle.

Their first child Mary Jane, was born at York Place, Portman Square, the Ouseley family home in London, on 28 March 1807. She was christened by the Reverend William Boldero and her sponsors were Mrs. Whitelock, Mrs. Hodges, Lieutenant-General Whitelock and Matthew Lewis. (She died at Frome in Somerset on 9 August 1861, aged 54 years).

In 1808, two years after his marriage, Gore Ouseley was created a baronet. In 1810, Lord Wellesley (now Foreign Secretary), appointed Gore as Ambassador to the Court of Persia. On 19 July 1810, Gore Ouseley and family set sail from Portsmouth on a journey that was to last almost eighteen months. They took the long sea route, bringing furniture and fittings for the palace Sir Gore was charged to build as a permanent residence for himself and his successors.

> Sir Gore was accompanied by his wife and-three-year old daughter, Mary Jane, together with his scholarly brother, Sir William, accompanying Gore as his private secretary. There was also an assistant secretary, four Officer members of the mission, two clerks, a butler, groom, coachman and boy, a head nurse, second nurse, lady's maid and a cow to provide fresh milk. (9)

This large party sailed on the sixty-four gun ship, HMS Lion, under the command of Captain Henry Heathcote, all passengers dining at the Captain's table. Travelling by way of Madeira and Rio de Janeiro, the ship sailed around the Cape of Good Hope and visited Ceylon, Cochin and Bombay, where they stayed for eighteen days. They finally disembarked at Bushire on the Persian Gulf on 5 March 1811.

By now, Lady Ouseley was some six months pregnant, and after a rest of three weeks, the party started out on the long overland journey to the Persian capital, accompanied by a large crowd of several hundred Englishmen, Indians and Persians. The transport arrangements were extremely primitive and only Lady Ouseley travelled on an Indian palanquin, carried by twenty stalwart bearers.

On 8 April 1811, the party arrived at Shiraz where they spent some months before travelling on to Tehran. While at Shiraz, Lady Ouseley gave birth to a second daughter, Eliza Shireen on 13 June 1811 and Sir Gore's Diary records: 'The Lady O safely delivered of a little girl at 3-30 am in the morning' (10) She was born in the Royal Palace of Fakhti Kajar at Shiraz. She was christened on 30 June by the Reverend Henry Martyn and her sponsors were the Honourable Mrs Spencer Perceval (by proxy – the Prime Minister's wife), General Kydd, Mrs Charles Ricketts and Captain Henry Heathcote.

> Being the first child of English parents born in Persia, the event was thus commemorated by giving her the name (Shireen) of a famous Princess of former days, who was married to Khuvri Parviz, a Persian Monarch of the Sassanian Dynasty and whose extraordinary loves and adventures have been celebrated in poems and romances by the best poets of Persia. (11)

By 9 November 1811, the family finally reached Tehran, almost eighteen months after leaving England. Lady Ouseley divided her time between Tehran and Tabriz, but with no other European female company apart from her three maids, she must have been very lonely. She must have felt even more isolated when her young baby daughter, Eliza, died in April 1812. Gore's Diary records this sad event. 'Eliza Shireen, at the early age of ten months and nine days, departed this life at Tehran on 22 April 1812 and was buried in the garden belonging to the Ambajeedon Palace. (12)

In 1813, Sir Gore's wife returned to Tabriz, the capital of Azerbaijan in Persia, where on 4 August, she gave birth to a son, Wellesley Abbas. The Reverend Mr Canning christened him on 4 September. His sponsors included the Marquess Wellesley, N.G. Prendergast, MP and Lady Champers. 'The name 'Abbas' was added at the particular request of the Shah and Prince Royal of Persia, Abbas Mirca, who, being a Moslem, was not eligible to be a sponsor at a Christian baptism.' (13) (Wellesley Abbas died on 7 March 1824 at the age of eleven years and was interred in the family vault in the church of Hertingfordbury in Hertfordshire.)

During his time in Persia, Sir Gore's extraordinary diplomatic abilities were every much in evidence and he is credited with bringing peace between Persia and Russia. He lived in Persia for four years, followed by a year in Moscow and St. Petersburg. He was decorated by the rulers of both Persia and Russia and the Shah of Persia presented him with a magnificent gold-enamelled inscribed plate. (see the chapter on Ouseley Mysteries)

Early in 1814, Sir Gore and his family left for Moscow. After their departure, the British Embassy in Persia was downgraded and did not regain its ambassadorial status until 1944. During their stay in Russia, another daughter was born to Lady Ouseley, and Sir Gore was proud to record that she had been christened in the Czar's winter palace with the Emperor (by proxy) and the Empress (in person) among her sponsors. The child was held at the font by the Empress Marie and named Alexandrine Perceval. (She died at Frome in Somerset on 2 December 1862, aged 48 years.)

On 1 July 1815, the family set sail from Russia to return to England, chartering a ship bound for Montreal for £ 225. Sir Gore's return to England was marked by the award of a civil pension by the Crown. (Joyce quotes a pension of £5,000 per annum (14) and Watkins Shaw (15) quotes one of only £2,000 per annum.) Whichever amount is correct, it was certainly a substantial sum in those days.

Sir Gore was a man of considerable attainments and on his return to England, was in great demand in society circles. He was elected a Fellow of the Royal Society in December 1817 and a Fellow of the Society of Antiquaries in January 1818. He played the violin and viola, besides other instruments. And his daughters had violin lessons from J.B. Logier, a noted teacher. At the Accession of George IV on 10 October 1820, he was sworn in as a member of the Privy Council and assisted officially at the Coronation in 1821. In 1822, he became a founder-member of the newly-established Royal Academy of Music. He was also a member of various Oriental Societies such as the Society for the Publication of Oriental Texts, among many others.

Apart from a house in London, Sir Gore first lived at Woolmers, a house near Hertingfordbury in Hertfordshire (later used by his son Frederick as the title of a hymn tune), and later at the Hall Barn Park estate near Beaconsfield, which he purchased in 1832. In June 1837, Sir Gore attended the Accession of Queen Victoria as a member of the Privy Council and later at the Coronation in Westminster Abbey in June 1838. He also managed to spend much of his spare time constructing elaborate genealogical tables of his family, which attempted to trace his descent not only from numerous noble families, but from the Kings of England and France, and in copying these out in albums, accompanied by his own heraldic illustrations. In Hereford Cathedral Library, there are Sir Gore's bound volumes, giving a vast amount of information about the nobility, their heraldic emblems and how they were related to the Ouseley family. One such paper shows a common ancestor (William de Arden), between the Ouseley family and William Shakespeare, and others attempt to show a relationship between the Ouseley family and many of the European Royal Families. (16)

While in Persia, Sir Gore had become skilled in ivory turning and he continued this hobby after his return to England. Also, during his extensive time abroad, he had bought many art treasures and curios, as well as many beautiful pieces of inlaid Persian furniture and objects which later passed to his son, Frederick. He had also collected the basis of what was to become the wonderful Library at St. Michael's College, containing many rare and beautifully-bound books and other material.

Although Sir Gore and Lady Ouseley had five children, only three survived to maturity. By the time the last of the family was born, there were only two daughters still living, Mary Jane and Alexandrine. On 12 August 1825, their youngest child, Frederick Arthur Gore Ouseley was born into a family of assured social standing and financial independence, proud of its history and service to its country. All this is clearly reflected in those who attended Frederick's christening. He was named after the Duke of York (Frederick), the Duke of Wellington (Arthur) and Gore after his father. Both these Dukes were present and acted as sponsors at his christening, together with the Marchioness of Salisbury and his eldest sister, Mary Jane. Frederick was christened by his uncle, the Reverend Spencer Whitelock.

REFERENCES

1. HCL D483
2. Watkins Shaw, p.1
3. HCL D483
4. HCL D483
5. HCL D483
6. HCL D483
7. HCL D483 (extract from Marquess of Wellesley Despatches, Vol.4 (1810-1815)
8. *Diary of Sir Gore Ouseley* Bodleian Library
9. Ibid.
10. HCL D483 (Sir William Ouseley's *Travels in various countries, including Persia.)*
11. *Diary of Sir Gore Ouseley* Bodleian Library
12. HCL D483
13. *Diary of Sir Gore Ouseley* Bodleian Library
14. Joyce, p. 3
15. Watkins Shaw, p. 5
16. HCL D483

Frederick Ouseley aged 7-8 years, c. 1832-3
Photo courtesy of Ouseley Trustees

CHAPTER TWO

CHILDHOOD AND EDUCATION

CHILDHOOD

One of young Frederick's two elder sisters, Mary Jane, was seventeen years old when he was born. It is clear that he was treated as the 'Benjamin' of the family, being the youngest child and showered with affection by his mother and sisters. To call the young Frederick Ouseley 'The English Mozart' (1) is not an understatement, but would surprise many people. He showed exceptional musical abilities at a very early age as Mary Jane recalls. 'At the early age of three months, he showed not only a very unusual love for music, but even the power of distinguishing particular tunes, listening attentively to every tune his sisters played.' (2) She further recorded soon afterwards that when he was in great pain from teething, any tune on the piano was sufficient to calm him down and this may have been an important contributory factor in his later great love of music.

His ear for music was so developed that, even before he could speak, he could sing tunes in the same key in which they had been played, a long time after he had heard them. By the time he was seventeen months old, he could sing in perfect tune, invariably pitching any tune in the correct key. At two years old his left hand would pick out the tonic and dominant notes as his sisters played a melody and soon after his third birthday, his sisters were committing to manuscript his earliest composition, called a Sauteuse, possibly an early form of dance tune.

While walking with his nurse near the coachhouse, his acute ear could distinguish the second tone in the sound of a clock chime and he remarked that the double tone was in the key of B flat minor, a fact later confirmed by his surprised mother. In 1830 when he was just four years old, he was listening with his father to a wind band outside their windows and casually remarked that what they were playing was 'A kind of F but neither F natural or F sharp.' (3) When his father went to the piano in the next room, he found that what Frederick had said was quite true. The band were playing a quarter tone too sharp for F natural and too flat for F sharp. On another occasion, when his father had a heavy cold, Frederick was heard to remark, 'Only think, papa blows his nose in G.' (4) It is clear that they were an extremely musical family and his father, mother and elder sister were able to nurture and develop his amazing talent. However, it is true to say with Watkins Shaw that

Only Mary Jane had the technical competence to enter into and discuss with him, his precocious interest in harmonic progressions and only Mary Jane had the technical competence to enter into and discuss modulation. As such a child will, he soon began to make up little pieces at the piano and both his mother and his sister had the musical literacy to write them down before he was old enough to do so himself. Many of these transcriptions Ouseley himself preserved with his musical library to the end of his life. (5)

In 1830, a friend of Lady Ouseley's, the Countess Montalembert, asked her to give her copies of some of Frederick's earliest compositions to send to a musical friend. This friend, the Duchess of Hamilton, was reputed to be the most accomplished amateur musician and singer in England at the time. Two months later, the Duchess wrote back to Lady Ouseley from Holyrood House, expressing her delight and wanting to know much more about the young prodigy. After being sent some more of his early compositions, she spoke effusively of little Frederick. 'I am equally astonished and enchanted with Sir Gore Ouseley's child's talent. Pray tell Sir Gore I hope and trust that I shall one day have the happiness of hearing this second Mozart. Oh, the darling child. Heaven bless and preserve him.' (6)

In August 1831, the celebrated Professor of Music, John Baptist Logier, who had earlier taught musical instruments and theory to both Gore and his daughters, wrote to Sir Gore after receiving some of Frederick's compositions.

> The three pieces which are in minor keys are by far the best which the little musician has written yet. This proves (if anything were necessary to prove it), how truly this child is gifted with genuine musical feeling . No. 154 in C Minor is really a very elegant and pathetic little composition…. plaintive….and the merry little strain which follows immediately after in C major sets all to rights again. (7)

Havergal, in quoting this letter, comments on this eminent testimonial of Frederick's abilities. 'This testimony from such an acknowledged good judge proves the proficiency that the little Frederick had made both in his choice of melodies as well as harmonies, previously to having entered his fifth year.'(8) Although some of his earliest compositions had just been melodies, Frederick was by this time showing an instinctive grasp of harmony and astounded the most eminent amateur and professional musicians by his theoretical knowledge of complex harmonic principles, quite astonishing for his age.

When he was six years old, Frederick experienced what his first biographer (Joyce) describes as one of the proudest moments of his youthful life, when he played a piano duet with Felix Mendelssohn, who was staying with Frederick's family as a guest of his father. 'The very composer with whom, in after life, his own musical tastes and refined style of composition appear to have been most in harmony.' (9) A year later, the Duchess of Hamilton was able to meet the young Frederick. She later wrote about the meeting. 'The little fellow's countenance is a noble one, very delicate, with full dark eyes and a very prominent and expansive forehead.' (10)

It was about this time that Frederick had what appeared to be a serious illness, in the form of a fever which lasted for some weeks. After his recovery, he composed a piece of music which described the course of his illness. This took the form of the beginning of the disease, progress, crisis and abatement, followed by a period of convalescence. When completed, this was presented to Dr. Granville, the doctor who had attended him throughout his illness. *The Harmonicum*, a musical magazine of May 1833 described it as expressing, 'As well as inarticulate sounds are capable of expressing sensations, all the variety of feeling which would be experienced in the course of a long fever.' (11)

The same magazine printed a march composed by Frederick at the age of six and refers to

> The extraordinary, the unexampled genius of this little boy, now over seven and a half years old. He has received no instructions in music and though taught by himself to play with considerable skill on the pianoforte, does not know his notes on paper and trusts his sisters for writing down that which he composes....His organ of hearing is so fine that with his eyes closed, he instantly names any note produced. (12)

At this time, his musical skills enabled him to accurately state the interval between two notes and he could name every note when a four-note chord was sounded.

In the Bodleian Library, included as part of the Tenbury Collection, is a small volume of his early compositions, 200 pages in length and containing 243 examples of his compositions, the majority of which were written before he was six years old. Eighteen months later, he had written his first operetta, composed mainly of hunting and rustic scenes, with an English libretto probably supplied by his father. In 1833, at the age of eight years, he composed a much larger-scale opera, with solos, choruses, etc. with the Italian words taken from Metastasio's *L'Isola disabitata*. Writing to Frederick's father in July 1833, the distinguished church musician Sir George Smart commented after hearing him perform: I did your son but justice; though not much given to musical surprise, I was very much so at his extra ordinary talents. I shall be delighted to hear his new opera whenever you will allow me this gratification.' (13)

Apart from his natural abilities in music, his general education was now in progress and, possibly with some concern for his future well-being, his father decided not to subject him to the hurly-burly of life in a great public school, but to arrange to have him educated privately by tutors at home. Despite his parents doing everything to encourage Frederick's musical interests in every way possible, it was felt that

> There could be no question of deflecting the course of education proper to a young gentleman and a future baronet in favour of an early concentration on music. Sir Gore might have helped to found the Royal Academy of Music, but had no thought of sending his only son there.... Musical prodigy or not, Frederick Ouseley's position in life demanded the classical education proper to an English gentleman, an education which in the event would prove invaluable to him in the special work he was to do for his country in the Church and through the University of Oxford.' (14)

Despite these limitations on his musical development, his growing reputation as a child prodigy, together with his father's position in society, brought him into contact with some of the most outstanding people in the world of music. *The Harmonicum* Magazine of May 1833 gave an assessment of Frederick's abilities. 'His intellects are quick and declare themselves in a countenance remarkable for intelligence and beauty. His habits are suited to his age, and the activity of his mind does not appear to have operated unfavourably on his general health, which seems as good and well-established as is usual with children of his years.' (15)

He attended a Philharmonic Concert with his father in 1833 and casually remarked that Mozart's G minor Symphony was actually being played in the key of A minor. To his great surprise, the next day his father was able to confirm that this was so after speaking to some of his musical friends in the orchestra. In consequence of the great heat affecting the wind instruments, others had been tuned half a note sharp. When many of these stories of his childhood were recounted to him in later years, Sir Frederick is said to have remarked in what had become his characteristic modesty 'What an abominably disagreeable child I must have been.' (16)

In 1836, three Persian princes visited the Princess Victoria at Kensington Palace and with his Persian connections and experience, Sir Gore and Lady Ouseley were asked to accompany the princes. It appears that Frederick must have been mentioned during that visit and the very next day, the Princess recorded in her journal that 'At 2 came Sir Gore, Lady, and Miss Ouseley with their little 'musical prodigy' called Frederick, only ten years old. This boy is really the most wonderful child I ever saw; he plays and sings beautifully, and composes, songs, whole operas, etc. without knowing a note of music.' (17)

Every year, during his boyhood, Frederick had an interview with his godfather, the great Duke of Wellington. However, it is clear that Frederick was not in awe of this famous soldier and in fact it was the great Duke who was quite ill-at-ease on these occasions, as Joyce recalls.

> The contrast between the Iron Duke and the gentle, home-trained boy, with his highly-strung musical nerves, is a suggestive one. But

the godson declared that it was the Duke who was shy and stiff and awkward, and who, whilst invariably kind in his intentions, never seemed to know what to say next on these (to the boy) all-important occasions. On the whole, both godfather and godson appear to have regarded their annual meetings in the light of the ordeal of duty which had to be gone through, and which they were both glad to get over. (18)

However, it was those meetings with celebrities and men of eminence in the musical world which Frederick is said to have enjoyed most and Sir George Elvey, formerly Organist of St George's Chapel, Windsor remembered an occasion when he visited Sir Gore's estate at Hall Barn Park near Beaconsfield when Frederick was twelve years old. 'In my presence, a heap of notes being put down by the palm of the hand, the boy actually named every one of them without seeing the keyboard.' (19) Another instance of Frederick's musical abilities occurred one Sunday when one of his aunts, Miss Whitelock, found him playing the *Hallelujah Chorus* on the piano. When asked what it was called, he said that he didn't know; it was something that the organist had played as they came out of church that day. Frederick had heard the work once and then played it completely from memory.

It is difficult to trace anything definite in Frederick's early life that may have contributed to his later spiritual development. His baptism at eight months old might seem unusually late to us today, but in the early nineteenth century, it was often delayed even longer. In later life, Frederick always spoke of his mother with great tenderness and she must have been a woman of loving and gentle character. With an ageing father, still with many important national responsibilities, much of the responsibility for his spiritual upbringing would fall on his mother and elder sisters. His mother had strict ideas of keeping Sunday which had been little altered by their residence abroad. 'In other ways, her old-fashioned piety may have laid the foundations of that devotion to duty, and above all, that intense love and reverence for the service of God, which marked out the future life of her son.' (20)

EDUCATION

While he was still living at home, Frederick's education had been largely carried out by his mother and sisters, supplemented from the age of six years by a governess, who taught him French, and a tutor who taught him Latin. Despite Sir Gore's links with the musical world, work for the Royal Academy of Music and Frederick's musical gifts, it was unthinkable that he should consider a career in music. He was the heir to a baronetcy and, as such, must follow the prescribed path to a suitable career. Writing about these musical gifts, Watkins Shaw points out that

Consequently, these gifts were never conditioned by, or exercised in, the main stream of English musical activity, be it as composer, conductor, teacher, or man of affairs like Henry Bishop, Sterndale Bennett, Arthur Sullivan, Charles Halle or George Grove, all of whom were at work in his lifetime. Thus his musical proclivities were to be directed into a different channel entirely. (21)

Sometime during his fourteenth year, Frederick was sent as a pupil to The Reverend James Joyce, Vicar of Dorking in Surrey, to be educated privately. This was clearly Frederick's first real period of time away from the bosom of his family. There were members of the vicarage household who had fond recollections of his time there, as Joyce's son recalls:'

> Our recollections of him there are of a good and amiable boy remarkable by his musical genius....His voice was beautiful: he used to sing little Spanish songs. He would play on a comb if no other instrument was at hand....I remember all people who did understand music were wonderstruck by his beautiful extempore playing. All the time we knew him at Dorking, he was absorbed in music. – so much so that my father used to say that he ought not to take 'Orders', because music would always be the first interest to him. (22)

At some time during his stay at Dorking, Frederick had made the decision to take Holy Orders, a decision clearly influenced by his deep friendship with Joyce's son, the Reverend Wayland Joyce, who, thirteen years older than Frederick, was then his father's curate. In later life, he always acknowledged with gratitude what he owed to the Vicar of Dorking and his son. The years spent there were a great formative influence on his later life. Much of his education during this time was devoted to Classical Studies and preparation for Oxford, but despite his marvellous facility for languages in later life, it is clear that he found the technicalities of Greek and Latin Grammar difficult and at times, almost impossible. James Joyce was described by his son as the most patient of teachers and he needed it as Frederick became uncharacteristically exasperated over some dull intricacy of Latin prose or Greek plays. 'It is no use Frederick, the thing must be done.' (23)

Towards the end of Frederick's time at Dorking, James Joyce had purchased a second-hand one manual organ with an octave of pedals, built by John Avery in 1790. He had this placed in what had been his 'bolt-hole', a loft over the stables at the vicarage. Of course, the organ had been chosen by Frederick, who was already thought of as an authority on such matters, and he no doubt spent many happy hours developing his extempore playing and also his art of developing intricate fugues from a chosen theme. (Joyce's son, Wayland later became Rector of Burford on the Worcester/Shropshire border and corresponded frequently with Frederick, who visited the area on many occasions. Wayland's son, the Reverend Frederick William Joyce, later succeeded his father in the Burford benefice and it was he who wrote Ouseley's biography in 1896.)

REFERENCES

1. Letter from Duchess of Hamilton 13 April 1832. (Havergal p. 10)
2. Early years of Frederick A.G.Ouseley by his Eldest Sister (Havergal p. 5)
3. Havergal, p. 6
4. Havergal, p. 9
5. Watkins Shaw p. 8.
6. Letter from Duchess of Hamilton 1 December 1830 (Havergal p. 6)
7. Havergal, p. 6
8. Havergal, p. 7
9. Joyce p. 13
10. Letter from Duchess of Hamilton 13 April 1832 (Havergal. P. 10)
11. *The Harmonicum* May 1833
12. *The Harmonicum* May 1833
13. Letter from Sir George Smart 18 July 1833 (HCL D 863)
14. Alderson and Colles p. 6
15. *The Harmonicum* May 1833
16. Joyce p. 10
17. Royal Archives – Queen Victoria's Journal of 14 July 1836
18. Joyce pp. 14 – 15
19. Joyce p. 15
20. Joyce p, 6
21. Watkins Shaw p. 11
22. Joyce p. 26
23. Joyce p. 28

CHAPTER THREE

OXFORD

Ouseley went up to Christ Church, Oxford as an undergraduate with the rank (as the son of a baronet), of Gentleman Commoner in 1843. We do not know for certain when the idea of ordination had occurred to Ouseley, but he had been under the influence of Joyce's son for some four years and when he went up to Oxford, it is likely that the idea was already in his mind, 'Although it is clear that his father felt that he was destined for quite another calling.' (1)

Ouseley's years at Oxford corresponded with the events of the Oxford Movement. John Keble, author of *The Christian Year*, was no longer the Oxford Professor of Poetry but was still a name of power in the University, and Dr Pusey, Regius Professor of Hebrew, was a Canon of Christ Church where Ouseley was a daily worshipper. Christ Church also had Gaisford, the great scholar, as Dean, and Dr Hampden, Regius Professor of Divinity, who was later to ordain Ouseley as priest when he became Bishop of Hereford. Watkins Shaw comments on the theological ferment in Oxford at the time that Ouseley arrived there.

> To a young man in Oxford, these were exciting times, dominated by the immediate controversies of the Tractarian or Oxford Movement. The previous year, Newman had resigned the living of St. Mary's, the University Church in Oxford and in 1843, Pusey, though a Canon of Christ Church and Professor of Hebrew, was suspended from preaching before the University. In 1845 John Henry Newman seceded to Rome. There were anxious questions occupying the minds of many thinkers in the Church of England and these problems would have certainly made an impression on Ouseley. (2)

Another event that must have influenced him no less than the publication of *Tracts for the Times,* was the work of John Jebb, who became Rector of the village of Peterstow in Herefordshire in 1843. It was his contention that that the services in the Book of Common Prayer were intended to be sung, and in order to assist the clergy in this, any choir should be seated in the chancel. These ideas were to prove very influential and became greatly helped by Ouseley's work in this field. In 1841, Jebb had delivered a series of lectures in Leeds parish church and published as *Three Lectures on the Cathedral Service of the United Church of England and Ireland* and very soon afterwards, parishioners in Leeds were considering the introduction of a daily choral service. Before the end of that year, Samuel Sebastian Wesley was invited to become organist of Leeds parish church after giving the opening recital on the new organ on 18 October 1841. Wesley had already spent three years as organist of Hereford Cathedral (1832 – 1835), before spending the next six years in an acrimonious situation as organist of Exeter Cathedral. Arriving at Leeds in February 1842, he came under the influence and enthusiasm of the Vicar of Leeds, the Reverend Walter Hook, a great supporter of choral music and determined to introduce a cathedral-type service at Leeds and establish a choral foundation. Like Ouseley, Wesley was to become one of the most influential figures in English cathedral music in the nineteenth century: their careers overlapped and took a similar course.

At Oxford, Ouseley's natural gift for languages made his classical studies somewhat easier than they might have been and his memory meant that he could recall great parts of a book after only two or three readings. At this time, he devoted most of his efforts into his mathematical studies under the able guidance of Edward Hill, his mathematics lecturer, whom he held in high regard. Letters written from home at this time expressed their concern about his inexperience in the ways of the world and his impatience at the routine work of reading which might prejudice his studies at Oxford.

At this time, it appears that his father's income may have been greatly reduced by the purchase of the Hall Barn Estate near Beaconsfield and his younger sister voiced her concern. 'Pray remember in trifles that pence make pounds…Pray do not lose your money when you get it…I hope that you are as economical as you can be. Do not let Coe (his servant) be extravagant, and consider well if you really can do without a thing before you get it.'(3)

Letters from his mother expressed her concern about a number of matters, such as regularity of study being more important than prolongued and tiring study which she felt Frederick would be unable to cope with. She worried about his accommodation and it is clear that he had previously told her about the noisy students in his Quad. She also expressed her desire that he might be able to move rooms into Tom Quad and perhaps gain some peace and quiet. His mothers views were somewhat old-fashioned. She was prejudiced against railway travelling and had strict views on the keeping of Sunday, yet saw nothing wrong in expecting her son to write home during some of his spare time on a Sunday. She entreated him to work hard and secure his tutor's attention and approval and thus ' prevent the possibility of your being considered idle or frivolous. Such a character would stay with you for life.' (4)

Joyce also expressed his reservations about Ouseley's ability to cope with his Oxford studies. 'His lack of power to apply himself persistently to the dry details of any study was perhaps a weakness throughout his life.'(5) Although this was clearly Joyce's view, he is honest enough to quote people who also had extensive experience of Ouseley's abilities and whose opinions differed considerably from his own. Firstly, Mr. T. L. Southgate, who had known Ouseley for some years. 'Ouseley never struck me as being impatient or unwilling to work methodically and steadily to an end.' (6) and John Hampton, who had known Ouseley since his ordination and was to work with him for over thirty-five years, gives a similar view. 'No man was so patient and persevering when there was a particular occasion for it. He worked long hours every day to accomplish many an object upon which he had set his heart.' (7)

Although college discipline was no doubt much stricter in those days than at the present, it must have been a considerable shock to Ouseley to find himself more or less his own master at the age of eighteen years, particularly in view of his sheltered upbringing.

Just over a year after his arrival in Oxford, the news came to him on 18 November 1844 of the death of his father at the age of seventy-four years. Despite attacks of gout and rheumatism, Sir Gore had generally enjoyed good health since his return from Persia, but in the last two years of his life, his family had noticed a great change in him and his strength began to fail. He rode for the last time on 30 October 1844 and two days later, returned to his country seat at Hall Barn Park in Buckinghamshire. He was 'attacked' by the disease which we now know as ulcerative colitis and by 15 November, was confined to his bed. By the 17th, his medical attendant felt that his death was near and he died on 18 November. He was buried in the family vault in the church at Hertingfordbury in Hertfordshire.

The death of his father meant that Frederick succeeded to the baronetcy at the age of nineteen years. This was the first shock of this kind that had occurred in his life so far and it probably helped to give him a greater sense of responsibility, both towards his studies and also to his widowed mother and elder sisters at home, as he was now head of the family.

In Oxford, his qualities of good temper and modesty made him popular with his fellow students. He could also disarm any opposition by his real and unsolicited forgiveness. He hated to be at odds with anyone. Throughout his life, there were instances of people who had previously opposed him, but who were won over by his character and demeanour. On occasions he was not against playing practical jokes against his fellow students and Joyce quotes a contemporary's account of his and Frederick's defensive actions. 'No sooner had the enemy commenced operations than they found themselves half–suffocated with clouds of pepper, emitted by a hot blower and then squirted with a foul liquid.' (8) A fellow student, G.W. Kitchin, later to be Dean of Durham, characterized him as 'absolutely guileless, indeed a little more guile would have served him in good stead. His good nature made him popular in spite of certain peculiarities of appearance which might have made him rather a 'butt' among his fellow students.' (9)

Throughout his time at Oxford, music was never far from his mind and was his chief interest to such an extent that it must have hindered the achievement that he was capable of in his other studies. Despite this, his general abilities were good and he was conscientious enough to work hard enough to secure his university degree. Another of his contemporaries at Christ Church gives a graphic picture of the young baronet.

> When the time came to call him Sir Freddy, the pet name among us was 'The Bart.' He was a general favourite, though not apparently rich, which might partly be owing to the handsome allowance which I know he made to his two sisters, but he was always ready to play to us, and I can see him now, jumping from side to side on the piano stool, for he never sat still a minute, and his thin legs were never quiet, directly he began to get absorbed. Most of his playing was extempore, and it was our frequent amusement to make him play two airs at the same time, say, *God Save the Queen* with the right hand, and *Rule Britannia* with the left, which he did with the greatest ease and with many variations, sometimes quite in Bach's manner, with fugue-like character, but always, of course, in perfect harmony. (10)

Ouseley certainly made the most of the musical opportunities offered during his time in Oxford. Dean Kitchin recalls that one day, while walking down the High, he saw a man coming towards him with his palms extended in the air over his head and running quite fast. At last, realising that the figure was Ouseley, he asked what was the matter. 'I have just obtained permission to play on the organ in Magdalen College, and this is the only way I can keep my hands cool for playing, by preventing the blood running into them!' (11) Despite his intense need to play the organ, Ouseley also played in instrumental ensembles and sang. One of the highlights used to be on a summer's evening when he and his friends used to gather on the beautiful hall staircase at Christ Church and entertain members of the College with glees of various kinds.

> The staircase had remarkable properties; a chord sung clearly will often continue to vibrate for a few seconds : therefore to stand by the central pillar and shout an arpeggio was a favourite pastime of the men. But Ouseley completely beat off all competitors at this fun, because, owing to his use of falsetto, he could produce an arpeggio nearly three octaves in length. (12)

He organised large-scale concerts including Handel's *Samson* and in 1845, led a performance of *Messiah* to raise money for the benefit of Irish famine sufferers.

Joyce recalls the time when at a performance by the University Amateur Music Society, Ouseley and two friends took the *fortissimo* passage in Mendelssohn's Wedding March literally and, hiding behind the orchestra in a hidden passage, used two massive cymbals made of bell-metal and a large tin tea-tray, coming with a tremendous crash at the appropriate time and causing the conductor, Dr Stephen Elvey, almost to have a heart attack, though he later took the prank in good part after his initial shock. One of Ouseley's friends, Canon Rich, whose friendship continued in later life, tells of Dr Elvey's reaction. 'Dear old Dr Stephen Elvey, who was conducting, was at first as indignant as he was astonished; but, when he found that the audience were highly amused and pleased with the effect, he took it all in good part, and I am not sure that he did not himself *encore* the performance.' (13)

It is very evident that the Oxford influence of religion was very strong in Ouseley. Its main effect was to intensify his devotion to church worship, which was to become the dominant influence in his later life. The services meant much more to him than mere attendance at College Chapel.

> But music was the special gift with which God had endowed him. And so it was in this direction that the spirit of worship found its chief expression in his case. From the beginning to the end of his Oxford career, as undergraduate hardly less than professor, Ouseley sought to elevate music, and sacred music in particular, to a higher place in the university life than it had hitherto occupied. (14)

For a man in Ouseley's position as a Gentleman Commoner, this must have been no easy task by all accounts. From various sources, it is clear that the whole cathedral body, led by Dean Gaisford, was a distinctly unmusical one. By his own influence and example, Ouseley sought to dignify the worship and actively participated in making this happen. During his last year at Christ Church, Dr William Marshall, the College Organist, resigned and Ouseley immediately offered his services to the Dean until a successor was appointed. During his time as Acting Organist, he made himself responsible for the whole of the musical work of the cathedral and it was said that he never missed a single service until the new Organist, Dr Corfe, was appointed some months later.

His relations with the great Dean Gaisford were not always harmonious and on one occasion he incurred the Dean's wrath by asking to hold a concert in College Hall. The Dean brusquely refused his request and asked him to leave the room, but the very next day, Ouseley found the Dean in his customary good humour and was invited to dinner.

It was expected that Ouseley would do well in his finals, particularly in Mathematics, but Watkins Shaw surmises that his result may have been affected by the death of his father over a year before.

> As it was, his attainment at the end of 1845 was anything but distinguished. In those days, candidates for honours were examined in two disciplines, classics and the elements of maths and physics. The names of those in the first four classes were printed,

while only the number of those in the fifth class was indicated. Ouseley obtained a fourth class in Maths and Physics but in Classics, he was among the unnamed of his year in the fifth class. (15)

In 1846, at the age of twenty-one, Ouseley graduated with a B.A. degree. It had been expected that he would have done rather better, but a number of things perhaps prevented him from achieving his true potential: his father's death and subsequent interruptions, as already mentioned, an illness of his own at a critical time, and also perhaps his lack of application to his studies. Dean Kitchin sums this up succinctly. 'He had wonderful abilities as a linguist and as a mathematician, but his passion for music prevented the full development of the sterner pursuits.' (16)

REFERENCES

1. Sermon by the Reverend T.A. Ayscough given at a Commemoration Service at St Michael's on 4 October 1906, quoted in *Memorabilia–50th Anniversary 1906*
2. Watkins Shaw, p. 12
3. Letter from his younger sister (Joyce p. 32)
4. Letter from his mother (Joyce pp. 32 – 33)
5. Joyce p.31
6. Joyce p. 31
7. Joyce p. 31
8. Joyce p. 35
9. Joyce p. 36
10. Joyce p. 37
11. Joyce pp. 37-38
12. Stainer, *The Character and Influence of Sir Frederick A.G. Ouseley* (p. 31)
13. Joyce p. 40
14. Joyce pp. 42-43
15. Oxford University Calendar 1846 (quoted in Watkins Shaw pp. 13 – 14)
16. Joyce p. 45

St. Paul's Knightsbridge
(Ouseley's curacy 1849-50)

St. Barnabas Pimlico
(Ouseley's curacy 1849-50)

CHAPTER FOUR
ORDINATION AND AFTER

Ouseley came down from Oxford in 1846, and for the next three years, went to live with his widowed mother at their London house. Sir Gore's London address had been Upper Brook Street, Grosvenor Square, but we can only assume that his widow, Harriet had possibly moved to a smaller house shortly after his death as her address in 1846 was given as Lowndes Street, which was only a short walk from St Paul's church, Knightsbridge. By this time, Ouseley had made the decision to read for Holy Orders and he spent much of the next three years in serious academic study. St Paul's had only been opened in 1843 and the Reverend W J E Bennett had been appointed as its first Vicar.

In July 1847, Ouseley sold his father's estate at Beaconsfield, Hall Barn Park and deeds at the St Helen's Records Office in Worcester show that it was sold for £100,000, a considerable sum at the time. Further records show that by the end of 1847, Ouseley had recently purchased or owned land in Worcestershire and Hertfordshire, land which would later provide much of the income to sustain his College at Tenbury: 'at Eastham,Worcs, Highwood Cottage and gardens, Slate Hall farm, wood and quarry and Eastham Park farm and estate; in Hertfordshire, houses and a nursery garden at Churchgate, Cheshunt, Five House farm and Hay farm at Thorfield, and the Rectory in the Manor of Thorfield. (1)

By this time, Ouseley's friend and former tutor, the Reverend J. Wayland Joyce had become Rector of Burford on the Shropshire/ Worcestershire border, and during these years Ouseley made frequent visits to the area, often staying a fortnight at a time and getting to know the neighbourhood where he was later to build his church and College. Indeed, Wayland Joyce is sometimes given the credit for preparing Ouseley for ordination, but it is more likely that his regular visits to Burford served as a time of relaxation from his intense studies for ordination. Also, in addition to these studies, Ouseley was preparing to take his Bachelor of Music degree. 'This required him to submit an original work for choir and orchestra, displaying competence in the craft of composition, including of course counterpoint and fugue.' (2)

Ouseley's decision to take a music degree came as a great shock to the university authorities and every effort was made to dissuade him from his intention. In the three years since leaving Oxford, Ouseley had submitted a thesis and been awarded an MA degree, and the authorities pointed out that it was unfitting to take a lower degree after taking a higher one. Dean Gaisford had suggested to Ouseley that such a course of action was also quite unbecoming for a gentleman of his rank and independent means and did everything he could to change his mind. Watkins Shaw comments on the status of an Oxford Music Degree at this time

> The status of the degree was wholly anomalous. No residence in Oxford was necessary, for indeed the University provided no course of instruction. All that a candidate had to do, without preliminary examination, was to prevail on some college to allow him to place his name on their books for a short time, and, when registered, to submit his'exercise' to the approval of the Professor of Music, who himself was not required to live or teach in Oxford. After approval, the exercise had to be publicly performed in Oxford, a discouraging factor which put the candidate to the considerable expense of engaging performers. (3)

Ouseley's submission for this degree was a cantata *The Lord is the true God*, and this was later revived for the Three Choirs Festival at Hereford in August 1858. Sir Henry Bishop was the Oxford Professor of Music at the time and Ouseley's examiner and his letters to Ouseley offer a number of helpful comments on his composition. 'I have examined your sacred cantata very carefully and with considerable pleasure. Your concluding fugue in particular does you great credit…Whatever you may do in any other work may be regulated by your taste and opinion, but in my judgement of your exercise, I conceive that I am bound by orthodox principles.'(4) Sir Henry goes on to say that when he has seen an amended copy of the score, with the decided grammatical errors he has pointed out being rectified, 'I will, whenever you wish it, forward to you the required certificate of my approval of your exercise for the degree of Mus.B.' (5)

On 26 April 1848 his beloved mother died, aged sixty-one, four years after the death of his father. It appears that, some days before her death, she had suffered a slight accident while out riding (possibly in a carriage), and though not physically hurt, was obviously shocked and frightened. She was already suffering from a weak heart and the extra shock proved too great. Much of Ouseley's interest in music and his spiritual development can be attributed to the influence of his mother and elder sisters and her death must have affected him deeply. Shortly after his mother's death, Ouseley travelled to Europe where he visited many countries and played some 190 organs. He made a further tour in 1850–1.

ST PAUL'S CHURCH, KNIGHTSBRIDGE

By this time, the theological ferment caused by the publication of *Tracts for the Times*, (which was so evident in Oxford during Ouseley's time there), had moved on from university debate and the Tractarians, or followers of the Oxford Movement, had begun to spread their ideas into many urban parishes.

After Newman's secession in 1845, as both politicans and press began to take increasing account of Tractarian developments, public response veered from curiosity to aggressive intolerance; and many, who had previously shown no interest in religious matters, were persuaded to take issue, fastening upon the proferred symbol of 'advanced' church practice – a surplice, a lighted candle, or the practice of intoning – as representing a scandalous innovation to be put down at whatever cost. (6)

St Paul's, Knightsbridge, was situated in a wealthy and fashionable area of London and Bennett, introducing the new Tractarian ideas, believed that there was a distinct growth in reverence and devotion as a result. Shortly after arriving, he had introduced a surpliced choir which was situated in stalls at the east end of the nave, but just outside the chancel, a position which was currently being recommended in the magazine, *The Ecclesiologist.* The choir was formed from boys in local schools with altos, tenors and basses being drawn from members of the parish. Ouseley spent the next three years (1846–9) as a lay member of the choir.

In many churches, the influence of the Tractarians had contributed towards the improvement of the conduct of services and St Paul's was no exception. Bennett had no doubt as to the effect of these ideas and in a rather florid description, speaks of a re-awakening of much older but forgotten ideals.

Architecture began to stir in the external construction of a better order of the sanctuaries of God, music lent its aid, and the Songs of David began once more to be sung to the ancient choral services of St. Gregory; painting lent its aid, and the churches began to manifest the beauties of colour and art... thus all combined in a revival of devotion which soon began to make itself felt. (7)

Translating these general ideas into his own church in Knightsbridge was his main priority, and Rainbow describes how this was achieved.

The new church, designed by Thomas Cundy, has been described as little better than a great galleried hall, lighted by Perpendicular windows and furnished with a shallow chancel. But through Bennett's endeavours, it was soon equipped in a manner to enhance decent observation of the Church's ceremonies and as quickly filled with a wealthy and fashionable congregation drawn from the opulent squares and terraces of Belgravia. (8)

Already, Bennett had incurred the displeasure of his bishop, (Blomfield, Bishop of London), with his 'ritualistic' practices. This was the situation into which Ouseley was ordained on Trinity Sunday 1849 by the same Bishop of London. Despite the differences between Bennett and his bishop, Ouseley was licensed to a curacy under Bennett and soon threw himself wholeheartedly into parish life. In the difficult times of today in which the Church of England finds itself, often criticized from all directions and with falling congregations, it is difficult to appreciate the work and subsequent stress which fell upon the clergy of large urban parishes in Victorian times.

> The labour, anxiety and mental pressure...is overwhelming, occupied as we are with an average of 120 communicants every Lord's Day. We now begin the service at eleven, *[Matins, Litany and Communion following on consecutively],* and seldom conclude before half-past two. Then the congregation come in for the Evening Service, women for Churching, and children for Baptism; so that we are occupied with very little intermission for some six hours; and that, remember, with the most solemn offices to perform, requiring the utmost stretch of the mind, in the presence of a congregation seldom less than 1,700 persons in the morning, and perhaps 1,200 in the evening; and with the second Evening Service following closely after, at half-past six. Now I do not begrudge this labour. – God forbid. I rejoice in it. (9)

In the first few years of his ministry at St Paul's, schools, a Provident Society, a lending library and a Community of Sisters of Charity had been set up in the parish. Bennett was acutely aware of the problems of the poor, most of whom never saw the inside of a church, and in his parish saw a living example of the Parable of Dives and Lazarus. The wealthy of the parish went to St Paul's while the poor had nothing.

> At the southern extremity of Bennett's parish, lay the marshy district of Pimlico, bordering the Thames. There, to the east of Ebury Street, and stretching westward to Chelsea Hospital, lay a remote region of deplorable slums. Its streets unpaved and, undrained, its ruinous lodging-houses and tenements packed with impoverished wretches, the district presented an aspect of degradation scarcely to be exceeded in London...Bennett's plan was to urge upon his wealthy congregation the duty of providing a church in Pimlico for their poor neighbours. The principle of alms-giving was to finance the whole enterprise. (10)

ST. BARNABAS, PIMLICO

A large church was planned, with adjoining schools and, as the support of his parishioners gathered momentum, Bennett enlarged his ideas to include a college attached to the church to house four priests and to provide accommodation for twelve choristers, whose education, training and clothing was free. In June 1847, the schools were opened, providing 600 places for children of all ages, followed by the building of the church and college. While the church was being built, Bennett, together with his wife and family and his curates, had moved into the clergy-house which was already attached to the half-built church. Ouseley was joined there by the Reverends Laurence Tutiett, Henry Fyffe and G F de Gex, the last two becoming lifelong friends and closely associated with the future development of St Michael's. When the church was completed, Ouseley paid all the expenses for the building and installation of an organ to his own specification for the new church. This was undertaken by Messrs Flight and Robson in 1849. They were later to build the first (unsuccessful) organ for the new St Michael's College in 1856.

On 11 June 1850, the new church and College, dedicated to St Barnabas, was consecrated by the Bishop of London. There was a special service in St Paul's church at which Archdeacon Manning preached and over the Octave of Dedication, there were numerous services, attended by many well known figures of the time., Bishop Wilberforce of Oxford, John Keble, J M Neale and Dr Pusey.

As well as elaborate rituals, the music at these service was of the highest order, with most of the arrangements for the Dedication Festival being placed in the hands of Thomas Helmore, who acted as Precentor and who augmented the St. Paul's choir with choristers from the Chapel Royal, Westminster Abbey and several amateur singers.

During this week, there had been sixteen choral services, including a daily celebration of Holy Communion with a full choir, and the magazine *The Parish Choir* saw it as a great opportunity to see what high standards of choral worship could be achieved, as many clergy were seeking to introduce choral services in their own churches.

> The week was of great importance to the cause of church music, not only because some sixteen services had been celebrated chorally, but because it provided an opportunity to test and establish certain points valuable as evidence to those of the clergy and others disposed to establish a choral form of service in their own churches. Moreover, the week's services in St Barnabas had been conducted in the presence of very large and varying congregations...Most important in that aspect, must be reckoned the daily celebration of the Holy Communion with a full choir. (11)

To many people, it may have seemed strange that Thomas Helmore, the Founder of St Mark's College, Chelsea, and a champion of choral services, should have been brought in as Precentor to train the new choir at St Barnabas, when such an accomplished musician as Ouseley was already in post as an assistant priest. Ouseley's biographer (Joyce) claimed that 'Ouseley was busy with choir work especially, besides taking part in the general routine of a London parish.'(12) But, as Rainbow points out, Ouseley's involvement with the St Barnabas choir 'is more likely to have concerned pastoral rather than music affairs,' (13) 'and even Joyce himself says that Ouseley 'had not the patience, even if he had any of the other qualities requisite to make a good teacher.' (14)

Even when at St Michael's, Ouseley never took part in the normal education of the boys or even the musical instruction of the choristers. At. St Barnabas, which enjoyed choral services and which included both choir and congregational participation, it is more likely that Ouseley disapproved of the musical policy adopted.

> As a church musician, he was wholeheartedly in support of the 'Jebb' school of thought, maintaining that the choral service was something to be listened to, not joined in by the congregation. Moreover, he shared with S S Wesley – and a number of other leading church musicians of the day – an active antipathy to Gregorian chanting. Had Ouseley sympathised more with the musical policy at St Barnabas, he would at least have played the organ for some of the services during the Consecration Festival. But this was not so. (15)

It had also been noted that the Canticles at one service had been sung to Ouseley's setting in A, some people thinking that it had been written specially for the occasion. In fact, it had been composed during Ouseley's undergraduate days in Oxford, and dedicated to the Dean and Canons of Christ Church. It is clear that Helmore and Ouseley held strong and differing views on the conduct and content of choral services, particularly when they involved plainsong, but despite this,

> the two men became firm friends. Indeed, Ouseley dedicated a set of eight anthems to Helmore, and despite his admiration for the stern simplicity of Gregorian melody, subsequently counted among his favourite pieces, Ouseley's expressive anthem, *How goodly are thy tents.* Moreover, Ouseley and Helmore's brother, Frederick, had been associates during their Oxford days and had preserved their association throughout their subsequent lives.(16)

Within a few weeks of the consecration, trouble began and continued over the next few months. The effect of the new church is summarised in Carpenter's book, *Church and People.*

> W J E Bennett, Vicar of St Paul's, Knightsbridge, introduced the eastward position, flowers, altar lights, a surpliced choir and a sung service. In the daughter church of St Barnabas, Pimlico, set in what was then a singularly degraded area of the parish with a criminal population, there was like ceremonial. Also, during a cholera epidemic in 1849, cards were circulated for private use with prayers for the departed. The St, Barnabas clergy, including Lowder and Ouseley, were unsparing in their pastoral work during the epidemic, but that did not save the two churches from being very unpopular with the world at large and also being made the scene of intolerable rioting. Even the bells were objected to :

Hush-a-bye Bennett, on the church top.
When your bells cease the outcry will stop.
If you don't stop when reason shall call,
Down will go Bennett, bell-ringing and all. (17)

The unrest which was evident throughout the parish spread further, and was also exacerbated by the issue of a Papal Bull by Pope Pius IX in September 1850, when he announced the formation of a new Province of the Roman Catholic Church, with an Archbishop of Westminster and twelve bishops. 'This Papal 'Aggression', as it became known, aroused a perfect frenzy of indignation all over England.' (18)

Throughout the year 1850, it was clear that Ouseley was very concerned about the direction the Church of England was taking, and he was also very anxious about his own position within it. Joyce, his biographer, includes a series of letters between himself and Ouseley dating from early in the year which show Ouseley's developing concerns. Questions of Royal Supremacy, the relationship between Church and State, the erosion of the rights and liberties of the church, were all questions on his mind and occupying the minds of many clergy at the time. On 28 September, he wrote to Wayland Joyce at Burford, apologizing for his late reply to a previous letter.

I know I ought to have written; but I had neither time nor spirits. I am in great perplexity. I *must,* according to the invariable and tyrannical rule of my Bishop, take Priest's Orders at Christmas. But I cannot and will not consent to do so at St Barnabas, as it is only my being in Deacon's Orders which saves me from doing many things sorely *against my conscience.* It is therefore essential to get away; but I am loath to do so without something definite to go to – *not a curacy*, because of the scandal which it would give against Mr Bennett, who has enemies enough ready to take hold of any pretext to defame him. Bennett himself is quite willing that I should go at Christmas; and I am also sure it is necessary both for my health and happiness to do so. Can you advise me how to act? Of course, I must not take a holiday till then, but will make a point of coming and seeing you as soon as I can get away. Pray write to me about this. (19)

Within a few weeks, the situation in the parish had worsened and the manner of worship at St Barnabas had begun to attract a 'no Popery' rabble who began to cause problems at the church each Sunday. Due to threats heard at the morning service, the evening service was cancelled and on his way back to the clergy-house, Ouseley overheard groups of men planning what was going to happen at the church the next Sunday. Despite his own objections to some of Bennett's ritual observances and the use of Gregorian chants, he pledged his loyalty the his Vicar and his fellow curates. On 20 November, Ouseley wrote a letter to his friend the

Reverend John Rich, and his account of the disturbances make frightening reading.

> You have doubtless read in the papers, accounts of the outrageous attack which was made by the mob on St Barnabas' church last Sunday. But as the accounts in some of the papers are incorrect, it is possible that you and others may have been misled as to the facts of the case. I write this to tell you how it all happened, both because I know you will take an interest in this matter, and because I am anxious the truth should be widely known. On Sunday 10 November, just as the non-communicants were about to retire, a great hissing was heard in the church, with loud cries of 'Popery', etc. This was, of course, stopped, and the Service proceeded; but a multitude of men had collected outside, prepared to make a rush had any sympathy been evinced within. A great crowd had collected in the evening, but we avoided all disturbance then by omitting the Service at 7. Mr Bennett remained at St Barnabas to defend his family and property if necessary, and sent me to preach for him at St. Paul's at 6. When I returned at 8-30, I found the crowd, gathered in knots of men, threatening what they would do next Sunday. I had been insulted and threatened the night before in the street and Mr Bennett too had received several threatening letters. We had every reason to be certain of a more violent attack on the Sunday the 17th, so we took every precaution to be prepared for it, nor were they superfluous. The 8 am and 9 am Services went off quietly; but at 10-30 am, the mob began to collect, but luckily our own congregation were seated in time. Nothing in the church happened before the Sermon, but during it a prodigious yell was heard without, which frightened some of our people much. The church was crammed to suffocation, and a body of staunch friends were stationed up the body of the nave to prevent any attack on the chancel. When the sermon was concluded, a violent rush was made by the populace outside; and doubtless, had they succeeded in their attempt, our beautiful edifice would have been dismantled, and our lives endangered. We know that was their object; but it pleased God to defeat their sacrilegious intention. The well-affected within were too strong for them, 100 policeman succeeded in quelling the mob without, sufficiently to let the congregation retire. The organist, by my direction, played 'Full Organ' the whole time, to drown the row, which had no small effect in preventing the disaffected from communicating with one another. In about forty minutes, the church was at length cleared. It was truly gratifying to see the very large number of communicants who remained to thank God in this way for His Almighty protection. (20)

As his letter to Joyce shows, his mind was in a turmoil. He was unsure what to do and his health had been affected by all the troubles. Soon the decision was made for him when Bennett resigned in November 1850 rather than be disloyal to his Bishop. After almost a year's break, Bennett was appointed to the living of Frome in Somerset and Ouseley's two sisters, Mary Jane and Alexandrine, followed him there to help him with his parish work. As for Ouseley, he resigned at the same time, together with two of the other curates, de Gex and Fyffe. At the time, Ouseley was very conscious of an obligation towards the boy choristers of St Barnabas, Pimlico. He felt that it was in their best interests to get them away from the turbulent situation there and quickly arranged accommodation for them at Lovehill House, Langley Marish, in Buckinghamshire. He took on personal responsibility for their welfare and generously provided for their education and board and lodging, under the care of the Reverend Henry Fyffe, one of his fellow curates from St Barnabas. He also ensured that their musical education would continue, in the capable hands of the oldest of the senior boys, John Hampton, who was later to have such an influence on the life of St. Michael's. A small, temporary chapel was created out of an old hay-loft adjacent to the house where the boys stayed, and soon there continued a regular routine of sung services.

Once these arrangements had been put into effect, Ouseley was determined to travel abroad. 'His nervous, excitable disposition had undergone considerable stress during his brief but eventful curacy in Pimlico and he left the country to recuperate. He visited Portugal Spain, Italy, Switzerland and Germany, playing on noted organs in the greater churches, and listening to celebrated continental choirs.'(21) He had taken his other fellow curate, de Gex with him and together, they travelled widely over the next year. Ouseley was also keen enough to write down the specifications of most of the organs he heard and played and these formed the basis of what were to be a collection of organ notebooks.

At this distance in time, it is unclear whether he had any long-term plans for his little colony of boys at Langley, but it is certain that his thoughts and ideas became focused on what his future role in life must be, during his time abroad. A series of letters written to his friend, Joyce, back in England, reveals the way his ideas were shaping and what his future plans must be. They visited Lisbon and Cadiz before travelling on to Rome and Venice. In Spain, one thing that did impress him was an Franciscan Monastery at Mapa, which he noted as having a chime of 114 bells. 'He disliked Italian church choirs and became confirmed in antipathy to the Church of Rome.' (22)

Writing to Joyce from Rome in May 1851, he was still unsure as to what he should do. He felt that much depended on how the present situation in the church resolved itself. He had considered 'a sort of offer of the Precentorship of Winchester Cathedral which is soon expected to become vacant…Still, in spite of all this, I may, after all, settle down into a country parson. If so, I had rather be near you.' (23) Despite this, his mind is beginning to focus on one theme.

I have scruples about hiding my light under a bushel. I think I clearly ought, if it be possible, to devote it to God's service in His Holy Church. Now in a regular country living, this is impossible; for a large town living, I have neither health nor strength. A precentorship is more the thing, but it has its drawbacks and they are of no small weight. I am pulled all ways. (24)

By September 1851, his ideas were beginning to take shape and Joyce had clearly made some interesting suggestions for his consideration, particularly with reference to something being possible at Ludlow. It is clear that Ouseley's service to the Church must be through his musical gifts and he saw this as an opportunity for which he was ideally qualified.

I have determined to undertake it but there are difficulties still. I cannot afford to build the church and endow it too. My income will not do it, and I cannot touch my capital. What I have in my thoughts is a church in fourteenth century style, with collegiate buildings adjoining, for residences for myself, two curates and choir, and cloisters too, for enclosing a private portion of the cemetery. Now, this plan is expensive, and so I can only accomplish it by degrees. I will give £ 1,000 towards this building, if anyone else will help me in any degree proportionately. Then as to the service, I must have a daily choral service: my choir must be a *model* choir. (25)

Within a month, Ouseley was writing to Joyce from Munich, telling him that he liked the 'Ludlow Scheme' even more, the only difficulty being money and explaining why.

You see, my funds are rather reduced now in consequence of all that I disbursed at St Barnabas, both toward the church and choir…I will not do without a daily choral service. I have no talent for teaching, no powers of preaching, and no health for hard parochial work. But God has given me one talent; and that I am determined to devote to his service, and offer it up to adorn His Church. (26)

In this letter, he asked Joyce to tell Hampden, now Bishop of Hereford, about his plans. He had also received a letter from Fyffe, requesting that he return to Lovehill House in time for Christmas Day. Three weeks later, he wrote from Dresden and informed Joyce that

I am quite out of conceit with English chorister boys. I think every Precentor and choirmaster ought to come and hear the boys here, both in the Roman Catholic and the Lutheran churches. I have never heard anything equal or approaching to the excellence of their voices. The intonation is so true, and the style so tasteful and refined, and the quality so rich and round, that it leaves nothing to be desired. (27)

Ouseley had similar views about the boys' choirs he heard in Leipzig and felt that he never heard anything approaching such quality. In comparison with the English boys, he felt that the German boy choristers came from a higher class of society. Although there were some exceptions, in general he felt that the system of recruiting and training cathedral choristers in England was appallingly bad. This was borne out by the considerable research into boy choristers by the Victorian philanthropist, Maria Hackett, who had visited most of the cathedrals at this time and, like Ouseley, was determined to improve standards. Ouseley's particular aim was to raise the standard of accommodation, education and musical training for English choir boys.

> Now they are too often mere rabble, and what refinement of style can we expect from such materials?... Now, my choral scheme will tend, maybe with God's blessing, to improve this state of things. I hope also that by instituting a model choir I may supply another great deficiency, i.e. choir *men*, brought up as choristers, who shall know how to be reverent and devout in church; singing not for their own sake, but for God's glory...Now there is a great lack of good *chanting* clergy in Church of England. No man can be so fit to perform the Priest's part well in a Choral Service, as he who has been brought up as a chorister boy. (28)

After Berlin, Ouseley's travels continued through Germany, visiting Hanover and Cologne before travelling through Holland, looking at a number of organs on the way, before their return to England. By the time Ouseley had returned from his travels abroad, it appears that the 'state' of 'the national church' was not as important to him as previously and now felt that he had his own work to do. 'He kept apart from further controversy in which Bennett and others continued to be involved; and after some initial suspicion, his own conduct in later years at Tenbury aroused no hostile reaction on grounds of ritualistic practices.' (29)

REFERENCES

1. Worcester Records Office
2. Watkins Shaw p 14
3. Watkins Shaw pp 14 –15
4. HCL D 863
5. HCL D 863
6. Rainbow p 143
7. Bennett *A Farewell Letter* p 4
8. Rainbow p 149
9. Bennett *A Pastoral Letter* p 10
10. Rainbow p 152
11. *The Parish Choir* Vol. III pp. 116–119
12. Joyce pp. 49–50
13. Rainbow p 158

14. Joyce p 107
15. Rainbow p 158-159
16. Helmore *Memoir* p 91
17. Carpenter *Church and People* p 207
18. Carpenter *Church and People* p 208
19. Joyce p 64
20. Joyce p 66
21. Joyce pp 68–78
22. Watkins Shaw p 22
23. Joyce p 71
24. Joyce p 71
25. Joyce p 74
26. Joyce p 75
27. Joyce p 76
28. Joyce p 78
29. Watkins Shaw p 24

CHAPTER FIVE

THE FOUNDATION OF ST. MICHAEL'S COLLEGE

At the end of 1851, Ouseley had returned to England, re-invigorated and completely restored to health, with an absolutely clear conviction as to what direction his future life should take. He went back to live with the St Barnabas choristers at Langley Marish. At that time, they were led by Fyffe, Ouseley, and John Hampton, who at seventeen, had lost his treble voice and had been put in charge of the choir, together with six choristers and three probationers. John Hampton, remembered those days well.

> While at Langley, we were well employed in keeping up the grand Cathedral use besides concert work in madrigal and other secular music. Sometimes we had a man from Windsor as in Wesley's *The Wilderness*. We were badly off for basses. (Hampton himself was a tenor.) At that time, we had visitors such as Sir John Goss, Dr. E.G. Monk, Dr. Corfe, Mr. G. Cooper and then we attempted big things, such as *Israel in Egypt* and *Messiah*. (1)

It is also recorded that on occasions, Ouseley took his choristers across to Eton College, where they joined the boys of Eton College Chapel Choir, under the direction of Dr Elvey, Organist of St George's Chapel, Windsor.

At this time, Ouseley was also consolidating his links with the world of cathedral music and had many friends among eminent musicians. He had written to S S Wesley, organist at Winchester Cathedral, ordering copies of a new anthem Wesley had written, (possibly *Ascribe unto the Lord*) and Wesley's reply is very revealing as to his admiration for Ouseley and his own state of mind.

> The very kind compliment you paid me in ordering copies of my anthem cannot I fear be declined by me, but let me assure you that it required no mark of attention from you. Your fine musical taste and acquirements might command the respect and esteem of those musicians, to which I gladly belong and I can only satisfy myself at all when ordering off these books to you that they may perhaps be of some little use and interest to your choir. I have added a copy to the specified number (was it four?) which you must kindly accept from me. Indeed, I rather wish you to look at the things for some of them do not wholly displease me, for although I have unfortunately been long out of the musical world and might do better, with notice, I cannot forget my early indilection and use of so much paper and to only the very meanest purpose.

51

How I do wish that your engagements were less important and that you would come over to me, bring a few of those fat volumes that you named and your own publications. Is it possible? Might I hope for it? Our good Dean will be in residence at the end of next week and I am sure that he would be delighted to have you when you tired of me. I want to show you a few things of my fathers.

Now let me thank you for writing about our organ. I think that we shall succeed as we have got so much money promised.

One of our Canons (one of the brothers Prityman, distinguished in *The Times),* opposes the Dean, insultingly I believe, and gives great trouble. He will do nothing for music or for any other object requiring money. He gives great dinners and fills the Close with servants in the brightest yellow livery.

...I have no musical friends now. Leaving London is quitting the world. I have been many years out of London and my old allies have grown worldly and seem less addicted to friendship than formerly. But I must conclude. Pardon all this from a recluse...Our Dean will name your work in Chapter and then we shall be able to have the anthems, he says. (2)

Ouseley therefore began to look at ways in which his idea to form a 'model' choir school could become a reality. Over the next few months, he was to look at a number of possibilities. The first of these had involved a scheme to create a new district from the parish of Ludlow, but when this idea fell through, the idea was then put to him to rebuild Buildwas Abbey near Ironbridge in Shropshire, but this also proved impossible. Friends then suggested that his ideas would stand a greater chance of success if he established his College near a large centre of population. He therefore wrote to Bishop Wilberforce of Oxford, outlining his plans. However, Bishop Wilberforce, son of the great evangelical preacher, William Wilberforce, had lost two of his own brothers to the Roman Church and he declined to associate himself with someone 'tainted' by recent connections with St Barnabas, Pimlico. This was somewhat surprising when Ouseley's plans were similar to his own for the foundation of a theological college for the training of ordinands at Cuddesdon.

After these 'rejections', Ouseley went to Burford to discuss matters with his friend Joyce and seek his advice. Joyce had also been looking for a suitable site for Ouseley's scheme and in June 1852, was instrumental in persuading him to purchase a tract of land in the area of the Old Wood, situated on the outskirts of Tenbury Wells on the Leominster road and approximately two miles from the little market town on the Shropshire / Herefordshire / Worcestershire border.

June! Who would not buy land adjoining the 'Old Wood' who saw it in June? Its pastures, its springing crops, with wild roses in the hedgerows, its orchards when the fruit is firmly set; its prospects,

Clee Hill across the Common to the north, the woods and uplands of Worcestershire to the south, all call the traveller to stay.

Sir Frederick Ouseley was still a young man, not twenty-seven, when he made his purchase. Would he have been less precipitate if he had to make his decision in January? Others who have lived there since have at least wished that he had thought again. The country has its rare beauties in every season, but the disadvantages of this spot as a centre of education leap to the eye more readily in the winter. A college on the edge of a Common two miles from the nearest market town, and that not much of a town when reached; problems of transport, catering, and particularly those of the domestic and medical care of small boys; difficulties of finding lay clerks, alto, tenor, bass, of employing and keeping them when found; these and a thousand other considerations were not likely to be present to Sir Frederick's mind as he drove between rose-clad hedges, and wandered round his new estate, deciding on the site for his church, seeing in his mind's eye the stately collegiate buildings in the approved fourteenth-century style already rising from among the buttercups. (3)

At this time, Joyce's parish at Burford had George Rushout (later Baron Northwick) as its leading family, living with his two unmarried sisters, Harriet and Georgina, at Burford House. George was Lord of the Manor of Tenbury and it appears that they had been aware of the need for a church to serve the outlying districts of Tenbury and hamlets around the Common. In the Will of Harriet Rushout, made as early as May 1849, she had bequeathed the sum of £ 600 'towards the erection of a church on the Old Wood in the parish of Tenbury.'

Nothing of this was known to Ouseley until August 1852 when Miss Harriet died and the contents of her will were revealed. Suddenly, Ouseley could see a way to move forward his plans. Joyce was of course a great help in this and William Norris, a Tenbury solicitor, also offered his help. He was the first of five partners in the family law firm who later guided the affairs of St Michael's College throughout its existence. Further help came to Ouseley from two clergymen brothers living in the parish of Bockleton, Thomas and John Miller. Thomas was Squire of Bockleton and patron of the living, together with that of nearby Leysters and his brother John was the assistant curate of both parishes. Ouseley wrote to John Miller, outlining his plans, on 3 September 1852.

> My friend Mr. Joyce has informed me that he has acquainted you with the wish expressed by Captain and Miss Rushout, that I should join with them in building a church according to the Will of Miss Harriet Rushout, whose death we all lament. I suppose that he has told you that I have offered a certain sum towards building the said church on the understanding that I should be the

Portrait of Georgina Rushout, c. 1830
Photo courtesy of Ouseley Trustees

incumbent thereof and now I write to beg of you to give me the benefit of your kind and valuable counsel as to how I should proceed in the matter...There are some difficulties which I apprehend – certain neighbours of yours seem to entertain no small fears of propinquity and on a former occasion, used their influence but too successfully in utterly preventing me from building in

Tenbury Parish, a church and college to my own sole expense – for the particulars of this business, I refer you to Joyce, who will explain them better 'viva voce' than I can by letter. In the hopes of carrying out my scheme however, in spite of puritanical opposition, I quite lately bought some land which is in your parish, and by the Bishop's advice, I was intending thereon to build a church, or rather a college with a college chapel – without a district, hoping by this means to settle in the neighbourhood to which I am attached and not without some hope also, that at some future time, when rancour and the theological odium had subsided, to have my college chapel converted into a district parish – but Miss Rushout's legacy to build a church on the Old Wood alters the case. And what I want now is to have the church built in your parish – and this is because I am presumptious enough to hope that I should meet with encouragement from you, as well as because it is always an advantage to have one's own church near one's own property – for obvious reasons. (4)

On 7 September, Miller wrote back to Ouseley, first making two points. 'I do not really lose sight of your independent power. I am myself a person of *no* sort of authority in the business, but may be capable of being useful in it so far as the kind confidence of the parties -principals – may lead them to credit me.' (5)

He cites some local people who had criticised and condemned Ouseley's plan, one of them being the Vicar of Tenbury, instead of 'giving a cordial welcome to our benefactor', but is also anxious that whatever is done should be done in the best possible manner. He then goes on to suggest an alternative to Ouseley's scheme.

I venture to think that it is very desirable to give your good work the character of a public benefit as far as possible, as distinguishable from an individual fancy…A church is decidedly wanted in the Old Wood, or in that region, for a very considerable population, ill provided for, but it would be quite idle to pretend any such help is needed in Leysters, particularly in that part of the parish where your new property is situated. (6)

Miller advised Ouseley to obtain a site on the old Wood itself, hopefully with the support of the local population. He suggests that there were two possible sites that could be made available. Land belonging to the Bockleton Perpetual Curacy as one possibility, and Leysters Glebe, which might eligibly provide the second. He promised to write immediately to interested parties, to secure their support and also advises Ouseley to do nothing in a hurry. 'There are a good many irons in the fire and it could make the difference between success and failure.'(7) On 11 September 1852, Miller wrote again to Ouseley, stating that an exchange of land between the Bockleton estates was out of the question and it seemed that under the terms of the Rushout bequest, the land at Old Wood was the more likely option, with the possibility of exchanging land with the tenants of adjoining land. Ouseley wrote back to Miller on 16 September, agreeing the choice of Old Wood and said that he hoped to come and visit the spot as soon as he could get away. He had written to the Bishop and the Rushouts about his plans and to ascertain their views. He was also concerned as to whether Captain Rushout would accept his designs, believing him to be more in favour of parish schools. However, Ouseley was prepared to offer £ 1000 towards the church. He believed that this, together with Miss Rushout's bequest, would be sufficient to build the church, but not much more.

By 15 November, Ouseley had studied the plans after visiting the proposed site on the Old Wood and wrote to Miller from Christ Church, Oxford. 'I am only waiting to know where the Bishop is to write a detailed account of the whole matter for his Lordship's perusal.'(8) Wayland Joyce wrote to Miller early in January 1853, mentioning that Ouseley that received a most satisfactory letter from Hampden, the Bishop of Hereford, on the subject of the proposed church, stating that he would 'forward the plan very heartily.' (9)

By this time, local opposition to the scheme was beginning to surface, led by the Vicar of Tenbury. In May 1853, Joyce wrote to Miller, endeavouring to reassure him 'that the Bishop would be answerable for the soundness of Ouseley's doctrine.'(10) On 17 May, William Norris, a Tenbury Solicitor, wrote to Miller, enclosing a tracing of the Tenbury Parish, showing what area would be included in the new district and what areas would be taken from the other parishes involved. Mr. Norris felt that he was in a very difficult situation.

> It is very painful to me to be acting in seeming opposition to the clergyman of my parish, but when a great good is offered to be conferred upon part of that parish, I cannot understand the fact of Sir Frederick having formerly been a curate of Mr. Bennett, is sufficient reason for opposing the accomplishment of such a work. Ouseley is a good man in whose principles our Bishop is willing to guarantee. It is the bounden duty of every right-minded person in the parish to do his utmost to forward such a work. There are a number of families on the outskirts of Tenbury Parish, living in a state of practical heathenism. (11)

Over the next eighteen months, the opposition seemed to have died down, the plans had been approved and with the Bishop's support, building the church began, using local stone. Ouseley, staying at Burford Rectory in January 1855, writes to Miller's brother after visiting the new buildings, expressing his gratitude for their kindness in giving him the use of their stone quarry. The foundation stone of St. Michael's Church was laid on 3 May 1854.

Bishop Hampden (Bishop of Hereford 1848-1868)

Sometime previously, he had engaged a young architect, Henry Woodyer, to draw up plans for his church and college. The archives at the Royal Academy of British Architects show that Woodyer was the first pupil of the well-known architect, William Butterfield and had built the church at Highnam in Gloucestershire for Thomas Gambier Parry, father of the composer Sir Hubert Parry. Later in his career, he was responsible for the rebuilding of Dorking Parish Church, where Ouseley had spent his teenage years. Woodyer also built many fine houses in Hampshire and Surrey and also designed and built a number of buildings at Eton College. These included the Timbrells Boarding House (1865), the New Schools (1861 – 1876) and he also re-faced much of the stonework of the Eton College Chapel in the 1870's.

During the years 1853 to 1855, Ouseley was also able to turn his thoughts in other directions as his plans for the college began to be realised. Novello published *Cathedral Music,* his collection of five service settings and seventeen anthems and shortly afterwards, a second volume, entitled *A Collection of Cathedral services by English Masters of the 17th and 18th Centuries.*

Four years earlier, Ouseley had successfully overcome opposition to his taking the Bachelor of Music degree at Oxford and in 1854, he spent much time composing his submission for the degree of Doctor of Music. This was to be an Oratorio, entitled *The Martyrdom of St Polycarp.* Sir Henry Bishop. Who had previously examined Ouseley for his B Mus., wrote in glowing terms about the work. 'I can have no hesitation whatever in giving it my unqualified approval. Indeed it does you infinite credit.'(12) Sir Henry goes on to speak of the necessity for proper and sufficient rehearsals for the performance of a degree exercise, but reassures Ouseley that for him it would be a matter of form, whereas many recent exercises had been 'so frequent of negligent and insufficient rehearsals,'(13) that Sir Henry had had to postpone performances until he was satisfied that they were ready for a public hearing. On 9 December 1854, Ouseley's exercise was performed at the Sheldonian Theatre, Oxford, 'with unprecedented completeness and effect.'(14) The work was written for three soloists (STB), three angels (sung by trebles from the Chapel Royal at St James), and a chorus of pagans and Christians conducted by Dr C W Corfe, organist of Christ Church Cathedral. The orchestra and choir consisted chiefly of his personal friends from the University. 'The Theatre was crowded with "auditors" and the performance was pronounced perfectly successful.'(15) Joyce recalls a special moment at this performance. 'Great was the composer's delight when at the last moment, the unmusical Dean Gaisford walked into the Sheldonian to be present at the performance.'(16)

Early in 1855, Sir Henry Bishop died and the Proctors of the University had no hesitation in nominating Ouseley for the vacancy and this was confirmed on 8 May 1855 in his certificate of appointment. On 1 March 1855, Ouseley had received a letter from the Bishop of Hereford, offering him the post of Precentor at Hereford Cathedral, but also explaining the financial drawbacks if he accepted the post.

> The Ecclesiastical Commissioners have appropriated to themselves the revenues of the office, whatever they may have been...Still I think that it is important that the position should be preserved and

worthily embodied in some living person. All however I ask at present is, whether you would like the sort of thing. You will know generally what the duties are of a Precentor, and that he has an assistant in them under the name of Succentor, who performs hem in the absence of his chief. (17)

It is clear from this letter that the post could offer no financial benefits of any kind, yet Ouseley went on to give thirty-four years of faithful and devoted service to the Cathedral. On Trinity Sunday (3 June 1855), Ouseley was ordained priest by Bishop Hampden in Hereford Cathedral, six years to the day since his ordination as deacon and he was installed as Precentor two days later. In the space of a month, Ouseley had received his Priest's Orders, and been appointed to 'Two public offices of more responsibility than pecuniary worth.' (18)

At the same time as St Michael's church was rising on the peaceful Old Wood Common in rural Worcestershire, England was embroiled in the horrors of the Crimean War and there can be no greater contrast between these two events. The foundations of the College were completed in August 1855 and by January 1856, the church roof had been completed. Throughout this time, Ouseley had been shuttling between his choristers at Langley and Tenbury, keen to see his church and college completed. While he stayed at Burford rectory, Joyce recalls him being in the best of health and spirits. 'He would run up and down the rectory stairs, singing the up scale or the down scale, according to his destination. As the staircase contained seventeen steps. It would include the two octaves which would be essential for his vocal practice.'(19) By early 1856, he had rented a house called *Spring Grove* at the far end of the Old Wood Common and this later became the temporary residence of the boys from Langley when they arrived prior to the consecration of the church. In a letter from the Secretary of the National Society, the foundation of the Parish of St Michael's is recorded. 'The Ecclesiastical District of St Michael's is formed out of the parishes of Tenbury (Worcestershire), Middleton-on-the-Hill and Leysters (Herefordshire.) The Tenbury element included the whole of the hamlet of Berrington and that part of the parish known as the 'foreign' of Tenbury.'(20)

Now the church was almost complete, preparations were made for a Service of Consecration on 29 September 1856, the Feast Day celebrating St Michael and All Angels. The day started with a cold morning, but the weather improved and eventually resulted in a fine, sunny day. The event was to be of great interest to many hundreds of people. All accommodation in Tenbury and the neighbourhood was taken up. Joyce recalls the occasion.

> The roads were lined with carriages and carriage folk from far and near; so that only a limited number of those who came could gain admission to the church itself. Some of the London musicians who

were present made their first acquaintance with the Herefordshire mud. The choir was a mixed one, gathered from various sources, but it comprised representatives from several of the chief musical centres in England. There were fourteen trebles, ten from Langley and others included C J Corfe, later to be Bishop of Korea and a young chorister from the Chapel Royal called Arthur Sullivan, who became the celebrated composer of light opera with W S Gilbert; four altos including Ouseley, twelve tenors, including John Hampton and fifteen basses. (21)

Colonel Rushout marshalled a long procession of clergy and laity and at 11-30 am, Bishop Hampden, as Visitor, signed the Deed of Consecration and consecrated a splendid set of eucharistic vestments which had been given by Miss Georgina Rushout. After this Service of Consecration, there was Choral Matins, followed by a Communion Service at which well over 300 people received the sacrament. Ouseley chose one of his favourite settings for the Services of Mattins and Evensong, Rogers in D, which Watkins Shaw believes that to our ears and different tastes, would sound 'drably nondescript.'(22)

After these morning services, luncheon was served in the barely finished library of the incomplete College and 'the day ended with the first of those many evening services which have since been offered up from the Old Wood church of St Michael and All Angels for almost one hundred and thirty years.'(23) During these services, the lessons were read by the Vicar and Curate of Tenbury and the prayers were intoned by Ouseley himself, as well as singing as an alto in the choir. The music included the following anthems, Boyce – *I have surely built Thee an house,* Elvey – *O Praise the Lord of Heaven* (written specially for the occasion) and Goss – *Praise the Lord O my soul* (with the treble solo being sung by Arthur Sullivan).

The first choristers of the College, who came from Langley with Ouseley and Hampton were the following boys.

C.F.A. Sangster
A. Lockyer
P. Butler   (later a Fellow, who retired to live next to St. Michael's)
T.H.B. Fearn
C.S. Boardman
A.B. Sangster
E.K. Kirwan)   These brothers were the sons of
W.B. Kirwan)   the Dean of Limerick
H. Deane   )   Both these boys are listed as boarders in the first Register
C. Corfe   )   Corfe's is the first entry in the College Register. He became Bishop of Korea in 1889, the year of Ouseley's death and was a regular visitor to the College throughout his life.

Watercolour of interior of church (1856). Ouseley standing by lectern
Photo courtesy of English Heritage, National Monuments Record

The organ installed in the church was designed by Sir Frederick himself, but was in an incomplete state for the Consecration services. Flight and Robson had built the organ which Ouseley had designed for St Barnabas, Pimlico in 1849 and it is believed that their organ made for St Michael's was finished in the factory and perfect, two years before it was needed.

However, when the organ arrived at St. Michael's it appeared that the architect had asked for some changes to its intended position and these changes resulted in the organ not being finished in time. Dr. George Elvey, organist of St George's Chapel, Windsor, played the organ for most of the services, assisted by Ouseley, and John Jebb preached a sermon at Evensong entitled *The Principles of Ritualism defended.*

After the enthusiasm and euphoria of the Consecration services, there was a lull in proceedings as the College was not yet complete and the boys did not in fact begin the daily choral tradition until February 1857. Soon there evolved a pattern of services which included two 'parochial services' every Sunday, with both weekday and Sunday evening services being choral.

Perhaps in order to assure Ouseley of the goodwill of the local people, John Miller collected subscriptions in order to make a public recognition of Ouseley's benevolence and actions. Writing to Ouseley in March 1857, he presented him with the sum of £ 272 in order provide the church with a suitable west window of stained glass. In a private note in the same letter, Miller expresses his reservations about what was happening at the services. 'I hope you will be careful not to damage a cause by any such form of excess as might possibly lead to unthinking resistance.'(24)

NOTE: At the Consecration Service, a clergyman was heard to remark that St Michael's was 'The first Collegiate church since the Reformation.' This is incorrect and it is clear from Ouseley's intentions that his aim was to found a College, attached to a parish church. St Michael's has always been a parish church, never a collegiate church. However, for generations of schoolboys, the church was always affectionately referred to as 'College Chapel', although not the correct title.

REFERENCES

1. John Hampden –*Reminiscences* HCL D 483
2. Letter from S.S. Wesley to Ouseley (Maria Hackett Letters – Royal College of Music)
3. Colles pp 14 – 15
4. HCL D 483
5. HCL D 483
6. HCL D 483
7. HCL D 483
8. HCL D 483
9. HCL D 483
10. HCL D 483
11. HCL D 483
12. HCL D 863
13. HCL D 863
14. HCL D 863

15. HCL D 863
16. Joyce p. 85
17. Joyce p. 87
18. Joyce p. 87
19. Joyce page 88
20. National Society Archive
21. Joyce page 89
22. Watkins Shaw pages 35
23. Joyce page 90
24. HCL D 483

The College and Church in Victorian times

CHAPTER SIX

COLLEGE LIFE 1856-1889

THE COLLEGE BECOMES ESTABLISHED

In the Hereford Cathedral Library are the Service Registers for St Michael's, which start in February 1857. In the early days, Ouseley held a Service of Choral Matins, which Watkins Shaw presumes was in addition to the two parochial services every Sunday. These 'extra' services continued until June 1857, when the pattern reverted to Evensong as the only choral service held on Sundays throughout Ouseley's life, with very few exceptions. From the very outset, the services in the church took precedence over everything else. Both from a musical and a devotional viewpoint, Ouseley insisted on everything being done in a proper manner and to the highest standards. This not only involved the music, but also the manner of those taking the service and the attitude and deportment of those taking part. For a boy in the choir, this involved very strict standards of punctuality, discipline and routine in everything connected with the worship in church and gave a very good training for later life. 'It was not a cut-and-dried musical performance for the congregation to listen to. It was an actual offering up of prayer and of praise to God.'(1)

It is very evident that these high standards which Ouseley introduced in the mid- nineteenth century have become an essential part of the present-day music of our great cathedrals and collegiate churches. As one would expect, whenever a boy or girl becomes a chorister, even in the lowliest parish church, higher standards of punctuality, effort and commitment are required in order to produce music that will inspire those who desire to worship, and strengthen their faith in God. Many were inspired by Ouseley's gift of the college and church to donate gifts themselves and he never ceased to be touched by their generosity. His initial benefactress, Georgina Rushout of Burford, had continued to enhance the church with her gifts on a regular basis.

It was Ouseley's intention that the choir should be able to provide music for the great festivals of the church, and unlike their later successors, they only had two vacations during the year, the period after Christmas and a long summer holiday. Most of the choristers in residence at St Michael's had been trained with Hampton and Ouseley at Langley and as a result, they already had a large repertoire. A detailed investigation of the Service Registers, singing 13 services a week for 40 weeks a year, would produce a figure of around 16,500 choral services during the 32 years leading up to Ouseley's death.

At St Michael's, it was necessary for both Ouseley and Hampton to sing with the choir and it was usually a requirement, sometimes to the detriment of the educational side, for any Headmaster or assistant master to be able to sing as well, which often caused a conflict of interest. Alderson and Colles, in their later history of St Michael's, felt that this was of crucial importance throughout its history. 'Perhaps St Michael's as a school might have prospered more than it did in its Founder's day, had the masters' claims as good scholars and teachers been made the first consideration. Some of them were inexperienced, but they were certainly good men in the choir.'(2)

On occasions, the small number of regular lay clerks were not able to attend both daily choral services due to other commitments and often there was only one of each part. On some occasions, the small number of regular lay clerks was sometimes augmented by visiting music students or other adults, and the numbers were such that the choir was able to sing more difficult music for double choir, such as Walmsley's Evening Service in Bb or Ouseley's own double choir setting.

Ouseley's duties as Warden of the College and Vicar of the Parish meant that these were his major responsibilities. (His other work as Precentor of Hereford Cathedral and Oxford Professor of Music is described in Chapter Seven.) He never contributed to the normal educational work of the school, or in the musical instruction of the choir. It has been mentioned in a previous chapter that he had not the patience to be a teacher, even if he had some of the other necessary qualities, but he was diligent in carrying out the duties that he assigned to himself and which were later enshrined in the College Statutes. He assumed ultimate responsibility for the general management, discipline and character of the college. He had very strict ideas about manners and this aspect of his character had a profound influence on most of the boys. The *St. Stephen's Review* of 1883 described the school at St. Michael's as 'The manners of Eton with the enthusiasm of Leipzig.'(3) He would get to know each boy individually, often taking a small group on a country walk, or when he had to pay a visit to someone in the area of the college. He was always happy in their company and they were happy when with him. He took great pains to prepare boys for their confirmation, always undertaking their regular instruction himself. He was forever writing, being described by his biographer and friend as a 'voluminous correspondent,' not writing long letters, but a great many letters to a great many people. He was always keen to keep in touch with Old Boys of St Michael's, some of whom may have only attended the college a short time, but such was his influence that they loved and respected him and wished to keep in contact. Despite his very busy schedule, writing to boys took no small part of his correspondence and was usually given priority. Once, having just received a letter from an Old Boy, which contained nothing of importance and which was merely an expression of good wishes, he sat down and wrote straight back, even though he was just about to leave to travel to Oxford. 'I *never* leave a boy's letter unanswered: it is not fair to their good nature, and I do not know when I may have time to write if I don't do it *at once.*'(4)

Perhaps it is surprising that the boys knew Ouseley so well and had great affection for 'The Bart', as they called him, since he was often away from the college for considerable periods of time for a variety of reasons. He took on all the responsibilities, together with all the worries and anxieties, inherent in such a position as his, and his highly-strung nature often drove him to a state of agitation and distress when he had to do something unpleasant, such as giving notice to an unsatisfactory member of staff. He was always concerned about the financial well-being of his College and worried a great deal about this and other matters.

> My dear..., Certainly, my name should be connected with the...Memorial Fund. I feel however, that I can't be as liberal towards it as I could have been last year; for, like all landed proprietors, I have had severe losses of late, and am retrenching in every possible *personal* way, so as not to injure my College. Still, of course I will contribute something. We have had such a wretched Christmas. I was down with bad influenza for a whole week... Most of the boys have had bad colds, and there was more barking than singing in church. Twice we have had to have a monotoned service, and no anthem. We could not have our annual concert for the farmers, nor could we have our children's treat, because of the prevalence of whooping-cough in the parish. So you see we have been in a bad way indeed! And when you add to all these miseries, consequent on a change of Headmasters and the fact of my having to dismiss a page-boy at a moment's notice for gross negligence, you will agree that I have had a very bad time of it. (5)

Joyce mentions that it was the domestic side of college life that Ouseley always found irksome and although he attended to matters conscientiously as Warden of his own College, he had no head for business and relied very much on the help of his friend, John Hampton, who would be his support for the next thirty years, apart from his time at University.

To complete the staff of the College, Ouseley appointed eight Fellows, including his friends Joyce and Rich, and these were added to in later years, up to a maximum of twenty-four non-resident Fellows. Some were clergy, some personal friends, some laymen, and in later years, others were former Masters at the College or prominent people in the musical work, such as Stainer. Ouseley hoped that the Fellows would contribute by their attendance at the yearly Commemoration and at other important times in the life of the College and he gave them specific responsibilities under his statutes of 1864.

Following the Opening Service, the custom was established of holding a Commemoration weekend at the end of September, centred around the Feast of St Michael and All Angels. (29 September). This involved Festival Services on the Saturday and the Sunday, with an Organ Recital, sometimes a concert, meetings of the Fellows and various social activities. Throughout the College's history, the yearly Commemoration attracted many musicians and clergy of national standing and there were special Preachers for these services. The following are a selection from the early Service Registers during Ouseley's lifetime.

1856 Reverend John Jebb

1859 The Very Reverend S. Kirwan, Dean of Limerick, who had sent his two sons to the College.

1861 Ouseley and Reverend John Jebb

1862 Reverend Wayland Joyce

1865 Reverend Sir Henry Baker, the noted hymn writer

1866 The Dean of Canterbury and the Archdeacon of Exeter

1867 Reverend J.B. Dykes and the Bishop of Oxford (RR Samuel Wilberforce)

1868 Ouseley and the Bishop of Hereford (RR James Attlay)

1870 The Dean of Lichfield and the Dean of York

1878 Reverend W. Walsham How (later Bishop of Wakefield)

1881 Reverend Edward King (later Bishop of Lincoln who also preached in 1884 and 1911) & Reverend H. Scott Holland (also 1885 and 1910)

1883 Reverend E.C. Corfe (an Old Boy and later Precentor of Truro Cathedral, he also preached in 1906 and 1915)

1889 Reverend F. W. Joyce, Reverend John Hampton and the Bishop of Korea (the Right Reverend C. Corfe, one of the first boys at the College. he also preached in 1897, 1903, 1907 and 1911)

The list reads like a 'Who's Who' of the Church of England at the time.

During Ouseley's lifetime, the numbers of boys stayed fairly constant, with 8 choristers and 8 probationers, and a few Commoners who paid fees for their education but did not sing in the choir. On many occasions he was anxious about pupil numbers.

Within a few months of the opening of the church and college, there developed an undercurrent of opposition. Concerns were expressed to Ouseley by the Reverend John Miller of Bockleton about the quantity of music in the weekday and Sunday evening Services, and in what could be termed a justification or apologia for his plans, Ouseley responded in the following manner.

It has pleased God in his goodness to endow me with a natural taste and facility in music and from my childhood, I always wished to devote this gift to His service. this object I kept steadily in view throughout my Oxford career as an undergraduate and Bachelor. I determined, in prosecution of this object, to take a degree in the Faculty of Music and then be ordained a Minister of the Church, believing that by these means, I could best attain that object on which my dearest affections and hopes had so long rested.

ie. – to do something to the music of the Sanctuary
  – to devote to the service of God as much as possible of these gifts which he had given to me.

When circumstances which you know first put St Michael's church into my head, I saw as it were, the hand of God in it – plainly directing me how to act. I was in prospect of the realisation of all that I had hoped for.

I conceived that it was my special province to organise a model choir service – to try to devote the highest developments of that noble art and I was, and am prepared to sacrifice if need be, wealth, rank, comfort, everything in short, for the attainment of this object. I think rightly, that many men might build churches, but few are able or willing to found model choirs.

At the same time, I felt that more ought to be done to gather together a parcel of choristers. Accordingly, I determined that we should board, lodge and educate gratuitously eight boys – to be chosen according to their vocal fitness for the office of a chorister, but preferences always being given to the sons and orphans of clergymen. (6)

Later in this letter of 14 March 1857, Ouseley wrote about the cost of building a college, finding a Master and, although others had helped financially, Ouseley remained sole Trustee, bound to support a certain number of boys and choristers and to support a liberal education. Eighteen months after the college opened, he wrote about the lack of funds and the problems of trying to make the college self-supporting.

I have therefore determined to risk an experiment and start a larger school than I first contemplated – one to a great extent founded upon the model of St. Peter's, Radley, [Radley College], though at the same time, free from its defects of extravagance.

As to doctrine, I beg to state that I hate Puritanism, having seen too much of it in my youth. I have seen far too much both of Romanism and Romanizing Anglicanism not to hate this extreme quite as cordially. I therefore hope and pray that in St Michael's College, nothing but the pure and solid theology of the Church of England may be taught, and that it may be strengthened to resist successfully, the various baneful influences with which we are now vexed on all sides...You will see that I could not very well act otherwise than I have acted without a very considerable sacrifice of principle and conscience. (7)

COLLEGE LIFE

Shortly after the opening of the College, Ouseley had appointed J.C. Hanbury as organist of the church, but he left in 1857 to become Chaplain of Wadham College, Oxford. His successor, John Stainer, recalled his first meeting with Ouseley.

> I first made Ouseley's acquaintance when a small chorister boy in St Paul's Cathedral He came to examine the choir boys and a few words of kindness, advice and encouragement which he spoke to me on that occasion were valuable to me for the rest of my life. I saw no more of him for some years until one day I happened to be playing deputy at St Paul's Cathedral (sometime in 1856) in the unusual absence of both Goss and Cooper. It was fortunate that those great lights were extinguished for that day. Sir Frederick Ouseley had come to ask whether either of them could recommend a young organist, and he came up into the organ loft, where he found me getting on very comfortably, and so in the evening of that day, he wrote me a very kind letter, asking if I would play his organ. (8)

After his voice had broken, Stainer kept his association with St Paul's and received organ lessons from the organist George Cooper. In 1857 at the age of 17, the young Stainer travelled to Tenbury.

> I found myself, after a railway journey to Worcester and then twenty miles on top of a coach, settled in the charming building which he had raised at his own cost for the advancement of church music. From it, a short cloister led into a church of beautiful design, rich in carved woodwork and stained glass, containing a fine organ and served with an admirable choir. Here, day by day, choral services of a high standard of excellence were maintained. (9)

John Hampton, who later succeeded Ouseley as Warden, remembered Stainer's arrival at Tenbury.

> He looked too young for the post, which we considered to be very important. However, Sir Frederick assured us that 'he would do' and we soon found out that this was true. All the while he was here I believe that he was most sincerely loved by us all and he was forward to help everyone with whom he came into contact. The curate, a first-rate mathematician, read with him and formed a very high opinion of his capabilities. We thought him bumptious, but we sound found out that we were mistaken, for he was humble enough and seemed glad to be plainly spoken to by any whom he

conceived had a right to speak. We were all right sorry to lose him and sincerely glad whenever he came to visit us. (10)

Life at Tenbury must have been rather strange and primitive for the young Stainer at first as aged 17, he was only a few years older than some of the boys.

Meals were served for the staff at High Table with the boys in the main body of the Hall. He gave piano lessons to the boys in the afternoon and after Evensong, studied or practised, often spending the evening with Ouseley, who had him playing some of the music from his Library. Apart from this aspect of his studies, Stainer continued to work at the organ and piano and wrote a good deal of music, including several anthems. *I saw the Lord* and *The righteous live* being the most well known. He was fond of sporting activities and played cricket and tennis with the boys and masters. (11)

Sung regularly at College meals – Ouseley's Grace

(At the end of 1859, Stainer left Tenbury to take up the post of organist of Magdalen College, Oxford, where he remained for 13 years, before becoming organist of St Paul's Cathedral, Langdon Colborne succeeding him at St Michael's.)

Almost a year after the opening of the College, Ouseley managed to find time to take a holiday, and in August 1857 visited the Farne Islands off the coast of Northumberland with the Reverend J B Dykes of Durham and other friends.

In 1858, Ouseley wrote to S.S. Wesley, asking him to contribute an anthem to his *Collection of Anthems for Certain Seasons and Festivals* (1861-66), but writing to Dykes a little later, he expressed his misgivings. 'I will make an attempt on Wesley, but he is such a mercenary fellow that I fear

Ouseley, c. 1858
Photo courtesy of Ouseley Trustees

the worst.'(12) Wesley's reply was very negative and unhelpful and not what Ouseley expected. 'I fear the publication will do great harm…There have been only two men in my time who could publish such a thing; my father and Mendelssohn…It vexes me to resist your bidding thus.'(13) Four years later, Wesley was corresponding with the Precentor of Ely, the Reverend W.E. Dicks, about church music and making decidedly unpleasant comments about Ouseley's music. 'And what are the things bought? I know that Novello has raked up from its hiding-place all the discarded trash of former times and published it as novelty, and choirs have spent their money thus – Sir Frederick Ouseley's Services, etc. The money all goes into Novello's pocket.'(14) Ouseley's friendship with Dykes continued to grow and unlike Wesley, Dykes felt able to contribute an anthem for Ouseley's new collection and *These are they* was the result.

In 1858 Ouseley sought to put the College on a much firmer financial footing and drew up a Memorandum, outlining his plans.

1. Get the College clear of Mortgage (£ 15,000), then it could be conveyed to Trustees and be endowed. He recommended 5 Trustees, including Colonel Rushout..

2. The gift of the patronage of the perpetual curacy of St. Michael's be made over to these Trustees. To nominate such clergy as will be best qualified to keep up the daily choral services in St Michael's church as now conducted.

3. The endowment of the different offices. Thus and thus only can this College be considered independent and perpetual.

Remainder of Mortgage	£ 15,000
Building bills	£ 500
Build a tower and west cloister	£ 3,000
Endow Wardenship	£ 5,000
Headmastership	£ 2,500
Six choristers	£ 4,000
Organist	£ 1,500
Three Clerks	£ 4,000
Fabric Fund	£ 1,000
TOTAL	£ 23,000

I commend these objects to those whom God has blessed with the means and heart to do good to such church schemes. May he inspire them with such a love for the spiritual advancement of those who are to be trained here to serve it, as may induce them to help forward this good work for Christ's sake, in whose Holy Name it has been undertaken. (15)

After this Memorandum had been drawn up, one would have assumed that Ouseley would have promoted an appeal to raise the necessary funds and thus put the College on a much more secure footing, but this did not happen. Watkins Shaw comments on the failure of this plan. 'Whether from diffidence, or some active discouragement, or any other reason, no such Appeal was prosecuted. And here we have one of the fundamental weaknesses of Ouseley's College. Its funding continued to rest entirely on himself and the institution had no broad base of public support.'(16)

Despite the lack of endowments, but with Ouseley's financial support, the College was becoming established, and in 1859, Ouseley felt able to let John Hampton go to University. Stainer had gone to compete for the Magdalen Organship on October 1st, 1859, and Hampton departed for Cambridge on 25 October. He became an undergraduate scholar at Queen's College, Cambridge, and gained his BA in June 1862, before returning to St Michael's to read for his Ordination at Winchester in July. It says much for Hampton's abilities that even before he had completed his degree studies at Cambridge, he was approached to become the Music Master at Uppingham School. Ouseley was so concerned at this development that he hurried across to Cambridge and was successful in persuading him to return to St Michael's after the successful completion of his degree. He promised Hampton the same salary for Curate in addition to what he had been receiving as Choirmaster, totalling about £ 240 per annum and a 'round sum in his will', if he was unable to keep that promise. Within a year, Hampton was offered a Minor Canonry and Precentor at Manchester Cathedral and two years later a similar post at Bristol. In 1877, Hampton was offered a Canonry at Westminster Abbey and later, the Precentorship of Worcester. It says much for Hampton's loyalty to Ouseley and St Michael's that he turned down all these posts and remained at Tenbury, despite the broken promises at various times.

From 1859, Ouseley worked with E G Monk, a pupil of MacFarran and Organist of York Minster from 1859 to 1883. Monk took a special interest in anglican chanting and together, they produced *The Psalter and Canticles pointed for Chanting*, which was published in 1862.

In June 1861, Ouseley stayed with J.B. Dykes at Durham, and in a letter to his sister, Dykes wrote: 'Sir Frederick Ouseley left me on Friday night; I have enjoyed his visit thoroughly. We were always so fully occupied, while he was with us, that I never found time to make him write for the Juvenile Tune book (a proposed children's hymnbook); only he quite takes to the idea, and has promised to send his contribution.'(17) During this time, the University of Durham recognised Dykes' great contribution to church music by awarding him an honorary degree of D Mus. and it was Ouseley who presented him to the Warden and Proctors of the University.

The following September, Ouseley invited Dykes to stay with him at St. Michael's, but due to a family illness, he was unable to take up the offer.

Despite all his other responsibilities, Ouseley was always busy composing, and wrote the anthem *It came to pass* for the re-opening of Lichfield Cathedral on 22 October 1861. It was used for the Commemoration Services at St. Michael's in 1889, a few months after Ouseley's death. The year was important for another reason, both for Ouseley and the Church of England, due to the publication of the first edition of *Hymns Ancient and Modern,* soon to be followed by new and enlarged editions. This first edition contained some 273 hymns, mostly older ones, but with a number of new and different tunes, mainly composed by Dykes, Ouseley and Monk, under the general editorship of Sir Henry Baker. Stephen Carpenter, in his *Church and People 1789-1889* felt that 'although possibly displaying elements that the more austere elements of a later period found unduly sentimental, it which represented a great advance on what had gone before.(18)

On 11 September 1862, Ouseley wrote to Dykes, expressing his regret on hearing about Dykes' resignation of the Precentorship at Durham, but praising his abilities.

> I know no man better qualified for such an office. This is no mere compliment, but a genuine expression of strong feeling on my part, which would come out.
>
> I like to think of you as my best coadjutor in matters choral.(19)

On June 30th 1863, Hereford Cathedral held a grand re-opening Service to celebrate its restoration. Ouseley wrote the anthem *Blessed be Thou,* especially for the occasion. The anthem *Behold now praise the Lord* was written for a large choral Festival held in Peterborough Cathedral the same month. Both anthems being composed for double choir.

Later in the summer of 1863, Ouseley gave a well-received paper on Church Music to a conference held in Manchester but a reporter of *The Standard* newspaper thought that Ouseley's remarks were too technical for the general reader.

In January 1864, Ouseley was able to discharge the mortgage on the College and was able to convey the College land, buildings and contents, together with a tiny financial endowment coming from rents and the advowson of St Michael's parish to Trustees, with the provision that they should appoint the Warden of the College to the living of the parish. The Trust Deed promulgated a body of Statutes which formally recognised the establishment of the College and church and the body of Fellows, who were to be responsible for the appointment of future Wardens after the death of the Founder. These Statutes were revised in 1921, 1927, 1957 and 1966, to take into account the changing circumstances of the College at the time. 'The object of the College is...to form a model for the Choral Service of the Church in these realms...and for the furtherance of this object to receive, educate and train boys in such religious, musical and secular knowledge as shall be most conducive thereto.'(20) The income to be received by the Trustees included land rents, income from other estates, stocks, funds, securities or endowments and monies held in the College Account at the Ludlow and Tenbury Bank

The following list of regulations was found in the Founder's papers after his death in 1889 and refer to the situation in the College in the year 1864, being regulations for some of the servants. They appeared in the College Magazine in 1934.

HOUSEMAID
–agrees to keep that part of the College clean which is allotted to her, namely all Sir Frederick's apartments, Drawing Room and Study and the Bedrooms over them, to make all the beds in the Dormitory, write down their washing for all the boys and keep the whole College clean, with the assistance of the under-housemaid. To mend Sir Frederick's clothes and the house linen. To sit down to needlework as soon as she can in the day. To rise at 8 am and go to bed at 10 pm, to be neat and clean in her person, not to wear artificial flowers, to be obedient to the Matron, not to go out without her leave. If she wishes to leave, to give and receive a month's warning or wages.

SUGGESTIONS
The Matron to always dine in the kitchen with all the servants, carve for them, and not to allow the meat to remain on the table after she has left it. No one to have anything to eat without her knowledge; for her to be responsible for the provisions. No to engage young girls as kitchen maid or under-housemaid, never to leave one younger than 25 years of age in the College.

AGREEMENT WITH THE BUTLER
He is to take charge of the plate, lamps, china and everything belonging to the Pantry. All the casks and utensils connected with brewing. All the ale, small-bear and cider. To keep the lists and keys of them, and never to leave them with anyone except the Matron. To be careful of all ale, small-beer and cider, not to have more used in the family than their allowance. No tradespeople or servants' friends to have it without leave. he is to clean the plate, glass, lamps and china in the Pantry; the tables and windows downstairs, to assist in taking up the carpets during the vacation, to shut the shutters and see that all the doors are locked at night, all the lamps, candles and fires put out, to wait on Sir Frederick; and to clean his clothes. Nothing to be sent for without leave, and the things to be entered in their respective books. Not tradesman to be sent for to work in or out of the house without leave. If anything goes wrong in the house, always to inform Sir Frederick at the time, not to go beyond the ground without leave, nor to be away from the

College after 6 pm in winter and 9 pm in summer without Sir Frederick's leave, to rise early, to be neat and clean in his dress, punctual to hours; no perquisites allowed, to put coals on the fires, to answer the door, no to be out when people are likely to call; to brew, clean the tables (look after the work people). tea, sugar allowed. When he wishes to leave, to give or receive a month's warning or wages. Not to allow anyone to go into the Pantry except servant working under him.

ALLOWANCE OF DRINK

The men-servants to have a pint of ale at their dinner and a pint at supper, and what small-beer or cider they like. Boys probably only small-beer. The women-servants to have half a pint of ale *either* at their dinner or supper, or what small-beer or cider they like. Any persons dining with the servants to be on the same allowance. Tenants or Farmers to have a pint of ale. messengers and other persons, small-beer. (21)

In 1865, the new chapel at Hurstpierpoint College was opened for services. it was described by *The Guardian* as 'One of the noblest efforts of ecclesiastical art that have yet been set on foot even in these days of church-building and restoration.'(22)

Nathaniel Woodard and his growing group of Woodard Schools were becoming a force in the world of church music. At the services in his schools, Woodard allowed plain-chant, the use of metrical psalms, and with the persuasion of the noted hymn writer, J.M. Neale, hymns were allowed as well. Anthems and settings by modern composers were however, strictly forbidden. In 1865, at the opening of the Chapel at Hurstpierpoint, John Dayson, the organist, was brave enough to include choral settings of the canticles in the service. Woodard was furious at this innovation, and when he discovered after the service that the settings were by Ouseley, his rage knew no bounds, Ouseley being an outspoken critic of plainchant. After this, Woodard wrote an unpleasant letter to the Headmaster of Hurstpierpoint, complaining about the use of these modern settings. 'Ouseley is the sworn opponent of Church Music. I can make every excuse for secular men liking that kind of music. It is effective and brings credit to the performers. But that is not what we seek.'(23)

Despite Woodard's antagonism, the use of choral worship in his schools and colleges grew rapidly as more schools were opened and this became the norm in the rapidly developing public school system.

On 25 September 1867, J B Dykes travelled to Tenbury to be Ouseley's guest and to preach at Commemoration. Writing to his wife on 1 October, he tells her about St Michael's.

Sir Frederick and I met at the Tenbury Station, he having come from Worcester and I from Ludlow, so we walked together over the fields to the College, and had a quiet Friday dinner together, and then went to Evensong. Yesterday afternoon, I had a lovely walk to a village called Little Hereford, where there is an interesting old Norman church. In coming back, I missed my road; it was approaching 6 pm, and time for Evensong, and I ought to have been back at the College. But suddenly I discovered I was wrong; I heard in the dim distance the College bell ringing for prayers – then I lost it. At last I recovered my path, and made the best of my way home. But I was too late to go into the choir, so I went into the nave of the church, and very glad I was that I had done so, for I had no idea until then what a charming church St Michael's was. It was all vested in festal costume. There is a very high gilded metal Rood Screen, and some lighted candles on the top of it. The altar has a large Baldachino over it. Candles were arranged at intervals, on the top. There was a lovely white altar frontal and the whole effect was delightful...The bells are ringing for our grand Commemoration service. I must put on my surplice in a few minutes…The Bishop of Oxford left us yesterday. He was so nice and pleasant, and kind, and amusing. He preached a beautiful sermon on Sunday night on the Ministry of the Holy Angels. He intoned the Absolution and Benediction so well.(24)

The Choir Schools of today hold regular Voice Trials in order to attract new boys and girls to sing in their choirs. These take the form of singing, sight-reading and perhaps a small academic test, but in Ouseley's time, he actually travelled around the country himself, choosing boys for his choir. In a letter to a Mrs. Hoskyns written from London on 20 August 1867, he gives his apologies and explains his reasons. 'Many thanks for your kind invitation, which was forwarded to me here, where I am come for the purpose of choosing boys for St Michael's choir. We re-assemble on Friday next and I shall have guests – new boys' parents – to look after for several days – therefore I am obliged reluctantly to forego the great pleasure of paying you a visit at Harewood.(25)

Almost since the opening service in 1856, considerable problems had been experienced with the Flight and Robson organ in the church. Ouseley decided it would have to be repaired and entrusted the work to a new firm, Harrisons of Rochdale, (the forerunners of Harrison and Harrison, who now look after the St Michael's organ.). They carried out considerable repairs, rebuilding the organ and enlarging it to 65 stops, and on 8 October 1868, the organ was re-opened and the new Bishop of Hereford (Dr Atlay) preached the sermon. Ouseley composed the anthem *Great is the Lord* to mark the occasion. He had already gained a national reputation, both for his advice on organs and for his lectures on choral music, and on 28 January 1869, was invited to Norwich Cathedral to give a lecture on the choral service.

Ouseley's other responsibility at Tenbury was as Vicar of the parish of St Michael's. He now felt that the village should have a parish day school, and John Hampton took on the responsibility of raising funds, mainly by voluntary subscription. The school was built by 1870 and enlarged in 1876. 'Ouseley personally took on the responsibility of the entire management of the school, appointing the teachers, and was by far the biggest contributor to its financial support.'(26) A.S. Miles, a partner in the Tenbury firm of solicitors, was also the College Bursar and a former churchwarden of St Michael's. He became Treasurer of the school in 1888, and four local farmers were also appointed as additional managers in 1895. The school closed in 1937.

Ouseley was always keen to reply to Old Boys' letters and in late 1870, he had received one from Charles Tindall Gatty, a boy who had only been at the College just a year (1861-62), and who was now living in America. Ouseley had obviously made a great impression on him during his short time at the College and he had sent Ouseley the music of four hymns which he had composed. As ever, Ouseley's reply, dated December 13th 1870, was gracious, and offered much helpful advice and one felt that he was honoured to receive this letter from an old Boy.

> I am always glad to hear from former boys – and was therefore pleased to get your letter, and likewise to see that you still cultivate music. You ask me to tell you what I think of your four tunes – And so I will, although I fear my criticisms will not be satisfactory to you altogether. [Ouseley then gives a detailed criticism of each of Gatty's four hymn tunes]...And now that I have exasperated you sufficiently with my criticisms, let me tell you that there is that in your four hymns which proves to me that if you work at harmony steadily, you will one day be able to do right well as a composer. Only do not run before you can walk. Such errors as the above, if reviewed by a <u>hostile</u> critic in a London musical paper, would ruin your musical reputation by anticipation, so if you publish your tunes, pray correct the harmonies first. In a hymn tune, or a chant, which has to be often repeated, every little error is of worse effect than it would be in a song, or ordinary drawing room piece. Therefore in hymns, the strictest observance of rules is required.
>
> Forgive me speaking my mind – I only do so because you ask me – and because I wish to be of use to you in any way I can. (27)

Also in 1870, the College, helped by a grant from the Ecclesiastical Commission, built a vicarage on land which it owned outside the College grounds and across the road. This firstly provided accommodation for teachers, but was later occupied by Ouseley's successors as Wardens, Hampton and Swann.

The next year, the College was honoured by a visit from Lewis Carroll on 11 July which he recorded in his Diary. 'St Michael's is a very pretty place. We arrive in time for the evening service, which is choral. There are about 25 boys, meals in Hall, with a high table for masters.' (28)

Tenbury Musical Society.

THE

FIRST CONCERT

(FIFTEENTH SEASON)

WILL BE GIVEN IN THE

Corn Exchange Hall, Tenbury,

ON

WEDNESDAY · JULY · 1 · 1885.

WHEN

The Rev. Sir F. A. G. Ouseley's

SACRED ORTATORIO,

The Martyrdom of St. Polycarp,

WILL BE PERFORMED.

LEADER OF THE BAND - - - - MR. W. CLAXTON.
CONDUCTOR - - - - - - - REV. J. HAMPTON.

——:o:——

Doors open at 7.30; to commence at 8; Carriages may be ordered for 10.30.

15th Anniversary concert – Edward Elgar and F. F. Elgar listed on reverse

Hampton, Ouseley's choirmaster, was appointed as Sub-Warden of the College in 1869, but without stipend. He was able to involve himself in the local community and was responsible for founding the Tenbury Music Society in 1870. Each year, it was Ouseley's custom to bring his choir to Tenbury to join with a choir of local people in putting on some large-scale musical work. Over the years, these included works by many well-known composers and some of Ouseley's own compositions. On July 1st 1885, the first concert of the 15th Anniversary programme took place in the hall of the Tenbury Corn Exchange, when the combined choirs and orchestra performed Ouseley's *The Martyrdom of St Polycarp*. Ouseley himself sang alto, and the basses included his friends, F.W.Joyce and A.S. Miles. The College Organist, William Claxton was leader of the band and the Conductor was Hampton. The second half of the concert included a work by Walmisley and Mendelssohn's *Hear my prayer*. On the back page of the programme for this concert was a list of orchestral players who had played for the Society at various times, among whom were Frederick Elgar on oboe and his younger brother, Edward Elgar, playing the violin. The following year, the Tenbury Society produced a booklet about its history, listing the works which had been performed since 1870. They included Ouseley's oratorio, *Hagar* in 1874, his anthem *The Lord is the True God* and Stainer's *Daughter of Jairus* in 1883. Ouseley also contributed both instrumental quartets and marches and Claxton a number of madrigals.

LADIES AND GENTLEMEN

(NOT MEMBERS)

Who have assisted at the T.M.S. Concerts.

Violin.

Alexander, Mr. A.	...	Wigan.
Arkwright, Mr. J. H.	...	Hampton Court.
Claxton, Mr. W.	...	Algiers.
Colborne, Dr.	...	Hereford.
Elgar, Mr. E. W.	...	Worcester.
Glennie, Mr. W. B.	...	Wimbledon.
Mar, The Earl of	...	London.
Martin, Mr.	...	Knighton-on-Teme.
Powell, Mr.	...	Thame, Oxon.
Richmond, Mr.	...	Carlisle.
Rogers, Mr. C.	...	Stanage Park.
Salt, Mr. B.	...	Shrewsbury.
Teague, Mr.	...	Cheltenham.
Watkis, Mr. Theo.	...	Ironbridge.
Woodward, Mr. E. G.	...	Gloucester.

Viola.

Bartholomew, Mr. R.	...	Ludlow.
Cooper Key, Rev.	...	Stretton, Hereford.
Price, Mr. W.	...	Ludlow.
Teague, Mr.	...	Cheltenham.

Violoncello.

Hill, Mr.	...	Birmingham.
Morris, Rev. M. C. F.	...	York.
Symonds, Mr. R.	...	Hereford.
Teague, Mr.	...	Cheltenham.
Waite, Mr.	...	Bristol.

Contra Basso.

Brookes, Mr.	...	Worcester.
Hardman, Mr.	...	Ludlow.
Moss, Mr.	...	Tenbury.
Pimm, Mr.	...	Gloucester.
Teague, Mr.	...	Cheltenham.

Oboe.

| Elgar, Mr. F. F. | ... | Worcester |

Flute.

Bailey, Mr. R. C.	...	Ipswich.
Jones, Mr. T.	...	Ludlow.
Anstis, Mr.	...	Tenbury.
Yeates, Mr.	...	Onibury.

Clarinet.

Brooke, Mr. O.	...	Bristol.
De Brisay, Rev.	...	London.
Helmore, Rev. F.	...	Canterbury.
Whinfield, Mr. E. W.	...	Worcester.

Bassoon.

| Duncombe, Rev. W. D. V. | | Hereford. |
| Roberts, Mr. | ... | Birmingham. |

Cornet.

| Martin, Mr. | ... | Ludlow. |
| Page, Mr. G. | ... | Tenbury. |

Trombone.

| Hughes, Mr. | ... | Cheltenham. |

Harp.

| Hawkshaw, Mrs. E. B | ... | Weston, Ross. |

Despite the attentions of Harrison on the church organ in 1868, problems were still continuing and in 1873, Ouseley finally called in the famous organ firm of Henry Willis, in a last attempt to rectify what was a very unsatisfactory situation. 'He undertook to dismantle the entire instrument, take it to his London factory, and bring it back within five months. Willis agreed to use only the best parts of the old instrument.'(29) His work was so successful that, with the addition of a few tonal alterations and periodic overhauls, his organ of 1873 is that heard in the church today.

One of the new boys who started at St Michael's in 1873 was to become very famous in later life. George Robert Sinclair later became the first organist of Truro Cathedral before being appointed to Hereford in 1889, where he remained until his death in 1917. He was a great friend of Elgar and often included organ transcriptions of new Elgar works in the recitals he gave at St Michael's during the Commemoration weekends from 1889 onwards.These included Elgar's *Enigma Variations* and the Prelude and Angels' Farewell from *The Dream of Gerontius*.

Also in 1873, Ouseley edited *A Collection of the Sacred Compositions of Orlando Gibbons* from the original manuscripts and part-books. This was a very difficult and time-consuming occupation, but one which has been of great benefit to musicians ever since.

The famous Victorian cleric and diarist, Francis Kilvert, had a great interest in church music and paid a visit to Tenbury in 1873 and was pleased by what he heard. 'A full choral service, the Te Deum long and drawling, fine Venite and Psalms. Sir F. Gore Ouseley intoned part of the prayers in a high, cracked voice.'(30)

Ouseley addressed a Church Congress in Brighton in October 1874 and welcomed the progress that had been made in the development of choral music in parish churches, but queried why it was not happening everywhere.

In 1874, the Musical Association was formed and Ouseley gave lectures on a variety of topics over the next few years.

January 1876	Considerations on the History of Ecclesiastical Music of Western Europe
March 1879	On the early Italian and Spanish Treatises on Counterpoint and Harmony
February 1882	On some Italian and Spanish Treatises on Music of the seventeenth century
February 1886	On the position of organs in churches

On 11 February 1875, he wrote to Dykes, sending him a prospectus of the College and talking about its future prospects.There had obviously been some problems the previous year, both financially and perhaps also with staff and Ouseley was pleased that matters had been settled to his satisfaction. 'I am glad to tell you that I have got a really good and

efficient Headmaster and that the prospects of St Michael's College are fair. After the anxieties of last year, it is indeed a comfort to feel secure again.'(31) At that time, the fees were quoted as being £ 120 a year for Commoners, £ 60 for sons of clergy, who had preference for any vacancy as a probationer, £ 40 for probationers, with choristers paying no fees at all.

Choristers waiting to process through cloisters, c. 1870-1880
Photo courtesy of Ouseley Trustees

Later in 1875, a number of prominent musicians were hard at work writing articles for the *Dictionary of Music*, edited by Sir George Grove. These included Davison, Prout, Hullah, Stanford, Pauer, Sullivan, Dannreuther, Parry and Ouseley. 'He also contributed an article on *Augmentation* but soon became too ill to complete its counterpart on *Diminution*, so Grove turned to Parry, who quickly obliged.' (32)

As a well-known composer, Ouseley was always receiving unsolicited compositions from people in all walks of life, asking his opinion on their efforts. He wrote to a Miss Mounsey from Christ Church, Oxford on 14 November 1876 expressing his thanks at receiving her songs and admitting in a very diplomatic way that he has not heard them yet. 'Sir Frederick Ouseley presents his compliments to Miss Mounsey and begs to express to her how obliged and gratified he is by the songs she has been so kind as to send him. Although he has not yet seen them, he may confidently feel sure anticipations of the pleasure they will afford him.'(33)

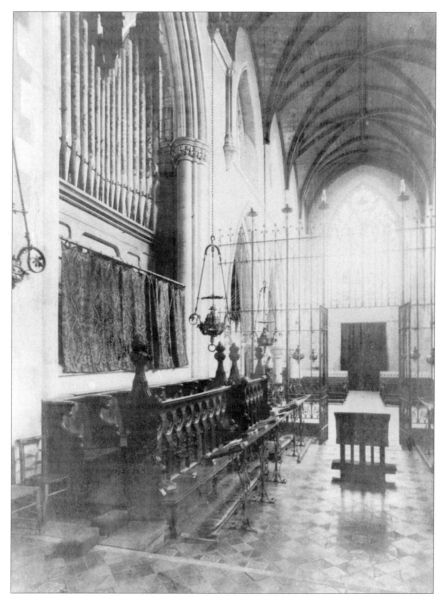

Chancel and Organ
Photo courtesy of Ouseley Trustees

In April 1879 James Turle, organist of Westminster Abbey since 1831, visited Tenbury. On his return to Westminster, he wrote to Ouseley, thanking him for his hospitality. 'My homeward journey is now safely performed. I now send you the promised 'photo' of my humble self. Let me seize the opportunity of thanking you again for your kindness and attention during my happy soujourn at St. Michael's – never to be forgotten' (34)

In September 1878, Monty Alderson had arrived at the College as a new boy and began an association that was to last until his death in July 1962. On 27 April 1883, Ouseley wrote to Alderson's father, Canon Frederick Alderson, expressing his concern that the Organist (William Claxton) had been negligent in his music lessons.

> He had not taken such pains as I think he ought to have done in his training of your boy in instrumental music (most likely to have been the piano).

> I am dissatisfied with him because I think that he has neglected his duties through laziness and one result has been that Monty's musical talents have not had proper justice done to them. I really do not like to lie down on him too heavily. Still, I feel that he must either devote more time and energy to his pupils, or reduce his charges, or leave St Michael's. (35)

(Claxton had been a boy at St Michael's, 1862 – 68, becoming Organist in 1877 and staying until 1886. He later took Holy Orders and was a Fellow of St. Michael's from 1894 until 1921.)

In a letter to Alderson dated 24 September 1883, just over two months since Alderson had left St Michael's to go to Winchester, Ouseley writes, expressing fears about his own health. 'I am sorry to say that I still cough and am by no means in strong health, which is a nuisance now that the hard work of Michaelmas is at hand...I see that you sign yourself as my "former affectionate pupil". I hope that does not mean that your affection as well as your pupillage has become a matter of history. (36) Six months later, writing to him on 26 March 1884, Ouseley apologises for not writing sooner. 'but in January I was very ill and I am supposed to be quite right now, though still in doctor's hands. It has made me feel permanently older and weaker than before...Here we are all well and everything goes on smoothly, the only drawback being that we are not full, having only five boys beside the choir. (37)

A few days later, Ouseley had recovered sufficiently to go away during the Easter holidays and went to Scotland with some friends. He received a letter from Monty, telling him that he had bought a piano. On his return to College on 26 April, Ouseley wrote back, expressing great interest in it and asking all sorts of questions. 'I suspect it is of short compass. If it requires much doing up, it will not be a very cheap bargain, but that may not be the case. You say that it is perfect order, but does that mean that

Photograph taken late 1870's or early 1880's (Ouseley 2nd from left on back row.)

nothing need be done to it? Is it not a tone below pitch? All these things have to be considered.'(38) Writing again on 6 May and giving further advice, Ouseley made a suggestion about raising the pitch. 'The best way to raise the pitch of a flat instrument is to shift the keys. ie. to put the C key where the E flat key should be, for instance. But this could cost money, perhaps a pound or so, and should only be done by an experienced musical mechanician. It is not safe to tune the strings to a higher pitch, for not only would they break, but the framework might yield under the additional strain...We had a delightful time of it in Scotland, barring the keen East winds and I enjoyed my ten days there greatly.'(39) On 26 October the same year, Ouseley returned from a visit to Hampshire, and told Alderson of the massive accumulation of letters [33] awaiting his attention on his arrival home. His letter to Alderson was the 19th he had written that day.

For Ouseley, the summer of 1884 had been an extremely busy one. There was a concert at St Michael's after the end of term and he had then to attend to his Precentorial duties at Hereford for most of the summer. At the beginning of September, he went to Worcester for the duration of the Three Choirs Festival, where his Canticles were sung at the Inaugural Service on September 6th. 'I was there all the time and enjoyed it thoroughly.' (40)

Ouseley c.1870's

In April 1884, the Edinburgh University Tercentary was celebrated and there was a gathering of all the distinguished men of learning in Europe. Amid such a company, Sir Charles Halle and Ouseley were both nominated for Honorary Degrees(LLD). Afterwards, Ouseley wrote to the Principal Sir Alexander Grant.

Now that your grand and most interesting Festival has come to a successful termination, I cannot refrain from writing not only to

87

congratulate you thereupon. but also to express my deep sense of the great privilege accorded me in being allowed a place among the number of distinguished and representative guests upon whom your University has conferred the honour of a degree. Among the many great successes of your Festival, I feel bound to refer to one which had special interest for me, the students' concert. It so happens that I have never before had an opportunity of seeing my old friend, Sir Herbert Oakeley, conduct a concert, and I was astonished to find in him such a complete mastery of the difficult art of judiciously and efficiently wielding the *baton*, an art not given to every musician. The zeal displayed by the students, the accuracy and heartiness of their performance, were also most delightful to witness, and contributed not a little to the success of the concert.(41)

On 10 October 1884, Ouseley wrote to a friend about the building of the new Liverpool Cathedral, but also expressed his doubts about the intentions of the Government towards the Church of England.

I am very much obliged to you for the interesting documents you have been kind enough to send me regarding the proposed cathedral for Liverpool. I presume the paper is written by yourself. No doubt, such a town as Liverpool ought to have a first class cathedral, but I fear that as soon as the money is collected for such a purpose, our church will be disendowed and all such monies confiscated to the state. (42)

Over the later years of his life, Ouseley was very concerned about the financial future of the College owing to a considerable reduction in his income due to the agricultural depression. Over the thirty years since the College opened, he had never managed to make it self-supporting, and its isolation and distance from large centres of population may have been another contributary factor. Land values had decreased, with a consequent reduction in rental income from his various landholdings and this meant that once again he had to look for ways of reducing costs in order to keep the College solvent. More than once, his good friend and neighbour, Georgina Rushout, was able to step in and assist him financially, as well as showing great generosity in providing Altar vestments, sacramental plate, the stained-glass windows of the apse, and many additions to the College Library. These financial problems were particularly noticed at the Commemorations of 1884, 1885 and 1886, when the College could expect to have many visitors. At each of the services, it was advised that Offertories would be given to the Sustenation Fund, 'for which they are urgently needed.' Such occasions as these helped to make visitors aware of the problems the College faced. Many of these people had been connected with the College for some considerable time and were perhaps able to offer some assistance. At the Commemoration Concert held on 29 September 1885, there were shouts of laughter from the audience when it was announced that ' the gentleman who was to have sung the *Romanza* from Donizetti's *Don Pasquale* is sick in Liverpool.'(43) A further handwritten annotation in the evening's programme also commented on the Bass aria from *Qui sdegno non s'accendo* from Mozart's *The Magic Flute*. 'Mr. Lambert was as heavy as lead!' (44)

REMINISCENCES

C. J. CORFE (1856 – 1857)

Of the Consecration Services I will not say much, the Bishop of Hereford (Hampden) was there of course and there were a number of clergy and members of other choirs which augmented our feeble efforts. The morning anthem *O Praise the Lord of Heaven* was written specially for the occasion by Sir George Elvey of Windsor and I have never forgotten the voice of the boy who sang the treble part in the verse *O pray for the peace of Jerusalem.* That boy was from the Chapel Royal Choir, and his name was Arthur Sullivan. He was then sixteen and the voice, wonderfully preserved and developed, was then at its best. I can hear it now, and have heard it, especially at Michaelmas – in all parts of the world. Sullivan was already recognised as a genius – he had won the Mendelssohn Scholarship, and was soon to go to Leipzig for his training in music.

The College not being ready for us, we were sent back to Langley for a time – leaving all the music books behind. When we reached Lovehill House and resumed our humdrum life, I remember that there was only one copy of Boyce, an organ copy, which Mr. Fyffe, who sometimes acted as deputy-organist, appropriated and treated us, for a whole week, to Rogers in D (morning and evening). How tired of it we were. After that we were able to sing it by heart. But though we returned immediately to Lovehill House, it was only to prepare for a final departure. Before the winter, we were divided into two parties, of which one was to spend, with the Head-Master, Norman, who became Warden of Radley, a few months at Tenby in Pembrokeshire, where we pursued our studies – again under picnic conditions. the other party of boys went to Spring Grove to remain there until the College was ready to receive us. This was not until the early spring of 1857, when we boys from Tenbury made our first acquaintance with a cubicle. The garden and grounds of the College were still strewn with the materials of which the College and church had been built, blocks of alabaster and stones taken from the quarry occupying what is now the ground where you play chevy and prisoner's base. *(the playground.)* No trees had been planted and there were no attempt at gardens, for the workmen were still about. This untidy spot was called *Balaclava,* the name of a battle which was much written about during the Russian War in the Crimea, which had come to an end the previous year. And so it came about that my name was the first name in the register of St Michael's College.

Let me only add that in the spring of 1857, my voice broke, and I left the College until my return as Assistant Master in 1865. (45)

MONTAGUE ALDERSON 1878

My arrival there on the Michaelmas Festival evening (1878) was peculiar. I was brought by my parents a month later than the beginning of the lst half of the School year (by permission of the Founder) and without rehearsal, dumped down in my seat, just below the Warden's Stall, arrayed in an open-fronted surplice, with singers all around me, fiddlers in front, masses of clergy from Bishops downwards, all pouring forth, to the accompaniment of the superb Willis organ, *Jerusalem on high, my song and city is.* I was a little fat boy of just over 9, parted for the first time from my devoted parents, and lost in wonder and amazement in the midst of so august an assembly, to begin what has proved to be the happiest period of my educational life. Ouseley, (we called him *The Bart.)* his memory is as fresh and green today as it ever was long ago. He still stands before me *colossal* and *unassailable.* He will ever be my life-long talisman to the end, for his merit and example. We glibly talk of waywardness and lack of stability in callow youth, but surely in this case it is untrue. Would that my feeble voice...in this centenary year of the Foundation of the College (1956)...might impart to this generation somewhat of the value of the glorious heritage bequeathed to us. The Reverend John Hampton was my teacher and the best voice and choir trainer anyone could possibly have had. Mr Rogers (the Head-Master) and Mr Hunt, his assistant, enabled me to develop my talents, such as they were, in scholarship. Mr Claxton (the organist), gave me pianoforte lessons of a somewhat desultory sort, although he was a most capable and accurate accompanist under the direction of the Sub-Warden who was choirmaster. (Hampton). Mr. Budinger, (the Village Schoolmaster), an outstanding calligraphist, doing all our choir book copying, gave us writing exercises. Monsieur De Vit, a dear old Frenchman, coming weekly from Bewdley, taught us French. My conscience now-a-days tells me how wrongly we took advantage of his inability to maintain order in class. His invariable punishment for our misbehaviour was writing out 100 lines, which we rarely did. The above was all the Teaching Staff needed for 16 boys and 4 non-singers (called by us choristers most unjustifiably *'Commoners'.*) Our pastimes out of school consisted of hockey on the playground and in the summer months, cricket on the school field.

Locomotion in those days was very limited. We had to rely on Shanks' Mare for walks across the Common, to the Poet's Stone at Leysters, or the Red Rock down by the River Teme. For wheel traffic, there was only a very high dogcart in the Village for hire, although at times a horsebrake from Tenbury could be obtained. Very occasionally, trips were taken by train, and these on a single line...We were just a lot of healthy lads – good mannered and well-behaved – coming mostly from country clerical homes. (46)

R T RICHMOND (1881)

It seems but yesterday that I stood at the front door of St Michael's, listening to the strident clang of the bell which my father had just rung. The bell seemed to shriek "Here's a new boy! a new boy!" I was very depressed, for I had seldom been from home before, and had travelled many miles from the North, leaving, as I thought, everything that was worth living far behind for ever. I was quite shocked that my father should be so jolly about it all; but then, he was going to renew his old friendship with Sir Frederick, and I was going to school for the first time. A tall footman in livery opened the door, and I shuddered as I passed the threshold, for the man reminded me of a prison warder I had once seen in front of the county jail at home. My Father went in to see Sir Frederick and I was handed over to a boy, who said he would look after me and introduce me to my new classmates. For some time I was the target of many questions, which I answered to the best of my ability. After a time, I was shown my cubicle, and that evening unpacked my box, shedding a few silent tears when I remembered that my dear mother had packed it. But I was very young.

I was given a locker in the schoolroom, and one in the corridor; also I was rigged out with a cap, gown and surplice; the surplice was very large, but then I was not very big. Not being a Chorister (for I had failed the voice test), I did more listening than singing; but the power at my elbow was my violin, on which instrument I had acquired some considerable skill, for I had previously been very well taught by a good master and an accomplished player.

We played rugby, but I do not recollect that we ever played any matches with other schools. Cricket was played in the season, but the team was generally augmented by the masters and some of the staff. We played Bromsgrove, Ludlow, Hereford Cathedral School and a local club or two.

The corridors and dormitory used to get bitterly cold in winter, for the heating apparatus was not very efficient; still, potatoes baked in their skins by the schoolroom fire counteracted this deficiency to some extent. Our food was sufficient, very plain, and sometimes very bad! Our differences were occasionally settled by fights – not vulgar rough and tumble scraps, but organised and properly-arranged combats, under the boxing rules, without the gloves. These combats were not interfered with by the authorities, unless brought to their immediate notice, and more than one lasting friendship was the outcome of a battle. We had a boys' library, a favourite book being Catlin's *North American Indians,* and this book was indirectly the cause of a conflagration. A wigwam of considerable size was built at the bottom of the playing-field near the Quarry wood. Being summer, it got very dry, and the chief 'brave', (feeling chilly I suppose), lit a fire in it. Well, he had just enough time to get out before the flames reached the tops of the trees. It was a glorious fire, did considerable damage to the trees, and required the help of nearly all the servants to put it out. The 'brave' fully expecting to be called upon for Investiture as a Companion of the Order of the Boot, spent the afternoon in tense, nervous uncertainty. The honour was not granted to him, and, with the exception of an inconvenience in sitting down for a few days, he resumed 'normal conditions,'

We held a remarkable licence as far as bounds were concerned, and we never abused this licence. The free country life which we were allowed to lead was the means of making a robust health in many of us who might otherwise have been delicate. I had an innate love of sport, and, together with a boy who is now my oldest and greatest friend, we fished the Cadmore Brook. Many a tasty little trout we did get – sometimes by fair means, sometime by foul...Those days were a veritable sportsman's delight. My friend and I also used to beat for the gentlemen who shot over the College estate.

I was hit by a stray ricochet pellet, but as it struck me on that portion of my anatomy on which there is more flesh than sunburn, I was none the worse. Occasionally, we would meet 'The Bart' on one of our walks and when asked if we liked the old music, I said that I did not like it because it seemed so much the same, but that it always ended up all right. The Bart replied that 'when you have heard more of it you will like it very much.' He was right, for years afterwards, when I lived within hail of two Cathedral towns, I often used to ride in to hear my old favourites, Byrd, Gibbons, Purcell, Croft and Boyce.

Alas! All good things come to an end. Towards the end of one term I was sent for. Sir Frederick wished to see me. With knees knocking together, I put on my gown and tottered to his study. At once I saw by his face (such a kind and expressive face), that it was 'nowt vara serious.' He put his hand on my shoulder and said, 'Your father has been made a Canon Residentiary of ———, and he has told me you will go to a new home when you leave this term? New home? Leave this term? I was stunned. When I realised it all, I wrote and expostulated with my father for accepting such a preferment, and his rashness in taking me away. 'Twas no good, for I left that term to go to a new home and a new school.

Did I learn anything at St Michael's College? A smattering of Latin and Greek and Mathematics, perhaps, for I was ever a lazy dog. Why worry about the unknown value of x when I was top of the school in Shakespeare. Why stare at Greek verbs when could practise my fiddle? Why thump Bradley's *Latin Prose* in despair, when I had *Darwin on Worms*, beautifully bound, as a prize for drawing?

But did I learn anything at St Michael's College? Yes. I learnt to keep myself clean, to rely upon myself, to appreciate and try and act up to all that was good; and last but not least, to keep my memory fresh for the best and happiest days of my life. (47)

REFERENCES

1. Joyce p. 101
2. Alderson & Colles P.44
3. St. Stephen's Review (quoted in Joyce p. 108)
4. Joyce p. 109
5. Joyce p. 112
6. HCL D 863
7. HCL D 863
8. RCO Calendar 1889
9. Stainer – *The Character of Ouseley* (Given to the Musical Association 1889-90)
10. Obituary in *The Musical Times* 1901
11. Stainer – *The Character of Ouseley*
12. Quoted in College Magazine December 1978
13. Quoted in College Magazine December 1978
14. Quoted in College Magazine December 1978
15. HCL D 863
16. Watkins Shaw p. 32
17. Fowler – Life and Letters of J.B. Dykes P. 74
18. Carpenter – Church and People P. 377
19. Fowler – P. 80
20. College Statutes 1864
21. College Statutes 1864
22. *The Guardian* (quoted in Otter p 176)
23. Rainbow – The Choral Revival in the Anglican Church p. 241
24. Fowler- pages 114-115
25. BUISSC LAdd 5209
26. HCL D 863
27. BUISSC Ladd 5206
28. College Magazine 1981
29. Roger Judd – St. Michael's Church Guide
30. Three Choirs Festival Programme – Hereford 1979
31. HCL D 863
32. Dibble – C. Hubert Parry – His Life in Music p. 128
33. MFCMCMLNY – Letter from Ouseley to Gatty, December 13th. 1870
34. Letters to Maria Hackett (Royal College of Music)
35. HCL D 863
36. HCL D 863
37. HCL D 863
38. HCL D 863
39. HCL D 863
40. HCL D 863
41. Oakeley pp. 190 – 191
42. HCL D 863
43. HCL D 863

44. HCL D 863
45. College Magazine December 1918
46. College Magazine 1956
47. College Magazine April 1919

CHAPTER SEVEN

HEREFORD, OXFORD AND ORGANS

HEREFORD

On 1 March 1855, over a year before his church was completed, Ouseley received a letter from the Bishop of Hereford, offering him the post of Precentor of Hereford Cathedral. Bishop Hampden, who had been Regius Professor of Divinity during Ouseley's time at Oxford, had been consecrated Bishop of Hereford in 1848, although his nomination the previous year had been opposed by no less than thirteen bishops on account of his liberal views. Hampden knew Ouseley; he knew the problems he had faced at St Barnabas's and was in no doubt that he would make a good Precentor. On Trinity Sunday (3 June) 1855, Ouseley was at last ordained priest by the Bishop in Hereford Cathedral. Two days later he was installed as Precentor and during his lifetime, a friend described this appointment.

> No more fitting appointment could possibly have been made; but whereas this office had, up to this time, been endowed with a sum of £ 500 a year for the benefit of the occupants, not one of them had discharged one particle of its duty for at least a century, or been qualified to discharge it, it was now under the operation of the Cathedrals Act of 1840, to present the unedifying spectacle of an entirely disendowed office, just when, for the first time perhaps since its foundation, it was occupied by a man not only anxious to do the work efficiently, but in every way qualified for such work; an accomplished musician, a man of zeal, energy, ability, and who by his courtesy to all no less than his influence and example, would soon have thrown new vigour and devotion into the choir and services, and been to his cathedral, as a Precentor should be, the centre of its life and action. (1)

Despite all these problems. Ouseley accepted the post and the Bishop installed him into 'the Dignity and Office of Precentor' ensuring that Ouseley occupied 'the Stall in the Choir and place and voice in the Chapter to the said Precentorship belonging.'(2)

In *Hereford Cathedral: A History*, the present Precentor, Canon Paul Iles, points out that Watkins Shaw is wrong to say that 'Ouseley ranked next to the Dean in Choir, and yet had no voice or vote in Chapter.'(3) from his own research, Canon Iles can state that 'Ouseley had *both* a voice and vote in the greater Chapter which preceded every meeting of the residentiaries, although attendance by its members was usually infrequent. Among the residentiaries, William Musgrave usually spoke and voted on behalf of Ouseley. (4)

Ouseley soon settled into cathedral life and carried out his duties as Precentor efficiently and responsibly, attending worship at the cathedral whenever possible. He obtained lodgings at 9 Castle Street and had overall charge of the choir and the music of the cathedral, although being non-resident in Hereford for the most part the daily supervision was delegated to the Succentor. Whenever he attended the cathedral, he listened intently to the singing, often putting his hand behind his ear to hear more clearly. If, in the course of a service he noticed a boy who was not singing properly, he 'collared' the boy after the service and proceeded to place a silver half-crown vertically in his mouth, in order to correct the singing technique, and letting the boy keep the money afterwards. These little gestures of kindness were common among the Hereford choristers as well as his own boys at St Michael's. He also entertained many of the choristers in his rooms for tea, playing the piano for their amusement.

Hereford Cathedral had a College of Vicars Choral, who were responsible for singing the lower parts in the choir. In the eighteenth and early nineteenth centuries, they had become very lax in carrying out their singing duties in the cathedral. Many of them held country livings around the county, and were often absent from the cathedral on Sunday mornings, taking services in their own parishes. In 1834, S S Wesley found that he only had one bass to accompany the trebles at the first performance of his anthem *Blessed be the God and Father*. The situation had become so bad by 1851, that lay clerks were appointed to ensure enough singers to maintain Alto, Tenor and Bass parts.

In 1863, Hereford Cathedral was re-opened after over twenty years of rebuilding and restoration. The official re-opening took place on 30 June 1863, with three choral Services, Ouseley composing a Service of Canticles for Evensong (for Double Choir in C) and the anthem *Blessed be Thou* to mark the occasion.

Ouseley and his colleague, John Jebb, a Prebendary of Hereford Cathedral, saw that the Cathedral kept up with the developments in liturgy in other cathedrals, and through their pressure on the Chapter, a weekly service of Holy Communion was introduced. 'Although more pedantic and unimaginative than Ouseley, Jebb was his considerable ally in the development of the cathedral's music and liturgy.(5)

Although a time of liturgical development came as a result of their efforts, the choir remained insecure until much later in the nineteenth century, when G R Sinclair, an Old Boy of St Michael's, was appointed organist.

When Ouseley arrived at Hereford, he was critical of the state of the choristers. Philip Barrett, in his book, *Barchester*, quotes from Dean and Chapter records of the time.

> Too many of them had difficulty in reading, let alone understanding the Psalms. No one seemed to be responsible for their religious and moral training. Further, they were subject to very vulgarizing, if not demoralizing influences when they were at home. The Dean and Chapter should do as much as they could to prepare them for their subsequent life, and thus they ought to be educated at the Grammar School. (6)

These remarks about the boys were Ouseley's first attempt to persuade the Chapter to start a boarding house for the choristers – which eventually happened 20 years later. In 1859, the cathedral organist at the time, George Townshend Smith, wrote to the Chapter about the problems still occurring.

> Boy after boy has left long before the loss of voice; in the present year the two seniors thus quitting have made it very difficult to provide for the services. He suggested that the Dean and Chapter should put aside an annual sum for each boy as an inducement to parents not to remove them from the school. In 1861, a start was made by boarding two senior choristers at the Cathedral School.(7)

The reason why the parents too often removed the boys before their voices broke was to obtain the valuable grant from the Tomson Fund which they could use as an Apprentice Fee for their sons when they started work and employment.

In order to make an accurate assessment of the situation, the Dean and Chapter held a formal visitation of the College, questioning each of the Vicars Choral and enquiring. 'about the choral foundation in general, about the lay clerks, and about the choristers and their education.'(8) The committee chaired by Ouseley looked into the relationship between the Dean and Chapter and the College of Vicars – who were all in priests' orders and therefore expected to be under clerical discipline, yet were resisting it. Between 1851 and 1918, there was a constant struggle between the Chapter and the College which affected the music, but which to a great extent was independent of the choir.

Nationally, the conditions and education of choristers were being championed by the redoubtable Victorian philanthropist, Maria Hackett, who for over thirty years, had made herself the bane of Dean and Chapters in most cathedrals by her determined efforts to improve matters.

> The admirable Maria Hackett, who constituted herself an unofficial inspector of choir schools in order to expose and eradicate the evil conditions under which choirboys lived, was, and had been for a

long generation by 1849, the scourge of every procrastinating Bishop and dilatory Dean. Beginning at St Paul's Cathedral in 1811, (which was her home church and where she worshipped regularly), she visited every cathedral in the country once every three years (there were 33 at the time.) She had made a considerable impression with her *Brief account of Cathedral and Collegiate Schools* (1827) and was still on her travels in the 1860's. However much she terrified Archdeacons and Chancellors, she became known as 'The Choristers' Friend.'(9)

When Maria Hackett died in 1874, her Obituary in The Times of 5 November mentioned in greater detail her annual visits to choirs and cathedrals.

In the autumn of each year, she made a six-week tour of the cathedral towns, always carrying presents for the choirboys, whose name she knew and kept in her diary, usually giving each boy a book, a purse and a shilling. Her interest and judicious exertions created great reforms in the schools and also in the treatment of choirboys, by which they are now, in the country as well as in the towns, receiving a substantial benefit...She was an ardent lover of cathedral music and the kindest friend to the young choristers of nearly all the cathedrals of England. For sixty years, she rarely missed the Sunday services at St Paul's. It had become so much a part of her life that she could not exist without her cathedral. (10)

It is probably not generally known, but at least one famous organist and composer would not have learnt his trade if it had not been for Maria Hackett. John Stainer was a cathedral chorister at St Paul's and after his voice had broken, he continued to be associated with St Paul's, receiving organ lessons from George Cooper, the assistant organist. These lessons were paid for by Maria Hackett, and Stainer's friend, Arthur Sullivan, a chorister at the Chapel Royal who had sung at the Opening Service at St Michael's in 1856, had organ lessons at St Paul's at the same time. It was while a young chorister at St Paul's that the young Stainer had first met Ouseley.

In 1870, the probationers at Hereford were examined by The College of Vicars and their musical progress was rated by them as unsatisfactory. 'More especially as to reading music from note – of this we cannot say that one seemed to have an idea; they all seemed to know what they do *entirely by ear*, which we cannot consider an altogether satisfactory or safe system.'(11) Ouseley did not actually agree with this criticism. The Vicars Choral were again trying to 'get at' the Chapter!

The publication in 1872 of *Essays on Cathedrals by various writers*, edited by J.S. Howson, Dean of Chester, was of great influence in the search for higher standards of worship, education of choristers and other aspects of Cathedral life. Among other essayists, Ouseley gave an important lecture on *The Education of Choristers in Cathedrals*. He looked at all aspects of a chorister's life, emphasising the need for better education, greater care of choristers' health, and the need for regular exercise and games. He recommended that education should not be just academic and musical, though these aspects should be of the highest standard, but should incorporate moral and devotional training. He wanted the moral training of the boys to be in two parts, both by instruction and example, and warned them about the 'proverbial carelessness of young lay clerks.' He made a number of recommendations concerning the conduct of rehearsals and where they should be held, and also felt that all choristers should be admitted to a choir using an appropriate form of service. 'It need not be an elaborate ceremony, nor need it be performed in the presence of a large congregation; but it should be of a nature to produce a deep religious impression, not only in the mind of the new boy, but also on the rest of the choir.'(12) He advised that each service should start and finish with a short vestry prayer in order to create an atmosphere of reverence, but strongly warned against possible irreverence in the conduct of services, for whatever reason.

Only a year later on 26 May 1873, F.T. Havergal wrote to Maria Hackett while staying at Tenbury, to tell her about the state of the choir at Hereford. With the choristers now being educated at the Cathedral School, a number of improvements and advantages were now apparent.

- The advantages of the whole school are thrown open to the choristers.
- During the last five years, on two occasions, choristers have finished their careers as Heads of School.
- Their studies are allowed to interfere as little as possible with their musical training.
- But little is done now, I am sorry to say, in teaching them instrumental music.
- The Subchanter or his deputy is responsible for the boys while in church.

Most of the boys are boarded now and well cared for. They are selected solely from musical ear, I merit, in public, by the Precentor.

I am spending a day or two at this delightful place of Sir Frederick Ouseley's. Doubtless you know about his sixteen choristers. It is a goodly sight to seem them at meals in the Hall, but to hear them sing – I know nothing like it, so sweet and refined are their voices that I have never heard the like elsewhere. They are very carefully trained and taught and their behaviour is remarkable good order. (13)

Later the same year, Maria Hackett visited Hereford for a second time. She praised the education that the boys were receiving and said that 'the standard of singing will bear comparison with any cathedral in England (14)

Ouseley photographed in early 1880's

Alongside his work at Hereford, Tenbury and Oxford, Ouseley served as a Proctor in Convocation for the Diocese of Hereford for over twenty years. Although not taking part in many debates, he was often consulted as a valuable authority when musical matters were being discussed.

Hereford was one of the venues for the Three Choirs Festival, held in turn at Gloucester, Hereford and Worcester in the early autumn of each year. Anthony Boden, in his masterly *History of the Three Choirs*, suggests that 'As Precentor of Hereford, Ouseley seems to have taken little interest in the Three Choirs Festival. In 1858, Ouseley absented himself from Hereford, along with Archdeacon Freer and Lord Saye and Sele, one of the Canons.'(15) The reality may appear rather different, although the fact that Ouseley's music was being performed did not guarantee his attendance at the Festival. In general, the Chapters of all three cathedrals didn't much care for the Festival and did little to support it. In 1855, shortly after his installation as Precentor, his Overture from *The Martyrdom of St Polycarp* was performed in the second part of the programme of the third morning after Mendelssohn's *Hymn of Praise*. At the next Hereford Festival three years later in 1858, his anthem, *The Lord is the true God* was performed and in 1861 at Hereford, Ouseley took the prayers at the Opening Service. In 1873 at Hereford, Ouseley composed a new work for the Festival, an oratorio called Hagar, with words from the Bible. The work was performed well and was favourably received. The 1878 Festival at Worcester, which included choral works by Ouseley and Stainer, and it is said that a young violinist named Edward Elgar was quite unimpressed with much of the 'new' music. 'We had been accustomed to perform compositions by Ouseley, Dr. Philip Armes (organist of Durham Cathedral) and others of the organists and professors who furnished meritorious works for Festivals, but they lacked that feeling for orchestral effect and elasticity in instrumentation, so obvious in the works of French, Italian and German composers.'(16)

Langdon Colbourne had been organist at St Michael's for fourteen years and then at other churches before becoming organist of Hereford Cathedral in 1877. Like others before him, 'Colbourne had found the behaviour of the Vicars Choral unacceptable ...and in the end, Ouseley's authority was needed to sort out the trouble.'(17) At the Hereford Festival of 1888, Colbourne's last, Ouseley's *The Martyrdom of St Polycarp* was performed, together with an early performance of Parry's *Blest Pair of Sirens*, which had been composed at the beginning of the previous year. Ouseley's work was considered a disappointment and is not mentioned in the *Annals of the Three Choirs* though the performance was considered one of the best of the week as Colbourne sought to do Ouseley justice in what was to be the last of the Three Choirs for both of them. Ouseley also preached at the Opening Service.

In 1886, on the death of John Jebb, a vacancy was created for a residentiary Canon at Hereford Cathedral and Ouseley was offered the post and accepted it on 9 February 1886. He always said that it was the only preferment he had ever received. It was also suggested at the time that others had been offered the post but declined it in order that it should be offered to Ouseley. As a residentiary Canon, Ouseley moved into a canonical house in the Cathedral Close, although he complained that he gained little financial reward from his new position as the house was ruinous and required rebuilding at his own expense. As well as his new residentiary post, Ouseley had been appointed Junior Claviger in 1886 and Master of the Fabric in 1887. These 'jobs' were shared out between the residentiaries in rotation – someone had to do the work of the Chapter. Usually the appointment was only for one year. 'For three years, Ouseley played his full part as a residentiary, taking his three months' residence in July, August and September.'(18) Despite his commitments at Tenbury, Oxford and elsewhere, Ouseley attended the cathedral on many more occasions than was required by his period in residence.

> Whenever there was any election of a Vicar Choral, an assistant Vicar Choral, or even of a chorister, he was invariably present, even making purpose journeys in order to be with them, and on all other occasions in anything connected with the cathedral and its well-being, he was always ready to be present, and to give them the help of his counsel, of his judgement, and of his musical experience. (19)

Indeed, his death occurred sometime after he had attended a Chapter Meeting in the morning of 6 April 1889 and was walking down Broad Street in Hereford. (see Chapter Eight.)

OXFORD

In 1855, the death occurred of Sir Henry Bishop, the Oxford Professor of Music, who had examined Ouseley the previous year for his D Mus. degree. The establishment and endowment of the post dated from 1626, and due to its poor remuneration, would have seemed a difficult post to fill. Later, at the time of Ouseley's death, it was felt that the first thing that must be done in order to attract candidates of sufficient calibre was to raise the salary to an equivalent amount to that of other professorial chairs. (Oxford paid £130 per annum, Cambridge £200, and Sir Herbert Oakeley at Edinburgh received £ 620.) Perhaps mindful of Ouseley's independent circumstances, the Proctors offered him the post. This appointment caused considerable consternation in professional music circles, as Ouseley could not be considered to be more than an enthusiastic amateur. However, as in other situations, Ouseley's manner and gentle disposition soon managed to dispel any jealousy or ill-feeling which may have arisen as a result of his appointment.

The post of Professor of Music was 'non-resident' and for many of the professional musicians who had held it in the past, was no more than a sinecure. Also on a wider basis, music had reached a very low ebb in Oxford, particularly in the University. Sir Herbert Oakeley, had gone up to Christ Church in 1848, and his biographer records his observations.

> Christ Church was at this time ruled, many still live to add, with a rod of iron from the 'stern captain' of Ruskin's *Praeterita*, who with rounded brow and glittering dark eye led in his thunderous Old Latin, the responses of the Morning Prayer. Few Christ Church

men of the time can forget the rasping and indignantly remonstrant tones of his 'Te rogamus audi nos.'

And those, who like Oakeley, were endowed with the excellent gift of the mimic, felt that this phenomenon awakened our dormant faculty. Such a heaven-sent subject is not to be lighted upon every day. So there arose quite a school of mimicry of Dean Gaisford, as in later years of Doctor Goulborn at Rugby; and he is thus almost as well known to a younger generation as to his own. (20)

Ouseley's position in society, together with his own achievements, soon began to have an effect on the position of music in the University. The study of music gained new levels of interest and prestige and in the first years of Ouseley's tenure of the Professorship, the Music Faculty was greatly improved and reorganised. The Professorship became a life-appointment, and the requirements of obtaining a Music Degree were made much more rigorous. Public examinations by three examiners were introduced. Candidates had to show a critical and historical knowledge of their art, as well as the submission of a substantial composition.

Jeremy Dibble, in his recent biography of Sir Hubert Parry, wrote of Ouseley's influence in this regard, and although he agreed with Ouseley's intentions, felt that the results were perhaps not what was desired or intended.

> The rather superficial method of submitting the Exercise was supplemented with written examinations which specified fluency in certain techniques: five-part vocal writing, an aria, an accompanied quartet, and a five-art fugue, as well as the rigours of species counterpoint, Undoubtedly, Ouseley's aim was to sift out those students who were less able to master the more exacting musical procedures; but because the specifications were so inflexible in their demands, many students were able to treat the examination as a series of mechanical problems in which they could devise formulas, and have their degrees virtually guaranteed. The inevitable result was a system where technical correctness was no longer the servant but the master; and consequently, the new examination system gave rise to the standardization of selected skills which stressed above all the furtherance of a contrapuntal stringency which seemed hardly relevant to the development of an original musical style. (21)

By 1871, Ouseley had succeeded in abolishing the requirement of exercises for the B Mus. degree to be publicly performed. (called by some the 'Unmusical Statute.') and in 1876, more reforms were introduced with the requirement for candidates for Oxford Music degrees to show that they had a good general education. As a preliminary to their music examinations, they were required to pass an 'arts' examination to show their competency in classics and mathematics. it appears that this reform originated in the University of Dublin, and was later adopted at Cambridge. In his address on *The Character and Influence of the late Sir Frederick Ouseley*, Sir John Stainer pointed out that these requirements would debar many experienced musicians of taking a music degree as they would have to satisfy these 'arts' requirements first. 'How many experienced and able musicians are now deprived of an honour which used formerly to be within their reach; and, worse still, it has encouraged the mushroom growth of all sorts of diplomas and hoods, and the importation, on a large scale, of degrees from Canada and the United States, many of which turned out to be suspect or bogus.'(22)

With these developments, Ouseley was beset on all sides by requests for degrees. Sometimes someone who happened to get a recommendation from some prominent person tried to persuade Ouseley to award him an honorary degree, and other musicians, unable to satisfy the new requirements for the award of a Music Degree, pleaded in vain to be awarded an honorary degree. From 1855 to 1889, the only Honorary Degrees in Music conferred were those given to Sir George Macfarren the Cambridge professor, Sir Herbert Oakeley the Edinburgh Professor, Sir Arthur Sullivan, Charles Villiers Stanford, who succeeded Professor Macfarren at Cambridge and Hans Richter, the well-known conductor – 'musicians' all worthy of this high distinction. (23)

One candidate submitted an exercise for a degree and Ouseley considered that within the requirements for the award of a degree, the exercise was hopeless and it was returned to the unsuccessful candidate. This candidate promptly berated Ouseley about his decision. 'Sir, your rejection of my exercise confirms the opinion I have long entertained of your utter incompetence for the office you hold.'(24) With Ouseley's wide reading, memory and knowledge of music, there was no chance of any candidate successfully passing the examination using 'cribbed' exercises. Studying one submission, Ouseley felt that it was not bad enough to reject and was on the point of passing it when he recognised that the exercise was in fact a rather indifferent passage from an indifferent oratorio, Russell's *Job*. Havergal's *Memorials* also recounts an occasion when another man, rejected for his B Mus. Degree, followed Ouseley around Oxford over an hour, crying pitifully all the time and waiting for him at every house he entered, until, making a call on another person, Ouseley was let out the back door and escaped his tormentor. As well as conducting the degree examinations, Ouseley's duties included giving music lectures at least once each term and these were enlivened with illustrations from Ouseley himself at the piano, organ or spinet, sometimes with a small amateur string band, or one of his Oxford friends, notably Sir Walter Parratt, at that time organist of Magdalen. These lectures were wide-ranging and certainly broadened the knowledge of those who attended them. Subjects from 1877 to 1889 included, *the Pianoforte, Church Music Anthems, English Ballads, History of the Organ, Spanish Music, German and Italian Composers, French and English Composers,*

Old Forms of Dance Music, Melody, Purcell and his Contemporaries, the Construction of Fugue, History of Fugue. These lectures were extremely popular although Ouseley was quite annoyed when one of his lectures was described by a local paper as a *Concert, Illustrated by a few remarks from the Professor!*

On 11 October 1865, Ouseley was at Oxford to hear Stainer's oratorio, Gideon, being performed in the Sheldonian Theatre to a packed audience. This was Stainer's successful submission for his D Mus. Degree. The work was well received but had a very short life. The year 1865 was a momentous one for Stainer in another way as he became engaged to Eliza Randall, the only daughter of Alderman and Mrs Randall of Oxford. On 27 December 1865, they were married by Ouseley in St Aldate's Church. A year later, Ouseley was in Oxford to oversee more degree submissions, and at a musical party in Professor Donkin's home, the young (18 year old) Hubert Parry was introduced to both Ouseley and Stainer for the first time. 'Sir Frederick and Stainer were both there. The Donkins performed a quartet of Sir Frederick's which he had composed for them.'(25) On 4 December the same year, Parry took his examination paper, which covered many aspects of musical knowledge, but did not complete the paper. 'However, when I had got a quarter of the way through the paper, they told me that I need not do any more and let me go. Sir Frederick was very kind and when they (Ouseley, Corfe and Stainer) came out about a quarter of an hour afterwards, I heard that ...I had got my testamur. Glorious! Sir Frederick asked me to come and stay with him at Tenbury.(26) In February 1867, Parry was only given a few days' notice to gather together the singers and instrumental players necessary for a public performance of his degree submission, a cantata, *O Lord, Thou hast cast us out* and after a rather chaotic rehearsal, the cantata was given a successful performance shortly afterwards.

For a musician, Oxford had much to offer, and Ouseley found many outlets for his interests. He had been responsible for the erection of a new organ in the Sheldonian Theatre and his skill on the organ was such that he could 'keep the noisy undergraduates in a good temper by his dulcet strains, or on occasion, drown the uproar.'(27) After one of his organ performances at the Sheldonian,, he was amused to receive a request for money from two 'blowists' who had 'blowed' for him at a lecture the previous Tuesday.

By the time of Ouseley's death in 1889, it was said that music was in a condition of healthy activity in the University city. The previous year Sir John Stainer had resigned as organist of St Paul's Cathedral, due to problems with his eyesight. These problems apparently stemmed from a visit to Ouseley at Tenbury in September 1875, when while playing on the fives court, 'a ball struck his good eye with such severity that the sight of it was for some time completely lost.'(28) It appears that Stainer had lost the sight of one eye after a childhood accident, and after his accident at St

Michael's, suffered recurrent problems with his good eye. This resulted in his decision to retire from St Paul's in June 1888. Later in 1888, Stainer and his family moved to Oxford, and when the vacant Professorship was advertised in May 1889, Stainer decided to apply. Sir John had been kept busy in his capacity as an Inspector for the Board of Education as well as still having many interests in London. In his lecture on Ouseley, Stainer indicated that Ouseley had felt that Stainer should succeed him, though Ouseley's recommendations carried no weight. When Stainer heard that Parry was considering applying, Stainer thought about withdrawing on account of his eyesight, but Parry wrote to Stainer in April 1889, urging him to stand. 'By chance, Stainer and Parry subsequently met on Gloucester railway station when Stainer told Parry that his eyesight was much better and that he would accept the Professorship if offered it. Parry decided in those circumstances not to stand, and their relationship continued to be close and harmonious.'(29)

It was apparent to many people that Stainer was the ideal candidate to replace Ouseley as Professor, his musical credentials were impeccable and he was already living in Oxford. On 18 June 1889, Stainer's election was announced in the *Oxford University Gazette* and met with popular acclaim. Sir Walter Parratt, lecturing in Oxford some twenty years later, said that 'no worthier successor to Ouseley could have been found than Stainer, who was not only Ouseley's friend, but to some extent also his pupil, whose vivifying personality had done much for music in general and for church music in particular.'(30)

ORGANS

Throughout his childhood, Ouseley had played the piano, but it is likely that at some point during that time, he was introduced to the sounds of a church organ and quickly gained some technical knowledge of its construction and operation. By his teenage years, he had clearly become quite knowledgeable about organs and it can be assumed that Ouseley had considerable say in Joyce's choice of organ at the Dorking rectory. A few years later, during Ouseley's university career in Oxford, William Marshall, the organist of Christ Church Cathedral retired and as an appointment was not made for some months, Ouseley offered his services as organist, taking complete control of the music of the cathedral. It is said that he played the organ for every service during that time, before Charles Corfe was appointed in 1846. (Both his sons were to be two of the first boys at the newly-established St Michael's.)

On 9 June 1847, St Peter's College, Radley was opened, founded by the Reverend Sewell. Like Ouseley and many others, he had been greatly influenced by the Oxford Movement and had already founded the College of St Columba in Ireland. His friend, the musician, E. G. Monk became Precentor of Radley College and the Reverend Singleton was appointed as the first Warden. By May 1848 the organ, which had been ordered from a Mr. Telford of Dublin, had been installed at Radley, although its power had been heard two months previously in the warehouse in Dublin where it had been temporarily erected. 'The largest, as well as the most perfect instrument of its kind ever made in Ireland, it being more than half again as powerful as the organ in St Patrick's Cathedral...and no expense has been spared to make it in every way creditable to the genius and mechanical excellence of Irish artisans.'(31) The organ was said to be one of the best in England, and Mr. Telford's reputation was such that he supplied organs to many English churches and Colleges, as well as all over Ireland. It was said to be equal to any imported from Germany. (For more information on this organ, see *The Organ*, No. 91 of January 1944.) It was intended that the services at the College should be modelled on those at the University of Oxford and it was no surprise when two of the first organists to visit Radley and play the new organ were Corfe of Christ Church Cathedral, Oxford, and Blythe of Magdalen College. With his interest in organs, it was not long before Ouseley visited Radley.

> Sir Frederick Gore Ouseley, a great amateur musician, came to dinner. He played splendidly on the organ, and has just come from a tour of organ inspection, 190 of which he has played on. I don't know exactly what he thinks of it. Some parts he certainly admires, but he says that the diapasons are too reedy. I imagine that he likes *sweet* diapasons, which I think is only to a certain extent, good taste. He was very surprised at the Chapel service being got up so well in so short a time. (32)

It is interesting to note with Ouseley's future foundation of St Michael's in mind, that Monk (1856), Sewell (1857) and Singleton (1868), all became Fellows of St Michael's. (E.G. Monk became Organist of York Minster in 1859.)

By 1850, Ouseley had been ordained as a deacon and had designed and paid for an organ for the newly built church of St Barnabas, Pimlico, where he was now curate. This organ was built by Flight and Robson, who were responsible for building the first, unsatisfactory organ at St Michael's. Ouseley's first tour of Europe had taken place in 1848, but after he had left St Barnabas in December 1850, he spent the next ten months visiting many of the major cities in Europe, listening to, playing, and writing down the specification of every organ came across. While in Dresden, as well as listening to some of the best boys' choirs he had ever heard, he heard the renowned Organist, Schneider, perhaps the greatest living organist of the time, play on one of the best organs in Europe. 'I really have not had the heart to touch an instrument since, so unapproachable does his excellence as a fugue-player and accompanist appear to be.'(33)

In 1853, Ouseley, R. Willis and J. Donaldson gave a preliminary report to the Directors of the Crystal Palace Company concerning the Grand organ and two years later, Sir Herbert Oakeley and Ouseley were at Romsey Abbey.

> About this time, Oakeley 'opened' the fine organ in Romsey Abbey. Sir Frederick Ouseley preached the sermon, and afterwards, the two paid a visit to Dr Wesley at Winchester. On this occasion, Dr Wesley had 'cut his finger', and could nor, or would not play. He gave his friends however, the run of the organ, and paid them the compliment of listening...Both Oakeley and Ouseley were of course ardent admirers of the man and his genius, and could make allowances for his idiosyncrasies, by which strangers were apt to be most upset. (34)

During the year 1856, as well as making final arrangements for the opening of St Michael's, Ouseley still found time to spend a fortnight in London, reporting on the condition of the organ at the Temple Church, prior to its enlargement and restoration. His advice was so much valued that he was given a substantial *honorarium*, which he spent on his College. Although he was in great demand as an organ consultant, some of Ouseley's ideas did not meet with universal approval and his ideas for the organ at Exeter Cathedral had been badly received. 'We view with some horror his historically insensitive actions at Exeter Cathedral, where he sanctioned the melting down of some of the Loosemore facade pipes and the alterations to the west front of the case.'(35)

In December 1853, the rebuild of the Wells Cathedral organ was being considered and Ouseley was asked to advise the Organ Committee. He wrote to Henry Willis, giving the following advice. 'Of these stops, the diapasons and mixtures are so very fine that they ought not to be touched on any account.'(36) Ouseley also suggested several other improvements, removing the present Great Trumpet and adding a Trumpet, Clarion and Claribella, together with the addition of an adequate pedal organ. His advice also included removing the Hautboy, Cornet and Trumpet on the Swell and replacing them with a Double Diapason, Fifteenth, Sesquialtera and Trumpet. On the Choir Organ, an Open Diapason and Cremona were to be added in place of the Fifteenth. Over two years later, Ouseley, after spending more time on considering the stops already available, wrote to the Chairman of the Organ Committee on February 11th 1856, stating that the following stops from the Green organ should be retained.

Great Stop Diapason, Open Diapason I, open Diapason II, Principal, Fifteenth, Sesquialtera and Mixture (or fourniture)

Swell Stopped Diapason, Open Diapason and Principal

Choir Stopped Diapason, Dulciana and Principal.

Ouseley wrote that 'Mr. Willis should be particularly cautioned not to alter in any wise the voicing of the Diapasons and Mixtures of the Great organ, which are very good.'(37) The booklet, *Organs and Organists of Wells Cathedral* (1998 Edition), points out that the contents of this letter were never brought to the notice of Mr. Willis, and on 2 June 1857, when the new organ was opened, Ouseley wrote somewhat critically of the end result.

> He (Willis) had departed entirely from the terms of his contract – in many particulars, but specially in his treatment of some very excellent portions of the old organ, to which the mellowing hand of time had lent particular beauty, and which I had carefully conditioned should be retained in their original place. Mr. Willis has transposed some of these portions to other places in the instrument, for which they were never designed by of *Greene*, their maker – but the greater portion, Mr. Willis has *melted down*, using the materials only, not the stops. Now I am free to admit that he has produced a very good organ. But it is an organ by *Willis only*, not by *Green, repaired and enlarged by Willis*. (38)

In 1855, there was published what many now regard as the Organ 'Bible', the magnificent book entitled, *The Organ, its History and Construction*, by E.J. Hopkins and Edward Rimbault. Hopkins, together with other friends, had undertaken European tours during the years, 1844, 1852, 1853, 1858, 1862, 1871, 1872 and 1888 and, similar to Ouseley, had played many organs during that time. By the third edition of their book in 1877, the large list of organ specifications given in an Appendix had grown to 342 examples. On his European tours, as previously mentioned, Ouseley had recorded all details and specifications of the organs he played in two manuscript notebooks. Although the book by Hopkins and Rimbault fails to give any acknowledgement, these organ notebooks were placed at their disposal by Ouseley and many of their examples were provided by Ouseley's own work. The edition of *The Organ*, No 19, Volume V, published in January 1926, states that these notebooks 'are now in the possession of Dr. Charles Vincent.'(39), a well-known composer of organ music. For many organ enthusiasts, advisers and historians, it would mean a great deal to discover the present whereabouts of these notebooks, if they have survived, but it has not been possible to trace them beyond their mention in *The Organ* in 1926.

In 1861, Ouseley was again involved as an organ adviser, this time at Llandaff Cathedral, where the organ was built by Gray and Davidson, in consultation with Ouseley. This organ is now in Usk Parish Church in Monmouthshire. The following year, Ouseley was consulted about the Gray and Davidson organ in Hereford Cathedral, which was much altered and enlarged for the re-opening of the Cathedral in 1863. As well as giving his advice, Ouseley contributed a substantial amount to the cost of this rebuild from his own pocket, and enlisted further financial support from others during the period 1861 – 1864. Through his own researches, Ouseley had collected much information on the organs at Hereford during the previous three centuries, which he intended to publish, but never fulfilled.

At St Michael's, the ten years since the College opened had seen mounting problems with the organ installed in 1856 by Flight and Robson, which was still incomplete at the time of the church's consecration in September 1856. This had been one of Ouseley's greatest disappointments in connection with St Michael's, as he felt that this original instrument had not proved worthy of the church and was also unsatisfactory in accompanying the choir. Partly due to a leaking roof and partly due to mechanical deficiencies the organ had become unplayable. In 1867, Ouseley called in the firm of Harrison of Rochdale (later to become the famous Harrison and Harrison of Durham), with a brief to reconstruct the organ and enlarge it from its original 56 to 65 stops. Harrison's workmen began the task but were largely unsupervised and stories abounded that they spent much of their time harvesting and fruit picking on local farms when they were lacking materials. There were also indications that Harrisons were experiencing a cash-flow crisis, with Ouseley being frequently asked for more money. Consequently, the rebuilding of the organ proceeded much more slowly than Ouseley had expected or desired and many complaints were made. With the approach of Commemoration at the end of September 1868, Ouseley decided to take decisive action and in a letter dated 7 September 1868, wrote to Harrisons of Rochdale.

> Having waited (as you have acknowledged) with great patience for many months, anxiously expecting the completion of my organ and feeling that I ought to wait no longer, now that our annual Commemoration is once more at hand; I must very unwillingly write to you to say, plainly that this system of slow work must go on no longer. Had you sent the pipes and other materials required, together with extra hands, some months ago, the organ would have been finished.
>
> I now put two alternatives for you to take which you please.
>
> THE FIRST ALTERNATIVE
>
> Send men and all necessary materials and pipes to aid your brother (who has done his part admirably well) and to get the organ finished out of hand. I will in that case (and not otherwise), do my best to pay what shall remain to be paid, as soon as the whole work is done. I ought of course to require also some understanding or guarantee that further delays on your part will forfeit a portion of your claims on me. Such understanding and agreement shall be drawn up and entered into at once, by my lawyer and yours, or if you wish it, give a distinct engagement on your part to complete the organ in...weeks on peril of losing some stipulated sum. Your reputation will then be saved and my future recommendation of you secured.

THE SECOND ALTERNATIVE

Let what there is of the organ hereby be put in order by you, made serviceable and the rest be given up entirely by me, and then let an arbitrator be called in to appraise the work already done and balance it against the money already paid by me, so as to be fair to both parties, and then let the whole matter be wound up and taken out of your hands. You may prefer even this to any further delay. it would of course be ruinous to your interests, but you need not adopt this plan if you will choose the former alternative.

I will keep a copy of this letter and shall not consult my lawyer until I get your answer. (40)

The fruit picking continued in the autumn of 1869 and as Roger Judd points out in his article on the St. Michael's organ,

This unsatisfactory situation dragged on into 1872, with the organ largely or completely unplayable...At last, in April 1873, Ouseley engaged a competent builder, 'Father' Henry Willis, to put the organ in good order. As previously mentioned he undertook to dismantle the entire instrument, take it to his London factory, and bring it back in playing order within five months. Willis agreed to use only the best parts of the old instrument. He revoiced the pipework, so that although the pipes were not made by Willis, they sound like Willis pipes, and it is this organ that, with a few small differences, the listener will hear today. (41)

Two years later, Ouseley was in demand as an organ consultant when a new organ was made for Alexandra Palace in 1875. When the rebuilding of the organ in Salisbury Cathedral by Willis was completed in 1877, Ouseley wrote enthusiastically to Richardson, the Organist. 'I honestly believe you have the finest church organ in the world – certainly the best in England, and I heartily congratulate you on the same.'(42)

On 1 February 1886, Ouseley gave an important lecture to the Musical Association, of which he was the first President. The lecture was entitled *On the position of organs in churches*. Ouseley was able to relate much of his experiences at home and abroad, giving examples of the different positions in which he had found organs. He pointed out that in some notable churches abroad, there were sometimes two, three or even four organs employed for the purposes of worship, whereas one usually suffices in English services. Speaking of the siting of church organs, Ouseley said the following.

'It is evident that there are several, various, and often conflicting interests to be consulted in the selection of a proper site for a church organ. There are first the interests of the clergy, who regard the matter, perhaps, from an ecclesiological point of view. Then there are the interests of the singers in the choir, who will view the question on its vocal side. Next we have the interest of the organist, who regards the position of the organ from a comparatively instrumental aspect. After him comes the architect, who chiefly looks at the appearance of the case, and too frequently hates the organ altogether, and would fain conceal as much of it as possible. Lastly, there is the organ builder, who knows how much better his instrument will sound with free space around it, than when boxed up in a small chamber, and who feels that his reputation is more or less dependent on the decision as to locality to which those who have the management of the affair shall finally come. Here is, then, a fruitful source of quarrels and differences, of contentions and recriminations, of jealousies and revilings, of grumbling and discontent.'

Sir Frederick protested that he must not be expected to lay down some general or applicable rule for finding the best place for an organ. As he said, what was suitable for a large cathedral would be unsuitable for a small country church. in cathedrals, he inclined to think that the best place *musically* was over the choir screen, though *architecturally* that position rendered it impossible to gain an uninterrupted view of the interior of the cathedral from west to east. He continued:

'Speaking as a musician, and lover of cathedral services, I am inclined to advocate in all such cases the retention of the organ on the rood screen; the bad effect to the eye can often be mitigated by dividing the organ, so as to keep all the middle part at low elevation, putting the tall pipes and all that tends to obstruct the view, on either side, as has been done at Westminster Abbey and at Rochester Cathedral. The other alternative was to place it over the choir stalls on one side, but this has its disadvantages, so far as antiphonal singing was concerned.'

Sir Frederick concluded his lecture by advocating a small but good and well-planned organ placed in the choir of small churches for choir accompaniment only, but 'in a large church where there was no choir, and where the whole congregation were in the habit of singing hymns at the top of their voices, what would be imperatively needed would be a large and powerful organ in a west end gallery to dominate and lead the singers, and to drown their shouts if the cacophony became intolerable. (43)

A few months later in June 1886, Ouseley came to Newton-on-Ouse near York to preach on the occasion of the opening of their new organ.

While standing with myself and others at the west end of the church listening to the instrument, while it was being played at full power, he suddenly remarked that there was a note (he named it) out of tune in one of the upper octaves of the mixtures. We were rather surprised, as the instrument had just been tuned throughout.

The fault, however, was there – it was a very slight one, but he had 'spotted' it at once. (44)

Ouseley's reputation as an organ consultant and tonal designer was another important aspect of his very full life and even though at times his advice appeared undervalued, he was considered to be at least as advanced in his ideas as W.T. Best on organ building matters.

REFERENCES

HEREFORD

1. Quoted in Havergal *Memorials* p.23
2. Canon Paul Iles in *Hereford Cathedral: A History*
3. Watkins Shaw p.28
4. Canon Paul Iles in *Hereford Cathedral: A History*
5. Quoted from Hereford Dean and Chapter records in Barrett *Barchester* page 204
6. Canon Paul Iles in *Hereford Cathedral: A History*
7. Canon Paul Iles in *Hereford Cathedral: A History*
8. Barrett – *Barchester* p.204
9. Routley – *A Short History of English Church Music* (1977) p. 62
10. *The Times* obituary of 5 November 1874 (Letters of Maria Hackett at RCM)
11. *Barchester* p. 406
12. Ouseley *The Education of Choristers in Cathedrals*, quoted in Howson 1872
13. HCL D 863
14. Canon Paul Iles in *Hereford Cathedral: A History*
15. Boden – *History of the Three Choirs* page 117
16. Quoted in *Three Pears Annual Magazine* – Worcester 1931
17. Canon Paul Iles in *Hereford Cathedral: A History*
18. Canon Paul Iles in *Hereford Cathedral: A History*
19. Havergal *Memorials*, p. 69

OXFORD

20. Oakeley *The Life of Sir Herbert Oakeley* pp. 26-27
21. Dibble *C. Hubert H. Parry* p. 12
22. Joyce p. 140
23. Joyce p. 143
24. Havergal *Memorials* p. 11
25. Quoted in Dibble, p. 43
26. Quoted in Dibble, p. 44
27. Joyce, p. 153
28. Charlton *John Stainer* p. 82
29. Charlton *John Stainer* p. 89
30. Charlton *John Stainer* p. 89

ORGANS

31. *The Freeman's Journal, Dublin*, 23 March 1848
32. Diary of Warden Singleton, 12 June 1848
33. Joyce, p. 76
34. *The Life of Sir Herbert Oakeley* pp. 53 –54
35. Clutton & Nyland *The British Organ* (2nd Ed.)1982, pp. 172
36. Letter from Ouseley to Henry Willis, December 1853
37. Letter to the Chairman of the Organ Committee at Wells Cathedral, 11 February 1856
38. Organs and Organists of Wells Cathedral (1998 ed.) pp. 13
39. *The Organ* No. 19, Vol. V, January 1926, p.140
40. Copy of Ouseley letter to Harrisons (in private hands) 7 September 1868
41. The Organ – in A Short History and Guide to the Church of St Michael and All Angels, Tenbury Wells (1993)
42. Matthews – *The Organs and Organists of Salisbury Cathedral*, pp.16-17
43. Paper given to the Musical Association *On the Position of Organs in Churches* February lst 1886
44. Havergal *Memorials* p. 60

CHAPTER EIGHT

OUSELEY'S LAST YEARS AND DEATH

By the year 1886, Ouseley's health had begun to deteriorate and he had been seriously ill on a number of occasions. Two things were causing him some anxiety. Firstly, he was greatly concerned about the financial future of the College. With so few boys, (and most of those on reduced fees), it had never become self-supporting and had relied on Ouseley's financial support throughout its life. Most of his income came from land rents. Since the late 1840's, he had owned properties and land in the Tenbury area and also in Hertfordshire, and as the agricultural depression took hold in the later years of the nineteenth century, so the income from agricultural rents declined and reduced Ouseley's available income to support his College. Throughout his lifetime, Ouseley had devoted an annual sum of around £1,800 from his own resources towards the upkeep of the College. At the same time, he was always generous to deserving charitable causes, especially widows and children and he was known to give donations to many churches, particularly when asked to support projects such as the building a new organ. In order to provide all this, he exercised self-denial very strictly and to such a large degree, that only his closest friends would have any idea of what was involved. In the last few years of his life, these financial problems worried him a great deal, particularly in view of his own ill-health and uncertain future. The other cause of his anxiety was his own position in the musical world. Perhaps his own feelings of 'neglect' from those in the world of music were in reality 'that dropping out of particular notice which comes to many men as they advance in years and as the best work of their lives becomes a thing of the past.'(1) However he may have exaggerated these feelings. He was unmarried, and in the later years of his life, all his close relatives had already died. He had many friends in music and the church, but he would not burden others with his own worries. Perhaps also, he was not conscious of the fact that his musical ideas had already become outdated and that he was considered to be somewhat boring and uninteresting to other musicians. Jeremy Dibble quotes one such example. On 19 October 1887, Parry wrote to his wife Maude. 'Tonight I have got to dine with Lloyd to meet Ouseley again. It will be a real bore and I look forward to it with despair. They will talk about what they call music, which is dull and scholastic shop; and probably after dinner, they will play Mozart Symphonies on the pianoforte as duets.'(2)

St. Michael's College, Tenbury.

TWENTY-EIGHTH COMMEMORATION FESTIVAL, SEPTEMBER 29th, 1884.

Matins & Holy Communion · · · · 11 o'clock.

Processional—(Psalm cxxii.)	*Rimbault.*
Service	*Smart in F.*
Anthem—(Hebrews i.—5. 6.)	*Handel.*

> RECIT :—"Unto which of the angels said He at any time, Thou art my Son, this day have I begotten Thee ?"
>
> CHORUS.—"Let all the angels of God worship Him."

Introit	Hymn 254.

Preacher:— *F. A. G. O.*

Evensong · · · · · · · · · · 6 o'clock.

Service	*Smart in F.*
Anthem—(Isaiah xlix.—18, 22, 23.)	*Sir J. Goss.*

> "Lift up thine eyes round about, and behold : all these gather themselves together and come to thee. "As I live," saith the Lord, "thou shalt surely clothe thee with them all, as with an ornament, and bind them on thee as a bride doth."
>
> Thus saith the Lord God, "Behold, I will lift up mine hand to the Gentiles, and set up my standard to the people : and they shall bring thy sons in their arms, and thy daughters shall be carried upon their shoulders. And kings shall be thy nursing fathers, and their queens thy nursing mothers : they shall bow down to thee with their face towards the earth ; and thou shalt know that I am the Lord : for they shall not be ashamed that wait for me."

Hymn during the Collection	243.

The Offertories at each Service will be devoted to the Sustentation Fund of St. Michael's College, for which they are urgently needed.

Commemoration 1884 (Note Preacher's initials, Ouseley's in his own hand)

It has already been mentioned in the previous chapter that Elgar criticised Ouseley and other contemporary composers whose works were performed at the Three Choirs Festivals as 'lacking that feeling for orchestral effect and elasticity in instrumentation,' in comparison with continental composers. Parry was also extremely critical of Ouseley's

Ouseley (Photograph taken after serious illness 1886)

oratorio, *The Martyrdom of St Polycarp,* when it was performed at the Hereford Three Choirs Festival in 1888, describing it as what he expected: 'purely asinine, antidramatic and ineffective.'(3)

In January 1886, Ouseley had received the only preferment awarded to him throughout his life, on his appointment to a Residentiary Canonry at Hereford Cathedral. A month later, Monty Alderson wrote to Ouseley congratulating him on his appointment. In his reply, Ouseley invited him to visit St. Michael's at his next holiday.

All goes on much as formerly, but you will find many new faces and miss many former ones. We have a new Headmaster, Mr. Fletcher, a new Assistant Master, Mr. De. Burgh and I have a new butler instead of Hill, so you can see there have been many changes of late. The Michaelmas Commemoration of the previous September was on the whole, the best we have ever had, which I am glad of as it completed our thirtieth year. I will soon be photographed again and will send you a copy if it turns out good. (4)

On 3 November 1887, Truro Cathedral was consecrated by Archbishop Benson, with Ouseley being present as one of the chief guests. (Benson had been consecrated as the first Bishop of Truro in 1880.) Ouseley's anthem *Great is the Lord* was performed at the Consecration Service and it is reported that Ouseley was visibly moved at the singing of the great Processional Psalm, *Lift up your heads O ye gates.* Ten years earlier, after the see had been established and services held at the Church of St Mary the Virgin, the Prince of Wales, in his capacity as Duke of Cornwall, had laid the foundation stone. It was noted that the ceremonies had been carried out with grand masonic honours. It was later revealed that Ouseley himself was a Freemason of considerable standing and a founder member of the St Michael's Masonic Lodge.

Despite Ouseley's own doubts about his standing in the musical world, many Old Boys of St Michael's held him in great esteem and during 1887, a Subscription Fund was started to pay for the installation of a bay of two stained glass windows in St Michael's, as a token of their affection and respect. F H Smith, then Secretary of the Appeal Fund, wrote to Monty Alderson on 23 July 1888, reporting on the progress of the Fund. During the previous year, a letter had been sent to 168 Old Boys with the following results.

4   have died
23   we cannot find
69   have not replied
72   have either promised or paid subscriptions

A newsletter sent to the Old Boys reported on the ordering of these windows.

As a result of this, an order had been given to Mr Hardman of Birmingham, a stained glass craftsman of national repute. (He had produced the windows for Eton College Ante-Chapel.) Two windows were to be placed in the North Aisle and he promised to have them ready for Michaelmas Day 1888. These were to cost £56 each. A brass plate, with an inscription, which, together with the working expenses, will bring the cost to around £120. The Appeal still hopes to get another £30 at least, which will enable us to add a third window, but in the event of not being able to do so, it proposed to hand the balance to Sir Frederick Ouseley for church repairs, or any other purpose to which he may think fit to devote it.(5)

The windows were in fact installed by Christmas 1888, and Ouseley took much interest in them in the three months before he died. He likened them to works of art and appreciated them all the more in that they were given by his Old Boys. At the time, opinions were expressed that both in colour and grouping, the windows were the best which Hardman had put in the Church. The bay of three windows depicted

1. Jesus healing the blind man
2. Jesus healing the deaf and dumb man
3. Jesus healing those brought to him as he left the ship

Towards the end of 1888, Ouseley was becoming aware that his hold on life was very uncertain and that his death was likely to be a sudden one. In a letter to Monty Alderson dated 4 November 1888, he writes of being 'so hunted and occupied during the last week that I have allowed your letter to go so long unacknowledged.'(6)

This was very unlike Ouseley as he always prided himself on replying promptly to the many letters he regularly received from his Old Boys. Shortly after this, Ouseley went to Hereford Cathedral for the November Chapter Audit and then had to travel to Oxford to judge two 'exercises' for Doctor of Music candidates on the Friday and Saturday. He was soon back in Tenbury and wrote to a friend on 18 December, expressing worries about his own health. 'I have not been at all well since May. My heart is all wrong and I cannot walk without horrid agony there very often. I fear that this is incurable as it is hereditary. It is a warning to 'put my house in order.'(7) Doctors had warned him three years previously that with his hereditary heart condition, he must beware of any excitement or violent exertion. This must have been very difficult for him as throughout his life, he had been a very good walker, but now, when walking with a friend up the long and not inconsiderable hill from Tenbury to St Michael's, he had to ask them to wait while he paused frequently to get his breath back. 'My doctor tells me to break any engagements, miss any train and suffer any loss or inconvenience rather than hurry. I suppose that I must have a weak heart, but I trust it is not a bad one.'(8) Ouseley's sisters had died in 1861 and 1862, and his friend Wayland Joyce in 1887, and Joyce, his biographer, always felt that Ouseley would like to die 'in harness.' In the last year of his life, Ouseley spoke frequently on the subject of sudden death and a friend reminded him of Bishop Wilberforce's explanation of the phrase in the Litany, *from sudden death, good Lord, deliver us,* which really meant 'from unprepared death....'

Joyce tells us that he preached his last sermon at St Michael's on 17 March 1889, the Second Sunday in Lent, and soon afterwards, went on what was to be his last journey to Hereford to stay at his residence in the Cathedral Close. He seemed to be in better health and spirits, and was looking forward to returning to Tenbury to celebrate Easter at St

Michael's, when the Choir would return from holiday. 'On Saturday 6 April, the day before Passion Sunday, Ouseley attended the 10 am Service in the Cathedral and read the lessons. Dean and Chapter records show that Ouseley attended a meeting of the Chapter after the service. He had lunch at his house in the Close and then told his housekeeper he was going out. 'I am just going to write a letter to Mr. Hampton, who is coming over on Monday; see that it is posted. Then I shall go over to the club or library, and come back in time for service.' (9)

As he was turning into Broad Street from the Close, he stopped to talk to a chorister, who was hurrying back in the direction of the cathedral, and asked him what was the anthem to be sung that evening. He called into the City and County Club for a few minutes and as he was walking back along Broad Street towards the Close, he stopped to talk to Prebendary Hawkshaw of Weston-under-Penyard, outside the library at about 3 pm. As they talked together, Ouseley was suddenly seized with agonizing chest pains. He was helped across the road by Mr Hawkshaw towards where Mr Kenrick, the Manager of the Birmingham, Dudley and District Bank was standing outside the door of the Bank. Both men helped him into a private room at the bank where he sat down, but continued to be stricken with a 'knife-like' pain and unable to talk. His Doctor was sent for and his servant, who was asked to help him home. Mr Kenrick had already given him some brandy, and Dr Turner then gave more brandy and a dose of ether, which seemed to reduce the pain and he was then able to talk to his helpers, telling them he thought he was going to die. He talked for about ten minutes after the restoratives had been administered and told the Doctor that he felt much better and would be all right in a few minutes.

> He mentioned that he was to have dined at the Deanery that evening, but Dr Turner said that it would not be possible to do so. He was immediately seized with an epileptic fit, and Dr Turner promptly shook him, cut open his collar and shirt band and asked Mr Kenrick to turn him over on his face. Mr Kenrick had him in his arms, and had half turned him over when he suddenly ceased to breathe. Mr Turner states that Sir Frederick had suffered from as weak heart for a long time and had recently been subject to spasms of the heart. The attack on the Saturday afternoon was undoubtedly the severest he had had, but the immediate cause of death was the epileptic fit. (10)

A cab was called to take the body to his house and the sad news was telegraphed to St Michael's College, where it was received with sadness and shock by all concerned. Two days later, the Reverend John Hampton travelled to Hereford to make arrangements for the funeral. His body remained at his residence until Wednesday 10 April, when it was taken into the Cathedral for a short funeral service, before being taken by train to Tenbury Station, arriving there in the early evening. The bells of St Mary's Church in Tenbury were tolled and the local people stood in silent tribute. Upon reaching the College, the coffin was taken into the College Library, where it remained until the following day. 'Shutters were closed and blinds drawn and the same signs of morning could be seen on the whole route to St Michael's. The coffin rested on a bier, covered with a purple pall in the centre of the Library and was surrounded by lovely floral wreaths and crosses sent by lamenting friends from far and near, eighty-seven in number.'(11)

The day of the funeral, 11 Thursday April, started off with rain, but by the time of the funeral at 3 pm, it was fine and the sun came out. Hundreds of people made their way across the Common to St Michael's Church. The St Michael's boys were away on holiday but had been due to return for the Easter Services, so a choir was made up specially for the occasion. This included the St Michael's staff, all the clerical and lay members of the Hereford Cathedral Choir and six choristers, the Precentor and four choristers from Worcester Cathedral and many other musicians and clergy. Shortly before 3 pm, the Procession formed in the corridor near the Library and led by the Bishop and over thirty robed clergy, the coffin was carried by six parishioners, followed by two cousins of Sir Frederick and the rest of the Procession. They entered the church through the west door, where the Bishop read the opening sentences of the Burial Service. The coffin was then carried up the centre aisle and placed in front of the chancel screen. The Bishop read the lesson from St Paul's Letter to the Corinthians on the resurrection of the body and then the chorus *Jerusalem on High*, taken from Ouseley's oratorio *Hagar*, was sung by the choir, conducted by the Reverend John Hampton. At the end of the service, the coffin was born out of the church to Handel's *Dead March* from *Saul*, and the procession made its way through the churchyard to the east end of the church where a grave for the Founder had been prepared beneath the east window of the chancel. Everything was done with love and care and reverence, to make his burial worthy of the man. The grave was lined with moss, violets and primroses, which had been gathered by children from the parish school which Ouseley had founded. After the words of committal and concluding prayers, the choir sang the unaccompanied hymn *They come God's Messengers of love*, which the Founder had composed for the Dedication Festival more than thirty years before. Over five hundred people attended the Service, representing all parts of Ouseley's life. On the following two Sundays, Palm Sunday and Easter Day, there were many references to him in sermons preached in Tenbury, Hereford, Oxford, London and elsewhere. A week after the funeral, John Hampton wrote to Monty Alderson. 'Many thanks for your kind letter. I could not write before. Hundreds of letters still to be written. The Tenbury paper will tell you what we did on Thursday last. The sun shone out brightly and everything in nature looked lovely and cheerful except us poor mourners.'(12)

[Over 140 years since the Foundation of St Michael's, the church still celebrates the Annual Commemoration on the Feast of St Michael and All

Angels. (The nearest Sunday to 29 September.) A visiting choir are usually present to sing at the morning Eucharist and afterwards, the choir and congregation process through the churchyard to stand beside the Founder's grave. After a few prayers and the laying of a wreath on the gravestone, the choir sings Purcell's quiet and reflective anthem, *Thou knowest Lord.* Standing in the churchyard on a sunny autumn morning with Clee Hill and the Welsh Border hills in the distance is a memorable and moving experience and one is able to experience the Founder's vision in establishing his College in such a beautiful spot.]

On Sir Frederick Ouseley's grave is a Memorial recumbent Cross, subscribed for by fifty of his friends. The grave was designed by Mr Aston Webb, and consists of a block of polished red granite, on which lies a cross of white marble, supported at the ends by four small pillars. The inscription is as follows:

In loving memory of the

REVEREND SIR FREDERICK ARTHUR GORE OUSELEY, BARONET;

Born the 12th day of August 1825; died the 6th day of April 1889

Vicar of this Parish:

Founder of the church and College of St. Michael and All Angels

This stone was laid on his grave by a number of his friends

On the upper edge on either side of the stone are inscribed the following verses from Holy Scripture.

He shall give His Angels charge over thee, to keep thee in all thy ways
and *The redeemed of the Lord, shall return, and come with singing unto Zion*

A brass cross was placed in the church, close to his stall, with a similar inscription. (13)

REFERENCES

1. Joyce p. 217
2. Dibble – *C. Hubert H. Parry* page 266
3. Dibble – page 270
4. HCL D 863
5. HCL D 863
6. HCL D 863
7. Joyce p. 222
8. Joyce p. 222
9. Joyce p. 226
10. Tenbury Advertiser – quoted in *Memorials* page 12
11. Tenbury Advertiser – quoted in *Memorials* page 12
12. HCL D 863
13. Joyce p. 233

CHAPTER NINE

OUSELEY MYSTERIES

This chapter attempts to explains three mysteries which have come to light regarding aspects of Ouseley's life.

THE GOLD PLATE

In 1812, Ouseley's father, Sir Gore, was British Ambassador in Persia. He had succeeded in arranging a treaty between Persia and Russia (The Treaty of Tehran), which was intended to strengthen the hand of both countries in rebuffing Napoleon's territorial ambitions, part of which was seeking a route to India through either country. The Shah of Persia invested Sir Gore with the *Star of the Order of the Lion and the Sun*, and among other honours, presented him with an engraved gold plate (about the size of a large soup plate), with an enamelled lion and sun. Ouseley inherited the plate from his father and kept it at St Michael's throughout his life, along with many other Persian artifacts from Sir Gore's collection of and his large Oriental Library, collected on his travels as Ambassador. Ouseley frequently crept downstairs with it hidden under his coat to show people, before hurrying it back to its place of security in his upstairs rooms.

On Ouseley's death, and under the terms of his Will, the ownership of the plate passed to the Trustees appointed to run the College, and at that point, the problems began, as Watkins Shaw relates.

> Very shortly thereafter, yielding to persuasion on grounds of family sentiment, the College Trustees, with innocent guilelessness, unwarily allowed the plate to be held for life by two distant Ouseley relatives, under covenant for its eventual return. When, on the death of the second of these, it was duly claimed by the Trustees, it was stated to have been lost and the College was able to claim only limited financial recompense. That was in 1907. (1)

For almost fifty years, nothing was heard of the plate, until 24 October 1953, when a lady called Miss Dolly Lowe sent a cutting from the *Daily Telegraph* of the same date, to Canon Monty Alderson at Salisbury. After hearing from Alderson, F S Miles, the College Solicitor at Tenbury checked all the details and it appeared that this was the missing plate which the Shah had presented to Ouseley's father in 1812.

The gold enamelled plate presented to Sir George Ouseley by the Shah of Persia in 1812
Photo courtesy of Ouseley Trustees

The mystery of its disappearance deepened as the *Daily Telegraph* article mentioned it in connection with the auction, by Sotheby's, of the Treasures of ex-King Farouk of Egypt, which had been put up for auction by the Egyptian Government, to be sold in Cairo in February and March 1954. Everyone connected with the College was amazed at its reappearance, but doubts were expressed as to whether the College would ever be able to claim rightful ownership and secure its return to the College. F S Miles wrote immediately to Sotheby's, informing them of the plate's provenance and history, and pointing out that the College held a photograph of the plate.

> Assuming that this is the identical plate, can you help us in any way, particularly as to how it came into the possession of the ex-King and whether there is any knowledge or history of its previous whereabouts during the past fifty years and whether, to your knowledge, it has ever passed through any London sale Room...

It may be a forlorn hope to think that the Egyptian Government would consider (particularly after the lapse of time), any representations which might be made on behalf of the College, but I and my Co-Trustees would welcome any suggestions you may care to make. (2)

What happened to the plate between its disappearance after 1889 and its reappearance in 1953? The distant relatives of Ouseley, who had been 'loaned' the plate were able to shed some light on the matter, and the following letter was forwarded to the College Solicitor by a relative in 1907 on behalf of their son, who had 'borrowed' the plate himself, though for whatever reason one cannot imagine, and took it with him on a tour of northern Europe in 1905.

My dear father,

I hope that that you will make it quite clear to the executors who are now asking for the return of the 'tray' that it was not sold. It was taken out of my kitbag when I was travelling between London – Brighton – London – Dover –Calais – Brussels to Charleroi more than two years ago. I was then taking it to Charleroi where I then lived. My bag was not examined at the frontier and I did not discover the loss till I had reached my room in Charleroi.

I am, I was, terribly distressed about it, but as I did not know where it had been stolen from my bag, it was impossible to trace it. Again, I am most sincerely sorry about it, but you know as well as I do that I can do nothing now. I am very very sorry about it, and you may be sure that no one was more worried about its loss than I have been.

always your affectionate son, (3)

Although from that point, the 'trail' would seem to have ended, it has been possible to trace the plate back from its appearance in the Sotheby's sale catalogue in 1953, back through various dealers. Also, unknown to the College, Sotheby's sale information revealed that it had been exhibited by H A Kazarouni of Cairo at Burlington House in London in 1931.

As a result of the efforts of a Reuter's Correspondent, who went through Cairo's famous bazaars to try to trace how the plate found its way into Egypt, it was learned that it was sold to King Farouk for £3,075 sterling by a rich Persian carpet dealer, named H.A. Kazarouni in 1939. Kazarouni said that he bought it from an Egyptian, Moussa Mishihi, owner of a curiosity shop at Khan Khalil in 1928, because Mishihi was selling out his business. He, Mishihi, had bought it from another Khan Khalil dealer called Shereki in 1925. The latter had bought it from an Armenian antiquary in Paris shortly after the 1914-1918 War. Kazarouni said that the Armenian had acquired it from the Persian Prince Firouz, who had bought it in Bombay at the turn of the century. There are still missing links in its history during the past fifty years.(4)

A valiant bid by the College Solicitor to assert ownership was initiated, but sadly, this failed on account of the lapse of time. On 17 March 1954, the plate was offered for sale at the reserve price of £5,000. As the bidding failed to reach even that price, it was withdrawn by the Egyptian Government and it is believed that it may now be held at the Cairo Museum of Arab and Islamic Art.

THE ABERLOUR WINDOWS

In 1978, Donald Findlay of Clerkenwell in London discovered a stained glass window, dedicated to Ouseley in a church at Aberlour in Banffshire in Scotland. He then wrote to Sir John Dykes Bower, who had been Organist of St Paul's Cathedral from 1936 to 1968, and who in turn on passed on this information to Watkins Shaw, the honorary College Librarian. His first reaction was that it must refer to some other Ouseley, as there was no evidence of Ouseley having anything to do with this church. The windows are in the Church of St Mary, Aberlour and are a pair of lancet windows in the south wall nearest the transept which houses the organ, one depicting St Cecilia and the other St Gregory. The inscriptions read as follows.

> St Cecilia   St Gregory

A.M.D.G. et in carissimam memoriam Rev. Can. Sir F A G Ouseley, Bart, Mus. Doc. Oxon. 1890

The church was built in 1878 and is part of the Episcopalian Church of Scotland. Over the years since the windows became known, it has been difficult to find any further information, but there is one possible link with Ouseley. At the time these windows were installed, a neighbouring window was also installed in memory of the parents of the Reverend F E Scott, who was Assistant Curate of the Parish and Headmaster of St Drostan's College, Aberlour, a private school whose existence was short-lived and which closed soon afterwards. Records taken from an early Crockford show that Scott was a student at Christ Church, Oxford from 1883 and graduated BA in 1886, being ordained deacon the next year. During his time at Aberlour, he was called the 'choirmaster' and it seems reasonable to assume that he was trained in music by Ouseley during his time at Oxford. Ouseley had clearly impressed Scott and he installed the windows in his memory of his teacher, shortly after the latter's death.

HURSTPIERPOINT COLLEGE

In August 1977, Christopher Dean of Hurstpierpoint College discovered from the College Register for 1853, that the Reverend Sir F A Gore Ouseley was mentioned as being on the staff of the school and another reference from an Old Boy, who had written in 1911, stated that 'Ouseley was the first Precentor at Hurstpierpoint College and taught me a great deal.'(5) Watkins Shaw examined all the available records held at St

Michael's College, including Joyce's biography of Ouseley, but failed to find any connection. 'It is noticeable that (as you say), Joyce's *Life* makes no mention of any such connection, and Joyce was writing from the most intimate personal knowledge of Ouseley, who he knew well, and who had been his father's closest and lifelong friend.'(6) Shaw believed that in spite of the register entry, any connection seemed unlikely, as by 1853, Ouseley was making plans for the building of his College, after purchasing the land in the Tenbury area in 1852. He was also frequently visiting his 'fledging' choir based at Langley near Slough, which was under the care of John Hampton. It is clear that Ouseley was very busy during this time and it seemed unlikely he could have spent any time at Hurstpierpoint College. However, there is a connection. When Ouseley's *Special Anthems for Certain Seasons* was published in 1861, one of the subscribers was listed as the Reverend John Rich, and his address was given as *New Timber, Hurstpierpoint.*

> Now Rich was one of Ouseley's lifelong friends from his undergraduate days at Oxford and was an original Fellow of St Michael's. Is it possible that Ouseley stayed with him in 1853 and took an interest in the nearby College? Also, Hurstpierpoint was the first of the Woodard schools to be built in new buildings, although Lancing is a few months older. (7)

Further research by Mr. Dean in the College archives showed that Ouseley was not a salaried member of staff during the period 1852 to 1854, which the ledgers make clear. One can only suggest some link between the Reverend Rich and the College and Ouseley's interest in the newly-established College as he prepared to establish his own. It is quite possible that he took part in some of the services while staying with his friend and a boy (E.S. Churton), who had been there in 1853, perhaps assumed that he was a member of staff. (The College Registers were actually collated much later and the assumption perhaps carried over into them as well.) It is impossible to be more precise.

REFERENCES

1. Watkins Shaw, page 117
2. Letter from F.S. Miles to Sotheby's, 24 October 1953.(HCL D 863)
3. Letter to F.S. Miles, 17 July 1907 (HCL D 863)
4. College Magazine 1954
5. Letter from Christopher Dean to the Warden 21 August 1977 (HCL D 863)
6. Letter from Watkins Shaw to Christopher Dean 19 September 1977(HCL D 863)
7. Letter from Watkins Shaw to Christopher Dean 20 October 1977 (HCL D 863)

CHAPTER TEN

A NEW BEGINNING UNDER WARDEN HAMPTON
1889-1917

COLLEGE LIFE

After the death of Ouseley, there was some uncertainty as to the future of the College and a number of difficulties quickly became apparent. Ouseley's will gave various personal bequests, with the residue of his estate being left to three Executors and Trustees, the Reverend M C F Morris, the Reverend John Rich, and the Reverend T Ayscough Smith. In his will, Ouseley had also left John Hampton the considerable sum of £8,000, which attempted to recompense him for the non-payment of his salary as curate of the parish and Sub-Warden of the College, an anomaly which had existed for many years, despite many previous promises from Ouseley to remedy the situation. It can be seen as an expression of Ouseley's gratitude for all Hampton's work for the College and, furthermore, for his complete and utter loyalty to Ouseley. The will had been made in 1878 and contained specific instructions about the future of the College, reported by Alderson and Colles.

> The letters of instruction warned the legatees that if legislation should prevent the College being confined to members of the Church of England or otherwise interfere with the ecclesiastical or musical character of the place, the testator would wish them to apply the money to other church purposes such as missionary and educational societies; so determined was he that the Church should not be robbed by an increasingly secularist state. (1)

After a number of other personal bequests, the residue of the Founder's Estate was used to form the basis of a second trust for the benefit of the College, although any income was small as most of the capital assets were tied up in land in different parts of the country. These estates were later sold by the trustees. As a result, the overall income of the College was severely reduced after Ouseley's death. It was clear that those at the College faced a time of uncertainty. When the vacancy for a new Warden was advertised, the Fellows effectively ruled out most outsiders from applying by announcing that there would be no stipend. In the circumstances, they turned to the only man on whose loyalty they could completely rely, and in May 1889, John Hampton was elected to be

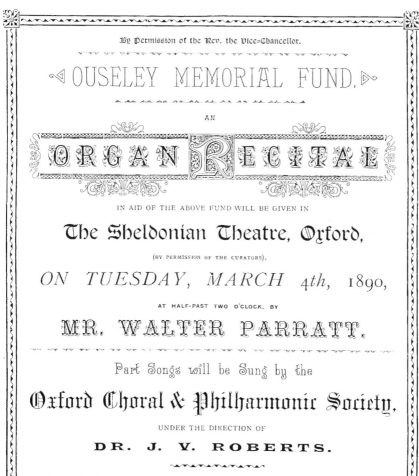

By Permission of the Rev. the Vice=Chancellor.

OUSELEY MEMORIAL FUND.

AN

ORGAN RECITAL

IN AID OF THE ABOVE FUND WILL BE GIVEN IN

The Sheldonian Theatre, Oxford,

(BY PERMISSION OF THE CURATORS),

ON TUESDAY, MARCH 4th, 1890,

AT HALF-PAST TWO O'CLOCK, BY

MR. WALTER PARRATT.

Part Songs will be Sung by the

Oxford Choral & Philharmonic Society,

UNDER THE DIRECTION OF

DR. J. V. ROBERTS.

Tickets : Semicircle and Area, 2s. 6d. ; Galleries, 1s., to be obtained only of Messrs. Russell and Co., 120, High Street, Oxford.

Doors Open at Two o'clock.   The Recital will terminate about Four o'clock.

J. T. Hall, Typ., Oxford.

Ouseley's successor as Warden and, in accordance with the Trust Deed, he also took on the responsibilities as Vicar of the Parish.

Hampton had thrown in his lot with St Michael's following his ordination in 1862. There is no doubt that Ouseley leaned on him heavily. From the start until going up to Cambridge, Hampton supplied the post of second master without payment. On his return, he received no remuneration as curate for about twenty years. In 1869, he was dignified with the appointment of Sub-Warden but this carried no salary. When one considers the numerous changes of headmaster, (to say nothing of assistants) and

Sir Frederick's unsuitability for direct control and administration, a good deal must have been owed to Hampton as a continuous anchorage and adjutant over some thirty years. It was not that he had no chance to move should he have so wished. Minor Canonries and Precentorships at Manchester, Bristol and Worcester Cathedrals might have been his and there was also some discussion of Westminster Abbey. But it was to St Michael's that he gave his loyalty.(2)

On taking over, Hampton was faced with a difficult situation. It was clear that severe economic cutbacks would be necessary in order to tide the College over what in today's terms would be called 'a cash-flow problem.' Two days after Ouseley's death, formal notice had been given to the entire staff, masters, organist and lay clerks. In Hampton's own words, 'The Hon. Fellows met and ultimately elected me to the Wardenship, expressly stipulating that I shall carry on exactly as Sir Frederick himself did and wished. Funds would not permit of the arrangements and two masters left and after the summer term we began with a new staff. All the lay clerks were dismissed, to be taken on again as funds improved.'(3) Within a short time, funds had improved and Hampton began to look to the future with something approaching confidence.

But Mr Hampton, at fifty-five years of age was not only buoyant of spirit and loyal to the memory of his former chief; he was generous towards the College. He was a man of no private means, yet from his well-earned legacy, he set aside £1,000 to be expended on the special needs of St Michael's as they arose and he was not long in finding needs to which his generosity could be applied. His personal effort was also supported by a fund raised by public subscription, headed by the Chancellor of Oxford University (Lord Salisbury) as a memorial to its last Professor of Music. This provided some £3000 for the present needs of Ouseley's Foundation. (4)

Over the years, Ouseley had spent much of his own income on maintaining the College and, on occasions, his finances had been quite stretched. With the choristers or probationers paying little or no fees, the College relied on the Warden admitting Commoners to swell the income, but the Trust Deed limited their number to sixteen and Ouseley had always regarded their admission as 'a privilege, given to a few sons of gentlemen.' Therefore, little effort had previously been made to increase the numbers.

Commemoration Services in 1889 and 1890 followed the normal pattern but a special request was made that the offertories were to be devoted to the fund for the completion of the endowment of St Michael's College. One popular event each Commemoration was the organ recital held in the church. G R Sinclair, a former old boy and now organist of

Hereford Cathedral, often played transcriptions of works by Elgar, who knew St Michael's well. A further link between St Michael's and Elgar was the publication by Novello of his four-part song *My love dwelt in a Northern land* in 1890. Older editions of the music state that the song is dedicated to 'The Reverend John Hampton, MA, Warden of St. Michael's College, Tenbury' and the first performance was given on 13 November 1890 by John Hampton and the Tenbury Music Society. He remained their conductor until 1900.

On 13 January 1891, Hampton followed further in Ouseley's footsteps when he was appointed Precentor of Hereford Cathedral. Hampton himself described his duties as Precentor as 'very light, involving a Sermon once a year and a special on the Sunday during the Music Festival.'(5)

Just over two years after Ouseley's death, an event occurred which was to have a marked improvement on the fortunes of the College and help to secure its future. In 1891, Miss Georgina Rushout died, and followed her sister in leaving money to St. Michael's, bequeathing the magnificent sum of £20,000 in trust to the church and College. She also left £ 4,000 for the restoration of Burford church. 'The Trust by which the Rushout Fund was created was drawn in such a way as to give the Trustees power to apply the income to any need of the institution which Ouseley had founded.(6) Over many years the College had owed an enormous debt of gratitude to the Rushout family of Burford House near Tenbury. From Harriet Rushout's original legacy, which had given Ouseley the impetus he needed to start building his church, to the many and varied gifts they had given to the church and College. These included the magnificent sacramental plate and altar vestments, the stained glass windows of the apse, valuable and extensive additions to the already well-stocked library. Miss Rushout had attached certain conditions to her bequest and her intentions are clear. 'It is my wish that no Warden be appointed who holds extreme views, nor the Masters or Curates under him, only the simple doctrine of the Church of England; Viability of the Sacraments, Baptismal Regeneration and Divine Life in the Eucharist (7)

At this point, being without any salary as Warden for the three years since his appointment, Hampton felt justified in approaching the Trustees to remedy the situation. The Trustees reluctantly agreed to his request, but pointed out that the College could ill afford such an expense. Hampton replied that he was already spending much of his own money on advertising the College, but after seeing that the College had a deficit of £ 300, the staff agreed to forego 5 % of their salaries, together with certain economies in running the College, notably the beer bill, and the deficit was soon cleared. Alderson and Colles, describing the College during the early years of Hampton's long tenure as Warden, felt that inevitably 'The place lost some of the glamour and personality with which Ouseley's personality and social position had invested it.'(8) This is perhaps unfair to Hampton, who had kept the College organisation running smoothly throughout Ouseley's frequent absences in London, Oxford or Hereford. It would also be right to state that when many eminent musicians and friends of Ouseley visited the College, it was Hampton's efforts in training and conducting the College choir which had produced such excellent results and impressed the many visitors. One of the original Fellows and a prominent church musician, E G Monk wrote to Hampton in August 1895, expressing his best wishes for the College's future success. 'I rejoice at St Michael's prosperity, given me in your interesting details. Long may it continue. Believe me always to remain an old friend and well wisher of St Michael's and the memory of its beloved Founder.'(9)

It has already been mentioned that Oxford University had started a Memorial Fund after Ouseley's death and the College itself had done the same. However at the same time, it was also thought appropriate to recognise his thirty years as Precentor of Hereford Cathedral by the provision of some memorial in the Cathedral, such as a stained glass window, and so a subscription fund was started. Sadly, many people had donated money directly to the needs of the College and the Hereford project did not get the attention it deserved. Ten years after Ouseley's death, the project had still not been completed. Accordingly, in February 1899, William Rayson, a Prebendary of Hereford and Fellow of St Michael's, sent out an Appeal Letter in order to obtain sufficient funds to provide a memorial window in the south aisle of Hereford Cathedral.

> I must apologise for addressing you as a stranger...I feel that I am in thorough sympathy with you in your reverence for the memory of our deceased friend Sir Frederick Ouseley and I therefore venture to send you the enclosed circular which will show you that we are desiring to make the Memorial in Hereford Cathedral more worthy of him whom we desire to commemorate than the two lights of a four light window. I shall be very glad if you can see your way to send ten shillings or any sum you like to Mr Sinclair, Canon Palmer or myself. I was the means of starting this completion fund nearly eight years ago but it hung fire at the time, many having contributed to the Memorial at St Michael's. But the Cathedral, of which for many years he was Precentor and afterwards Canon, ought to have a good memorial of him and in this I am sure many of his friends of the musical profession will concur. It is not large subscriptions we want, but many of them. (10)

This letter appeared to have the desired effect and arrangements were soon put in hand for a four-light window, designed by Powell, depicting four biblical characters with their musical instruments. Miriam (Timbrel), David (Harp), Asaph (Shawm), Deborah (her voice) and an inscription on a brass plate below the window.

Commemoration in 1899 included another organ recital by G R Sinclair, again featuring the music of Elgar. Sinclair had arranged some

The Ouseley window, Hereford Cathedral, South Aisle (1899)

of the Enigma Variations for organ, shortly after the first performance of the complete work in St. James Hall on 19 June 1899. Writing to his friend Jaeger at Novello's earlier in September, before the Tenbury Commemoration, Elgar comments on the possibility of these arrangements being published. 'Sinclair is playing some of the Variations at Tenbury. I think you published an arrangement by him of something. How is it done – practicable, saleable? And would it do to ask him to perpetrate an arrangement of some of them for organ?'(11) On 2 October 1902, Sinclair played the Prelude to *The Dream of Gerontius* at Tenbury, but it is unclear as to whether this was his own arrangement as on previous

ST. MICHAEL'S COLLEGE,
TENBURY.

FORTY - THIRD DEDICATION FESTIVAL, SEPTEMBER 29, 1899.

Holy Communion	8 a.m.
Mattins	11=30 a.m.

PROCESSIONAL.—Ps. cxxii ... ... *Rimbault.*
SERVICE IN G ... ... **Rev. W. Claxton.*
ANTHEM ... ... *Rev. Sir F. A. G. Ouseley, Bart.*

Ps. xlviii. 1.—"Great is the Lord and highly to be praised in the city of our God even upon His holy hill. Amen.

We wait for Thy loving kindness, O God, in the midst of Thy holy temple, Walk about Sion and go round about her, and tell the towers thereof. Mark well her bulwarks, set up her houses, that ye may tell them that come after. For this God is our God for ever and ever, He shall be our Guide unto death. Amen.

ANTHEM BEFORE SERMON ... ... *Rev. Sir F. A. G. Ouseley, Bart.*

Numbers xxiv. 5—6.—How goodly are thy tents O Jacob, and thy tabernacles O Israel; as the valleys are they spread forth, as gardens by the river-side.

Preacher, The Hon. and Very Rev. J. W. Leigh, D.D.
(DEAN OF HEREFORD.)

During the Collection ... ... Hymn 254.

Litany	3=30 p.m.

Evensong	5 p.m.

SERVICE ... ... *Smart in B flat.*
ANTHEM ... ... *Sir John Goss.*

Isaiah xlix. 18.—Lift up thine eyes round about and behold: all these gather themselves together and come to Thee. As I live, saith the Lord: thou shalt surely clothe thee with them all, as with an ornament, and bind them on thee as a bride doth. Thus saith the Lord God, Behold, I will lift up mine hand to the Gentiles, and set up a standard to the people: and they shall bring thy sons in their arms, and thy daughters shall be carried upon their shoulders. And Kings shall be thy nursing fathers, and their Queens thy nursing mothers: they shall bow down to thee with their face towards the earth, and thou shalt know that I am the Lord. For they shall not be ashamed that wait for me.

During the Collection - - - - - - - - Hymn 243.

ORGAN RECITAL by *Dr. G. R. SINCLAIR,
ORGANIST & MASTER OF THE CHORISTERS, HEREFORD CATHEDRAL.

1.—CONCERTO IN F (Allegro Moderato, Andante Moderato, Adagio, Allegro Pomposo) *Handel.*
2.—LARGO - - - (New World Symphony, Op. 95.) - - - *Dvořák.*
3.—MUSICAL MOMENT - - - (Op. 16.) - - - *Rachmaninoff.*
   Hymn 323.
4.—VARIATIONS ON AN ORIGINAL THEME (Op. 36.) - - - - *E. Elgar.*
   (i. iv. ix. xi. xiii.)
5.—ALLEGRETTO PASTORALE - "The Morning" (Op. 46.) - - - - *Grieg.*
6.—CAPRICCIOSO - - - Sonata in A major (Op. 188.) - - - *Rheinberger.*
   Hymn 136.
7.—CHORUS - - - "Thanks be to God." (Elijah) - - - *Mendelssohn.*

* Formerly a pupil at St. Michael's College.

Note: Organ Recital, Item 4 – Elgar's Enigma Variations

occasions, or whether he played the newly written transcription by Sir Herbert Brewer, Organist of Gloucester Cathedral, published by Novello in 1903.

Later in the year, before Commemoration began, a mural brass plate was placed over the Decani choir stalls in St Michael's church in memory of Sir John Stainer, Organist of St Michael's from 1857 to 1859. Presented by his eldest son (a former old boy of the College). 'It represented the distinguished musician in the attitude of prayer, together with a quotation from a poem by George Herbert.'(12)

During the summer of 1905, Edward Elgar had undertaken a Mediterranean cruise with some friends. One of the stops on the cruise was at Smyrna, where lay the Tomb of St Polycarp. In the Cathedral Library at Hereford, there is an envelope addressed to Dr Sinclair, the Cathedral Organist. Inside is a broken piece of card carrying part of Elgar's address in Malvern, *Craeg Lea*, inscribed in Elgar's own hand and dated 3 September 1905. 'In Memory of F A Gore Ouseley. Brought from St Polycarp's Tomb above Smyrna for G R Sinclair by his friend Edward Elgar.'(13) The card also carries two bars of music which were later authenticated by Sir Percy Hull, Sinclair's successor as Organist at Hereford and an Old Boy of St Michael's, as the 'Fellowship' theme from Elgar's *The Apostles.*

There are two ways of learning about the daily routine of College life, the more 'official' version by someone connected with the College and the more subjective reminiscences of former pupils as given later in this chapter. In an extensive serialised article in the magazine *The Architect and Contract Reporter,* the distinguished ecclesiologist J S Bumpus gives an 'official' account of life at St. Michael's during the year 1903 and this is worth reproducing in full.

> Twice daily in term time, at 9 am and 6 pm, Matins and Evensong, with the accompaniment of the choicest music, are as reverently and punctiliously performed in this remote spot as they would be in the midst of a crowded city. On Saints' days, the morning service is at 11 am. On all such days, and on certain Sundays, matins are followed by a choral celebration of the Holy Communion. The selection of music is large and representative, and comprises the finest specimens of the English school of cathedral music from the period of Tallis to the present day...The daily musical routine comprises an hour and a half in church and an hour's vocal practice in the hall with the Warden and Choirmaster, the Reverend John Hampton. There is a rehearsal with the full choir in the same place every Wednesday evening.
>
> There is schoolwork each weekday morning from 7 to 8 and from 10 to 12; in the afternoon, from 4 to 5.30; and again, in the evening from 7.45 to 8.45. Saints' days are half holidays from schoolwork. Boys who are taking lessons on the organ and pianoforte attend the

organist after morning school at 12. So from this timetable it will be clearly seen that musical work is a prominent but by no means an indispensable feature. Examinations are held at Christmas. (G R Sinclair acting as the Music Examiner.)

The boys have excellent cricket and football fields, a fives court, playground, gymnasium and a good school library. Recently, a carpenter's shop has been started and has proved a great source of interest. There are adequate facilities for bathing in a large pool, formed out of the Cadmore Brook, a narrow stream dividing the County of Hereford from that of Worcester, just below the cricket field. Attached to the College is a Foundation for eight choristers, to which boys are admitted only as vacancies occur after having served as probationers. The choristers receive their board and education gratuitously. probationers are elected after a competitive trial of voice and ear – preference being given to the sons of clergymen. They receive their education at an almost minimal cost. A certain number of Commoners, or boarders, are admitted on much higher terms. All boys wear the academical cap and scholar's gown in hall and the surplice in church. The last named is only worn by the commoners on 'surplice days' – ie. Saturday evenings, Sundays, Saints' days and the Eves of Saints' days. The adult portion of the choir is composed of the Warden, Headmaster, the second master and four professional lay clerks resident in the neighbourhood. The educational staff of the school consists of the head and second masters, both in Holy Orders, the organist, for instrumental music, and masters for French and writing. The vocal training is in the hands of the Warden. To his long experience and careful tuition is due the admirable and natural way in which the boys produce their voices and pronounce their words. Their uniform excellence of conduct and sobriety of demeanor in church is very noticeable. The adult members of the choir (both clerical and lay) sing with thoroughly artistic feeling, and with that hearty love for their noble art which alone makes it possible to produce such music adequately. (14)

Commemoration in the year 1906 was a special occasion, celebrating fifty years since the Foundation of the College. It took the form of an Octave of grand musical services and series of notable sermons by eminent preachers. (29 September to 6 October.) The first Evensong was a breathtaking occasion.

The church stood forth in its festal array. The altar was vested in a beautiful white frontal, with lighted tapers flanking the cross and vases of choice flowers. The church presented a most beautiful appearance, many lingering after the service to admire the long line of pendant brazen lamps (copies of those in the Holy Sepulchre at Jerusalem)...and the choir screen with seven lights on its summit.

Rarely has Woodyer's chaste and beautiful interior been seen to a greater advantage.(15)

Unlike the Day of Consecration fifty years before, when it was cold and wet, this anniversary fared much better. John Hampton wrote: 'From first to last, it was a typical day of late September, with a flood of golden sunshine and a sky of cloudless blue. The foliage was only just beginning to assume its autumnal tints, the flower beds in the picturesque grounds of the College were still ablaze with bright blossoms and the lawns were in the normal state of shaven trimness.'(16)

One person who attended the morning Communion on the 29th, noted as the choir and clergy entered through the west door that the church was still lacking a processional cross and that one or two 'richly-worked banners would also have enhanced the scene.' Sinclair's organ recital, during the evening of 30 September included the Prelude from Elgar's oratorio, *The Kingdom*. This was a special occasion as it actually took place three days before the first performance of the work in Birmingham on 3 October, surely a great honour for St Michael's. Tuesday 4 October was celebrated as Founders' Day, the choir singing Ouseley's anthem, *And it came to pass,* which had been written for the re-opening of Lichfield Cathedral in 1861. At other services, anthems by Boyce, Handel, Tallis and Ouseley were sung, together with service settings by Elvey, Ouseley and Rogers. There were many favourable comments about the standard of the music over the whole Festival. Edgar Broadhurst, the organist, was described as 'presiding at Willis's noble organ (the pride of the College), with consummate ability.'(17) The beauty of the boys' voices was also noted. 'The natural and unaffected way in which they pronounced their words, qualities all due to the sound musicianship and excellent training of the Warden, with his fifty years of experience.'(18)

Many people attributed the success of the Festival to the efforts of the Warden and it was noted:

> How earnestly and intently he throws himself into the work at St Michael's. His utter unselfishness and thoughtful kindness for the welfare of others, his careful planning of the most minute details. One and all must congratulate him on living to see not only the Jubilee of the Foundation, but also that of celebrating his connection with the work from the very inceptive stage, first at St Barnabas, Pimlico and subsequently (1851 to 1856) at Langley, near Windsor.(19)

The tomb of the Founder, situated in the churchyard centrally beneath the East Window, was neither forgotten or left unvisited. The beautiful flowers and wreaths covering the tomb were admired by many during the week.

On 30 September the Commemoration Sermon was given by the Reverend Canon E C Corfe, Precentor of Truro Cathedral and a Fellow and former pupil of St Michael's.

It is perhaps difficult to realise now, what obstacles and discouragements our Founder had to meet and overcome. The establishment of such an institution as this was regarded by many as at best a piece of quixotic folly, foredoomed in the nature of things to uselessness and failure. We know how Frederick Ouseley answered his critics; he simply went his way and did his work and put his trust in the Almighty. There is now no possible room for doubt or hesitation as to the result. God has shown plainly that he has accepted and blessed this College. In these fifty years, the children of this little school have made their way all over the world; not only in the ranks of the ministry, and in most of the English Cathedrals nor in the noble profession of music, but in the navy, army, scholastic work, letters, colonisation and commerce. Wherever they have been, whatever they have been, St Michael's boys have carried with them a deep reverence for music and an undying affection for their College.(20)

Canon Corfe spoke realistically of the last fifty years, that St Michael's could not hope to, and had not fulfilled literally, all the hopes and expectations of its Founder. Indeed there were times when 'disappointment and anxiety pressed heavily upon him.'(21) He spoke of St Michael's as not achieving success as the world views success. Its work passes comparatively unnoticed and is not widely spoken of. In the long run, the work that tells is that done without advertisement, that done quietly and unostentatiously. 'God has blessed these first fifty years, the first Collegiate church built in England for many centuries and in the future he will continue to bless us, if we look to Him with reliance, courage and hope.' (22)

In another sermon, preached on 4 October by the Reverend T A Ayscough Smith, he acknowledged the deep influence of the Oxford Movement on Ouseley and his College.

It was but natural, that a temperament so warm, so impulsive, so deeply spiritual as his, should have been affected by that great Movement, which, commencing at Oxford, had spread with what result is known to all throughout our land. And so it was that at the time of his college life at Oxford, corresponding with what may be termed the crisis in that Movement, its influence should have showed itself in him by directing his musical and religious instincts into that devotion to church music which became the absorbing motive of his whole afterlife.

Endowed as he was to an extent far beyond that almost divine gift of music, it was his desire to consecrate that gift by employing it in God's service, himself taking Holy Orders, although his in his father's mind, he had been destined for quite another calling. And then, as time went on and he became possessed of amply means, by devoting all to the formation of church and College which he raised on this very spot. (23)

Commemoration, c. 1916
Seated (l to r)
Canon G C E Ryley, Canon E C Corfe, Bishop C J Corfe, Reverend T A Ayscough, G R Sinclair
Photo courtesy of Ouseley Trustees

St. Michael's Church, 1913-18

Founders' Day was also noted for a meeting of Old Tenburians, held in the evening in College Hall, with the aim of forming an Association consisting of the Warden, Fellows and Old Boys of St Michael's, to be called *The St Michael's College Society*. John Hampton presided over this first meeting.

Some years later, the College was able to celebrate the Coronation of King George V which took place on Thursday 22 June 1911. It was a great honour for two boys from the College choir to be asked to go to London and sing with the Westminster Abbey Choir. The boys chosen were L S Mann, J W Hampton, the son of the Warden and Harold S Denton, the writer of the following account.

> We rehearsed regularly with Mr Hampton during the glorious weather of that Coronation summer. Our repertoire in church at that period contained little contemporary music and in the Coronation music we had our first introduction to Elgar, Parry and Stanford. The Stanford Gloria, specially written for the 1911 ceremony (repeated in 1937 and 1953), was considered by the late Dr Fellowes to be one of the finest examples of English church music.
>
> We left St Michael's on a Friday morning (16 June) in a waggonette for Tenbury Station. We were met at Paddington by Mr John Bumpus, the College Librarian. We stayed the first night with him and his brother at Stoke Newington. Next day he took us to Harrow where we were shown over the school by Mr Broadhurst, a former music master and organist at St Michael's. Our first rehearsal was in Church House, Westminster. Sir Hubert Parry conducted his own works and Sir Walter Parratt his own contributions. We attended two other rehearsals, one at St Margaret's and the other in Westminster Abbey.
>
> I do not wish my readers to suppose that the choir were in the best position for seeing the ceremony, because most of them were not. I myself was in row five on the Cantoris side, and had the organ case in front of me, but I could see in a diagonal line down to St Edward's Chair. I could also see the choir stalls (where numerous foreign Princes and Envoys were sitting. I could also see the chair which the Prince of Wales was to occupy and also the Royal Box where the other Royal children were...At about 11 o'clock, Parry's anthem, *I was glad* was sung, the 'Vivats' of the Westminster boys being included in this; they were sung as the Queen passed by and repeated in the King's Procession...I could not see the crowning or the anointing as there was a great pillar in the way. I saw the King sitting in St Edward's Chair. After the ceremony was over, I saw the King and Queen splendidly as they walked down the Nave. The Service ended at 1-50 and we got out of the Abbey by 2-30 pm. I saw a great many more people, but I could not take much account

The Reverend John Hampton – the second warden

of them as there was such a lot more to see. For our services, we were given one guinea each from His Majesty's Privy Purse and as a permanent memento, His Majesty's Coronation Medal.(24)

At the College, the Coronation festivities were many and varied and embraced the College and the local community. A luncheon for men and youths over 14, was followed by a short Consecration Service in Church and a tea for women and children. Later, everyone was able to enjoy a variety of sports and the day ended with a huge bonfire and firework display.

In the magazine *The Cathedral Quarterly,* written about 1913, The Right Reverend C J Corfe, former Bishop in Korea, a Fellow of St Michael's and one of the first boys there in 1856, compared the music presently sung at the College with that sung at the Consecration Service in 1856.

> During the fifty-seven years which have since elapsed, the daily Cathedral services, morning and evening, have been continued without interruption, except during the boys' summer and winter holidays. During the Michaelmas Festival which has just been commemorated, the Service setting was that of Smart in F, and the anthems were *Sing unto the Lord* and *How goodly are Thy tents* by Ouseley and *The glory of the Lord* by Goss. This may suffice to illustrate the conservative character of the music which prevailed during this long period.(25)

From 1913 until the time of Hampton's retirement as Warden in 1916, there is little actual material about the life of the College. Everyone's minds would soon be focused on the First World War and, like many other institutions, St Michael's would quite likely lose most of its younger staff to active service, replacing them with older, possibly retired schoolmasters, who were able to keep the College functioning during these extremely difficult times, having to cope with shortages of food, materials and manpower as well as continuing with the training and education of the boys at St Michael's. At the time of the Jubilee in 1906, Hampton was already 72 years old and had given most of his life to St Michael's. By 1916, the year of the College's Diamond Jubilee, Hampton was suffering problems of increasing age and failing health and, due to illness, was unable to attend what would be his last Commemoration as Warden. It is indicative of the dedication, hard work and loyalty of John Hampton that the College had managed to survive those sixty years. 'For the whole time I was connected with the College, it was a fight against expenditure for until three years ago, I was under the impression that the College was living up to its income and I so often put my hand into my pocket to save or keep expenses down.'(26)

Sadly, Hampton's retirement brought an exchange of letters between him and Norris and Miles, the College Solicitors. Many of his friends had assumed that in view of his long service, the College was paying him a pension and were amazed when they were told this was not so. Hampton wrote, giving details about all the money promised to him but never given and the attempt to correct matters through Ouseley's legacy. 'It gives me great pain to write all this. People will not believe that after 66 years in one service, I could retire without pension.'(27) The letter was given added poignancy as it was written on 29 September 1917, the feast day of St. Michael and Hampton's thoughts were very much with his old College!

REMINISCENCES

The following are shortened accounts written by boys who attended St Michael's between 1903 and 1918. It is noticeable that there is quite a distinction between their recollections of the Warden, John Hampton, and their accounts of the spartan conditions that existed at St Michael's during that time.

IVOR POWELL (1903)

In the spring of 1903, I arrived at St Michael's. A sheltered home life had not prepared me for the impact of boarding school. Even today, St Michael's is isolated, but think of it in the days when telephones were few and motor cars hardly seen. The school doctor, on his occasional visits, rode up from Tenbury on horseback. All rules were strict, particularly the out of bounds rules. The forbidden territory of the Common, our Berlin wall, separated us remorselessly from the rest of the world. It was a monastic existence, with an almost complete lack of the feminine touch, though you must meet our matron later on.

By present day standards we led a spartan life. I cannot forget the horrid sound of the handbell at 6-30 am on wintry mornings, the ice-cold dormitory, the chilblains and chapped hands, the lack of hot water for washing and the last minute scamper to get dressed in time for early morning school (before breakfast!) After that came prayers in the library, and at 8 am we were marched into hall for breakfast. Plates of stale bread, smeared with what must surely have been some experimental form of margarine, stared coldly at us from the long refectory table. The tea had a sullen look, and was dispensed from a battered enamel pitcher. Once a week we got a plate of thin porridge, and on Easter Sunday, we could count on an egg, appropriately hard-boiled. That was all, though I admit that breakfast was helped out by pots of jam from home. But as the term drew on, the pots of jam were few and those who had them were much envied and courted by the rest.

Our 1 pm dinner by no means atoned for the breakfast. Gristly, sometimes high, bits of meat swam in a watery fat. For second course it was a toss up between stewed rhubarb of the sourest variety and a deadly form of boiled pudding inevitably known as 'stodge.' The menu for tea, the third and final meal of the day was the same as for breakfast, but without the weekly porridge.

Once when I was head boy, I ventured to approach the Warden as he presided at High Table and drew his attention to an exceptionally nauseous brew of tea, 'Hampy' would have none of it and I retreated in confusion, pursued by angry Victorian rumblings. There was nothing wrong with the tea he spluttered, very red in the face and 'we all deserved to be horse-whipped.'

Austerity was indeed the order of the day. Except in emergencies at night, there was no permitted access to indoor sanitation. To meet the demands of nature during the daytime, expeditions had to be made to primitive earth closets well away from the College buildings. Now and then, in class time, a hand would be raised and a shrill treble voice would pipe out ' Please Sir, may I go down by the fives court?' These austerities, coupled with our meagre rations and the strict discipline, tended to make the boys themselves somewhat tough in their treatment of one another. Bullying was on the decline when I joined the school, but there was still a tendency to give a new boy a slight roasting in front of the schoolroom fire.

It was around the choir that our lives revolved. It is indeed surprising that time was left for ordinary schooling. On Wednesday evenings, the whole choir, men and boys assembled in the hall. It was a memorable scene, the masters and lay clerks seated at high table under the hanging oil lamps, the boys grouped at their music stands in front, the organist at the piano and 'Hampy' facing us, baton in hand. His expression was grave and mild, and if every he chided one of the lay clerks for a wrong note, it was in the gentlest of tones. A touch of Sir Thomas Beecham, perhaps, might have increased our virtuosity, but if anyone had hinted to us that a better choir was to be found in the whole of England, I, for one, should have felt deeply hurt...We were a little bulwark of Victorianism in a changing world...'Hampy' resolutely refused to move with the times, and though our young headmaster – whom we had to thank for an excellent grounding in Latin and Greek- was more progressive than 'Hampy', he certainly did not lack a proper Victorian faith in the virtues of the cane. Happily for myself, I had a good memory, but woe betide the luckless wretch who failed to memorise a Collect on Sunday morning!

As for the domestic staff, they exuded a positively Dickensian quality. Bob Tunadine, the butler, was a jolly old heathen, who never in any circumstances attended divine service, a remarkable feat of abstention, considering the ecclesiastical atmosphere in which we moved. Now and again on his afternoon off, he would celebrate a bit too freely in Tenbury. At the evening meal, his tottering gait and flushed face excited consternation at High Table, but delighted the rising generation. Bob was assisted by a page boy when one could be got. One engaging youth, like the rest of us, was often hungry, and succumbed to the temptation offered by any tuck to be found in our schoolroom lockers. He never polished off the entire contents of one locker, but took a large, semi-circular bite of jam sandwich, now here, now there.. No doubt he felt it cruel to rob one nest of all its eggs.

The most notable character of all was our elderly matron, who lived in a frowsy den down a short flight of steps at the end of the corridor. Here she would administer black draughts and paint sore throats with unrelenting hand. Now and then she would creep out like some embittered spirit, ever on the look out for juvenile delinquency. 'Now then, you boys' was her customary opening sentence. Many a parent tried to persuade 'Hampy' to get rid of her, but he would not. Somehow, I could not bring myself to dislike her. Once, after it was found that I had been in contact with a case of measles during the holidays, I was segregated from the other boys, and for a fortnight, was allowed to roam the countryside more or less as I pleased. One morning, I decided to pick wild flowers on the Common, and shyly presented the Matron with a bouquet of love-in-a-mist. She was clearly unused to attentions of this kind, and I was rewarded with a long whinneying laugh, not without a maternal warmth in its cadences. Some years after my time, she was found to have been juggling with the laundry accounts, and so at last she had to go. Poor old lady, she came to a tragic end, being burned to death when the house in which she was living caught fire.

We counted the days to the end of term with an even more heartfelt longing than most schoolboys. Term always started on a Sunday and ended on a Monday. As often as not, the anthem for the last Sunday night of term was Maurice Green's *Sing unto the Lord*, chosen for the aptness of its concluding words, 'Heaviness may endure for a night, but joy cometh in the morning.' (28)

CLIFFORD PRICE 1904 – 1906

I suppose that the question of food looms largest with any normal boy and after the substantial, if plain, food that one was accustomed to at home, the fare at St. Michael's was my main grievance. Such food most certainly would not be tolerated anywhere today. The bread almost always had whiskers on it. One got nothing for breakfast in the shape of egg, fish or meat without a special payment being made and quite a number of boys had to do without…The only occasion on which really excellent food was provided was at Michaelmas, and that more than the special music, was, I fear, the highlight to us of the festivities.

Tenbury without a car is still an inaccessible spot, as I know to my cost, and horse transport was all that was then available, so visits from my parents were much fewer than they are now. The Sunday afternoon walk comprised the whole school and the variations of route were few. For the same reasons our school outings were very limited and matches against other schools were almost non-existent, apart from matches against Lucton and Ludlow. Bathing in those days was a burden to my flesh. We had to go to a pool in the Cadmore Brook, frequented by four-footed creatures as well as ourselves and I can only suppose that chlorinated water is not as essential to health as one is now led to suppose.

Nearly half of those who were at College with me failed to survive the 1914-1918 War. For myself, I shall always believe that my time at the College gave me a better start in work and play than I should have had elsewhere, and that what I think would be regarded by the boys now at St Michael's as grave hardships did one good. (29)

MICHAEL THOROLD (1912 – 1918)

When one thinks of the pre-1914 days, the figure standing out most vividly in one's recollections is that of the Warden himself...He was a most kindly man. With this however, went a great dignity. He never needed to assert his authority – I don't think anyone ever questioned it, or, if they did, I am certain they did not do so a second time! His chief concern was with the music of the College and the training he gave us was remarkable and thorough. He took great pains over voice-production and (again like the Founder), would often insert a coin into a boy's mouth to ensure that it was properly opened. He would afterwards give us the money. He was amazingly active and very much 'on the spot.' If there was any musical catastrophe in Chapel, he would strike the side of his stall sharply – 'smacking his baby', we used to say.

I recall the pleasant scent of his cigars; the time when I, coming back from 'Tombo's, (the local post office and tuck shop), and meeting him going down from College to the Vicarage, offered him a sweet, receiving the reply, 'What! sweets on Ash Wednesday!' The pleasant Sunday evenings at the Vicarage, when he, with Mrs. Hampton and their family, entertained two of us in turn each Sunday night for supper – and what a delicious supper it used to be! – the sadness of his illness and resignation. When he finally left St Michael's, I used to go over to Eye in Somerset to see him when I could get permission, and when I said good-bye to him for the last time, on my leaving St Michael's, Mrs. Hampton gave me 2/6 from him, after we had come downstairs from his room, 'because he did not think he would see you again.'

Those of us who were there in these years were unfortunate by reason of the many changes of staff that took place after the end of 1916. These were partly due to the Warden's resignation, partly to the war. (30)

REFERENCES

1. Alderson & Colles p. 52
2. Watkins Shaw pp.50-51
3. Hampton mss, HCL D863
4. Alderson & Colles p. 53
5. Hampton mss, D863
6. Alderson & Colles p. 54
7. Alderson & Colles p. 53
8. HCL D863
9. Maria Hackett Letters, Royal College of Music

10. HCL D863
11. Percy Young, *Letters to Nimrod* p. 61
12. HCL D863
13. J.S. Bumpus, *The Architect and Contract Reporter*, 3rd,10th,17th & 24th July 1903
14. HCL D863
15. HCL D863
16. Memorabilia 1906 HCL D 863
17. Memorabilia 1906 HCL D 863
18. Memorabilia 1906 HCL D 863
19. Memorabilia 1906 HCL D 863
20. Memorabilia 1906 HCL D 863
21. Memorabilia 1906 HCL D 863
22. Memorabilia 1906 HCL D 863
23. Memorabilia 1906 HCL D 863
24. Memorabilia 1906 HCL D 863
25. Article in *The Cathedral Quarterly* c. 1913
26. Hampton mss, HCL D863
27. Hampton mss, HCL D863
28. College Magazine December 1978
29. College Magazine 1956
30. College Magazine 1956

Cubicles in big dormitory

The dining hall, looking west, 1920's
Photos courtesy of English Heritage, National Monuments Record

CHAPTER ELEVEN
COLLEGE LIFE UNDER WARDEN SWANN
1917-1936

At the end of 1916, the Trustees met to elect a new Warden. They chose the Reverend G C E Ryley B Mus., MA, who had worked at the College for a short time as assistant master some years ago and was now a Fellow. However, within a few days of taking up the appointment, a sudden and serious illness compelled him to resign. The only action he took in his time as Warden was to appoint two new Fellows, his immediate predecessor as Warden, John Hampton, and Ernest Breffit, an Old Boy of the College who became the first Secretary of the St Michael's College Society. There was now an interregnum of some months and Canon Corfe, another old boy and now Precentor of Truro Cathedral, became Sub-Warden and temporarily took charge, although he made it clear that he would not be able to accept the post of Warden on a permanent basis. A few months later, the Trustees appointed the Reverend Ernest Henry Swann as the new Warden. A former Cambridge Exhibitioner and Organ Scholar, he had taught at Great Yarmouth Grammar School for some years before being appointed as a Minor Canon of Ripon Cathedral, later becoming Precentor. From his varied experience, he was well qualified to take charge of St Michael's, although at an unsettling time due to the First World War. The Headmaster and Second Master were ready to leave and the Organist had already been 'called up' for war service. It was a time when parents were wary of making what could be heavy financial commitments for their children's education and as a result, future numbers at the College were uncertain. Nevertheless, he looked forward to the challenge. One of the first matters to take his attention was the condition of the original College buildings, which were in urgent need of refurbishment and improvement. At the time the College had no electricity, was in desperate need of improved plumbing and a hot water supply, and needed much re-decoration.

With the small number of boys at the College (23) on his arrival, Swann realised that the school could not function economically unless the number of 'commoners' or non-singing boys was considerably increased. Such a move would place impossible demands on the limited amount of teaching accommodation available. Watkins Shaw explains how the Trustees planned to finance substantial building developments. 'To pay for these developments, most of Ouseley's remaining family possessions were sold, thus converting one kind of trust property into another. Engravings, silver, glass, Persian furniture and other 'art treasures' as well as some few selected volumes from the non-musical library.'(1) Another of Swann's early developments was the institution of a College Magazine, which ran on a termly basis for some years, before reverting to two editions a year, in December and July and finally, a yearly edition which continued until the closure of the College in 1985. Swann justified this development in the following way. 'Every boy who takes a pride in his school and its future likes to have a record of his achievements, and every old boy who remembers what he owes to his old school, likes to see what his successors are doing, and how worthily they are carrying out its traditions. Therefore we confidently hope for the support of both present and past members of the College.' (2)

Other changes in the buildings began to take effect. A new boiler was fitted, radiators were placed in the dining room and classroom and a second bathroom was added, with a much improved hot water supply and the large dormitory was cleaned and re-decorated. The boys revelled in the luxury of hot water at any time of the day, particularly in the early mornings. New equipment was provided for the newly-refurbished gymnasium. The heating in the church was also improved with a new boiler and sixteen new radiators, in addition to the seven already there, with the pipework being laid under gratings on both sides of, and across the nave.

Despite all these difficulties, the choir, under temporary organists for the period up to the end of the War, managed to add 17 new services to their repertoire as well as learning 31 new anthems. On 7 Sunday July 1918 a Memorial Service was held in the church for those who had laid down their lives in the War, ending in a short recital of Tallis' *Funeral Music.*

Another difficulty was that the Willis organ of 1870 was a large four-manual one which had always been pumped by hand, requiring two people to do the job properly. Sadly, with a shortage of labour, much damage was being done and it was decided to launch an appeal for the provision of a mechanical blowing apparatus, which was going to cost about £ 450. The Trustees promised £ 200 and £ 120 had already been raised by the College with the hope of the remaining £ 130 being donated, particularly from Old Boys. It was later reported that Bishop Corfe had donated £ 100 towards the appeal and plans were made to install the new blowing equipment the following summer.

After the death of John Bumpus, the College Librarian, the previous year, followed by the sudden death of his newly-appointed successor, the Reverend G Surtees Talbot, the Fellows appointed the Reverend E H Fellowes as Honorary Librarian. It was Fellowes' intention to sort, repair, and catalogue the complete Music Library, a task which was to take him some thirty years, and after the bookshelves in the College Library were extended, the whole of the Music Library as well as the General Library is now in the same room.

By the end of 1918, many more changes had taken place with the provision of cassocks for the choir for the first time, red for the boys and black for the men. It was also felt that a number of items were needed for the church, including a Processional Cross, a carpet for the Sanctuary, a St Michael banner, green and red altar frontals and seven sanctuary lamps. In February 1919, on his return from War Service, Dr Ernest Bullock was appointed as Organist and Music Master of the College, after being Assistant Organist at Manchester Cathedral before the War.

The main talking point throughout the term was the installation of electricity. 'We not only install, but talk electricity. – volts, watts, currents, switches, bulbs, controls, and other technical jargon are now becoming familiar as ABC and we shall see the result when we return next term. Gone are the smelling oil lamps and the flickering candle. All you will have to do is to press the button and, as you know, we do the rest.'(3)

The electrification of the organ was installed in memory of Dr G R Sinclair, Organist of Hereford Cathedral, who had died in 1917 and was an old boy of the College. The new organ blower had already been used on a few occasions. However, it had to be used directly off the engine until the accumulator batteries were installed. July 1919 was a notable month, with three Organ Recitals in the church. Sydney Nicholson (Westminster Abbey) on 8 July, Ernest Bullock on 17 July and Edward Bairstow (York Minster) on 30 July. (Bairstow's son attended the College from 1926 to 1930.)

The summer of 1919 was the first one since the end of the War and there were many peace celebrations in the area with teas, bonfires and fireworks.

Many of the boys were keen on improving facilities at the College and with adult help, an organisation called the Odd Jobbers Company was started. Some of their first jobs included providing racks for the boot room, a 44 ft flag pole and the construction of 26 steps from the west bank of the terrace down to the cricket pitch. (Built in 1919, they are still very much in use today!)

By September 1919, the provision of electricity in the College had been completed. The editor of the College Magazine spoke eloquently of its arrival.

Not even Sinbad ever experienced the delight we feel when, by pressing a switch, we illumine gross darkness with a flood of brilliant light. Have you Ever seen a young child with a new toy? Then you have seen us turning on the electric light. And the fun of it is that there are switches everywhere. I should like to go on a voyage of exploration, and turn on every switch there is on the premises – but I haven't the time between now and Christmas (4)

Commemoration in September was rather uneventful due to a railway strike, as only one Fellow managed to attend and there were very few other visitors. However, many residents came from Tenbury to hear a fine Organ Recital from Dr Bullock, with another one taking place in November. The music at these recitals compares favourably with many of today's recital programmes, and included works by Bach, Jongen, Bairstow, Debussy, Stanford, Franck, Harwood, Karg-Elert, Reubke and Saint-Saens. Sadly the November Recital was to be his last, as it was announced that Dr Bullock would be leaving at the end of term to take up the post of Organist of Exeter Cathedral. The College had greatly appreciated his work. 'He has delighted all those who have been privileged to hear him, by his brilliant talent and he has added materially to the advance made in the musical rendering of the choral services in Chapel as well as the progress which the boys have made in instrumental as well as vocal music.'(5) Dr Bullock's successor at St Michael's was to be Heathcote Statham, who had attended St Michael's some fifteen years previously and whose musical studies at the Royal College of Music were supervised by Sir Walter Parratt (organ), Sir Charles Stanford (Composition) and Sir Frederick Bridge (Counterpoint). He obtained a Cambridge B Mus. Degree and was ideally qualified for St Michael's.

Generally, facilities for the boys had greatly improved after the end of the War and there were many interesting activities available for their leisure hours, including a Cub and Scout Troop, a model railway layout, a fully equipped gymnasium and the many sports and games, part of the life of any lively preparatory school.

The school numbers were encouraging and had risen from 23 in 1918 to 36 in April 1920, a testimony to the efforts made by Warden Swann to get the school on a sound financial footing. Another modern innovation was an application to the Post Office for the installation of a telephone line to the College, which was completed during the summer holidays and proved of great benefit to all at the College.

Musically, the College went from strength to strength, learning particularly the difficult Brahms *Requiem,* which was being given two performances with the help of the Tenbury Music Society at the end of term. Heathcote Statham, the College Organist, was also congratulated on being awarded his FRCO, and the boys were awarded a half-day holiday in honour of this success. Towards the end of term on Good Friday, the College choir performed a new choral work, *The Passion of Our Lord according to St Mark* by Charles Wood, intended for small choirs unable to achieve the heights of Bach's Passion music.

After looking at a number of suggestions for a War Memorial to old boys, it was decided to have a Processional Cross made for the church, to be made of solid silver, with five gilt medallions, the Agnus Dei in the centre surrounded by four Warrior Saints, St Michael, St George, St Aidan and St Martin, costing about £70, of which £50 had already been raised. The Cross was completed in time to be used for the first time on Easter Day.

At a meeting of the Fellows early in 1921, the College Statutes were revised and approved by the College Visitor, the Bishop of Hereford. They took into account the various changes that had occurred in the organisation of the College since the death of the Founder. Sir Ivor Atkins, Organist of Worcester Cathedral and a great friend of Sir Edward Elgar, was appointed as a College Fellow.

The College was saddened to hear of the death of Bishop Charles Corfe, who died in London. He had been one of the first boys at St Michael's in 1856, coming with his brother from Langley. He was an assistant master at St Michael's from 1865 to 1867, before becoming a naval chaplain, serving on a number of ships until 1889, when he was consecrated as Bishop of Korea. He spent most of his retirement in England, helping particularly with Confirmations, and had confirmed boys at St Michael's, some years previously. A Memorial Service was held in the church on 4 July, Bishop Corfe's executors sent the College a cheque for £50, 'to be used for the College, church or parish at the Warden's discretion.' After some consultation, this money was spent on the purchase of a handsome Persian Sanctuary carpet, which has added considerably to the dignity and beauty of the East End of the Church.

More developments took place with the purchase of a gramophone, enabling the boys to hear many of the works of the great masters although it was reported that many of fell asleep on the floor while listening to the music. By now, the numbers in the school had risen to 41 and accommodation was becoming rather crowded. It was decided to remove some of the partitions between the cubicles in the big dormitory, so that four sets of two cubicles were converted into four larger ones, each containing three beds. What was called the chapel dormitory, used for the younger boys, had the cubicles taken out in order to provide more room and one of the windows was enlarged in order to provide an additional fire escape, with an iron balcony and ladder being fixed to the outside wall.

4 December 1921 was a very sad day in the life of the College with the announcement of the death of the Reverend John Hampton at his home in Somerset. He had been unwell for the previous two weeks and died peacefully, surrounded by his family.

His death removes from St Michael's a link with the past, but his memory will long be cherished by all those who are connected with the College, where he spent practically the whole of his long life, and which he loved so dearly and so well. His body was laid to rest on Thursday 8 December at the east end of the church, next to the grave of the Founder, as was right and fitting. After a moving funeral service, the choristers sang the hymn, *They come, God's messengers of love,* to the Founder's tune *Woolmers.* There was a large gathering of friends from the parish and from Tenbury and many floral tributes, testifying to the affection in which the late Warden was held. 'Now that his grave, beside our Founder's, looks towards the sunrise, the love that we have given him is his still.'(6)

A fund was started to provide a church clock in memory of the late Warden, and within a few months, donations had reached over £250 with the fund remaining open for further donations.

Since April 1922, the choir had not learnt any new music, but instead, were becoming familiar with some of the great music of the sixteenth and seventeenth centuries. The choir planned to make a special study of the music of one of the great church composers each term, starting with Henry Purcell in the summer term. In the Michaelmas term, the choir studied the music of S S Wesley and also that of his father and sang many of their services and anthems. In December 1922, the College choir again joined forces with the Tenbury Music Society to sing Mozart's *Requiem* in Tenbury parish church on the evening of 13 December, and again at St Michael's the following afternoon. One significant change in the choir was the introduction of *The English Hymnal* to replace *Hymns Ancient and Modern*, justifying the decision in the following way. 'It was believed to be the best hymnbook in existence and we feel sure that, on account of the words and tunes to which they are set, we shall soon learn to appreciate it.'(7) With the larger number of non-choir boys or Commoners in the school, it was decided to form a Commoners' choir and on Friday mornings, they were able to sing some verses of hymns themselves without the support of the College choir.

The Trustees' decided to build on the old playground site, four modern, well-equipped classrooms, changing rooms on the ground floor, and above them, rooms for masters and visitors. Work was due to start over the Easter holidays and was planned to be complete in time for the start of the Michaelmas Term. As the College was spending £4000 on the new accommodation, it was felt that the cost of providing a new playground on the south field and which would require substantial levelling could be met by voluntary subscription. (£ 100).

The choir made a special study of the music of Charles Stanford and Charles Wood during this term and also added six anthems by Wood to their repertoire, *Hail gladdening Light, Expectans Expectavi, and O Thou the Central Orb.* The Bishop of Hereford also made two visits to the College within the space of six days during March 1923, first ordaining Mr Hayter, a member of the college staff as a Deacon, (the first ordination held at St Michael's for 48 years), and then a second visit to confirm nine boys. (One of the boys confirmed was Noel Kemp-Welch, who became Warden of the College many years later.) During the summer term, the choir made special study of the music of William Byrd to celebrate his Tercentenary. All members of the College congratulated Heathcote Statham on the award of a D Mus. degree by Cambridge University, a great achievement, as only five Doctor of Music degrees had been awarded in the previous 25 years.

During the term, the new buildings were completed at last. The general view was that they were bright and cheerful, well ventilated, well lighted and well heated. Schoolwork was now able to be done under the best possible conditions. The new playground was levelled but would need to settle before the top layer was applied. At Commemoration, a new set of oak fronts for the boys' choir stalls were dedicated in memory of Bishop Corfe and which replaced the previous open metal fronts. The workmanship was excellent and embodied designs from the old stalls.

The new buildings were now in full use, especially the changing rooms and it was hoped that the new playground would be ready by Michaelmas. Mrs. Crowther, widow of a former master of St Michael's Church School, presented electric roll lights for the pulpit, lectern and organ. They were a great improvement on the not-altogether beautiful and decidedly domestic oil lamps.

On 13 December, Dr Statham gave an organ recital and there was also a number of items sung by the combined College choir and the Tenbury Music Society, including Parry's *Blest Pair of Sirens* and Wood's *Hail gladdening Light.*

The boys were acquitting themselves well in choir and towards the end of the term, Kemp-Welch, Ensor and Hare accompanied part of the service on the organ and did so very creditably. During the Summer term, they accompanied the weekday services on several occasions and occasionally played one of the voluntaries after Evensong on a Sunday. 'It is not often that the choir has had three such splendid musicians at the same time and their work has been of great value to the choir as well as a shining inspiration to the other boys. It is sad that they are all leaving together, but we hope that they will keep up their organ playing.'(8)

During this term, the number of boys had reached 49 and facilities were further improved. During the summer holidays, two larger 'dormer' windows were put in the roof of the big dormitory, one at each end, providing much needed lighting and better ventilation. The Governors installed a third window during the next year.

News reached the College of the publication of Dr Fellowes, 'magnum opus', the editing of *English Madrigals of the 16th Century Composers*. This was published in a series of thirty-six volumes by Stainer and Bell, the last appearing during 1924. 'It is thanks to Dr Fellowes that we are now able to sing both sacred and secular music of the sixteenth century as the composers undoubtedly intended it to be sung.' (9)

On the educational side, the teaching of French was vastly improved by the introduction of a new department, equipped with wall pictures, etc. to introduce the Linguaphone method of teaching. By hearing the French language spoken in the correct accent by mean of a series of gramophone records, it was hoped that the teaching would become far more effective and add much interest to the subject. At the end of term, the choir were saddened to be losing Dr Statham, who had been organist and choirmaster for the last five years. 'He has shown unremitting interest in the musical life of the College as well as other departments and his valuable help and advice is responsible for St Michael's continued high position in the musical world and we are proud to think of him as an old boy of the College. He has edited many of the services and anthems in our Music Library.'(10) Dr Statham moved to be organist of St Mary's, Southampton before becoming organist of Norwich Cathedral in 1928.

In the church, the term was marked with a very important Organ recital. The distinguished French organist and composer, Louis Vierne (Organist of Notre Dame Cathedral in Paris), toured England and gave a series of Recitals. St Michael's was extremely fortunate in obtaining his services and the Warden appealed for donations to cover the heavy expense involved. (£30) Vierne gave his long-awaited recital at St Michael's on 7 May. He was almost sixty, nearly blind, and played all his pieces from memory. Everyone spoke highly of his masterly performance, the church being filled to capacity and the expenses being more than covered.

Commemoration in September 1925 was of special significance, celebrating the hundredth Anniversary of the Founder's birth. As a consequence, much of the music performed was Ouseley's and included *Jerusalem on High* from his oratorio *Hagar* and his Evensong Canticles in Bb. The anthem sung was Ouseley's *Give thanks O Lord*. One of the oldest members of the College, Canon Corfe, was able to come and preach, and naturally, made many interesting and touching references to the days when the Founder was still alive. Percy Hull, now the Organist of Hereford Cathedral, gave an excellent Organ Recital to one of the largest audiences ever seen in the Church.

Christopher Hassall, aged 13 and a half and later to become a famous poet, was appointed as one of the Choir Monitors. In the College Magazine for December 1925, he wrote the following poem to celebrate Christmas.

CHRISTMAS DAY ELSEWHERE

Everyone who walks this earth
Does nearly always say,
When bubbling o'er with Yuletide mirth,
'How spend you Christmas Day?'

Some will take it as a joke,
And talk of indigestion,
But let me ask some fancy-folk
To ease you of your question.

The early morn is spent in prayers,
At ten we go to Chapel,
Whilst Grandmama meanwhile prepares
Our tart of plum and apple.

At dinner-time a goodly meal
Lies spread upon the table.
And, having satisfied our fill,
We romp if we are able.

At tea we simply feast away
On cake or toasted crumpet,
Whilst Uncle Joe attempts to play
Upon his big bass trumpet.

But grandma is growing grey,
And early does retire,
Whilst we remain to end the day,
And gossip round the fire.

When twelve o'clock sounds deep and clear
We all retire to sleep;
And that's the way, O reader dear,
Good Christmas Day we keep.

A merry Xmas to all ye
Who read this magazine,
I hope this dawning year will be
The best you've ever seen.

(11)

When the boys returned to College at the beginning of 1926, one new innovation for the College was the purchase of a Wireless Receiver, consisting of a three-valve set and a loudspeaker, which was placed in the Library with an extension in the reading Room. It was much appreciated by the staff and the next term, it was brought into full use for the boys, giving them the opportunity of listening to some of the excellent talks to Schools.

Commemoration was the usual well attended affair in September 1926 and Dr Edward Bairstow, organist of York Minster gave a splendid organ recital to a very large audience. By the end of term, the number of boys had dropped to 42 as older boys had left, but numbers were expected to increase in the following year. On the last night of the Michaelmas term, the choristers, probationers and the Tenbury Music Society gave a performance of Handel's *Messiah* to a large audience.

Captain Butler, one of the first choristers, died at the age of 82, and was buried in the shadow of the College he loved so well. His executors kindly presented two church bells to the church, but it was found impossible to hang them. Instead, it was decided to sell them and with the money raised, two fine carved oak organ screens were made, one for the front of the organ in the chancel, and one for the side in the south aisle.

One of the Governors' development plans was the provision of a swimming pool in the College grounds. With a promised yearly donation of £5 from the Reverend Monty Alderson, the Warden appealed for donations as it was vitally important that all boys are taught to swim. For many years, some of the senior boys had gone to the river in Tenbury, but owing to problems with transport, their visits had been infrequent.

During the year, the Governors spent much time on revising the Statutes and the following extract represents what in modern phraseology would be called a 'Mission Statement'.

> The Object of the College is to prepare a course of training and to form a model for the Choral Service of the Church in these realms; and for the furtherance of this object, maintain two daily Choral Services throughout each term and to receive, educate and train boys in religious music and secular knowledge. It is enjoined on all who shall at any time be connected with the College, that they carefully bear in mind the main object of the Foundation and that they be mindful in all that they say or do to promote that and as far as in them lies; thus, and only thus can they best carry out the wishes and intentions of the Founder. (12)

News of note during 1927 was the announcement of the appointment of Dr Ernest Bullock as Organist of Westminster Abbey. Dr Bullock had left St. Michael's at the end of 1919 on his appointment as Organist of Exeter Cathedral and congratulations were sent by everyone at the College. Commemoration Services in September were notable for the visits of so many prominent figures in the world of music and the church. These included the Bishop of Hereford, the Deans of Windsor and Hereford, Dr Fellowes, Sir Ivor Atkins, Dr Percy Hull and Sydney Nicholson, as well as Old Boys such as Monty Alderson, F. Bennett, and A F de Gex.

During the years since Reverend Swann's appointment as Warden, and the increase in number to around 50 boys, the College became more securely established on a sound financial footing and as a result, was able to put some income aside into a Reserve Fund to cover any financial problems or unexpected expenses which may occur in the future. Also, the College, although still concerned with its own well-being and survival, was able to look outwards and encouraged the boys to support deserving charitable causes. This was done through a collecting box in the College 'tuck-shop'. For a number of years, money collected in this way was given to the Melanesian Mission by a yearly donation of £ 10. Earlier in the year, the Travelling Secretary of the Mission had visited the College and, by means of an Interesting Lantern Lecture, aroused the enthusiasm of the boys to do even more for the Mission. Two of the boys were appointed as Secretaries and with the help of the Committee, organised a Jumble Sale on behalf of the Mission, while the Warden's wife, Mrs Swann, raised more money by selling photographs of the College which she had taken herself.

Commemoration on 3 October was attended by many visitors, the Bishop of Winchester preaching and the Organist of Salisbury Cathedral, Dr Walter G Alcock, gave a fine Organ Recital. Later in the term, on 3 December, the Tenbury Music Society invited Dr. Ernest Bullock to give an Organ Recital, and this included various choral items from the Music Society Choir and the College Choir.

The College was pleased to hear the news of an Old Boy and former organist, Dr Heathcote Statham, who had just been appointed organist of Norwich Cathedral, a position he was to hold for almost thirty years.

On 14 May, the College choir were asked to sing the services in Hereford Cathedral on the occasion of the Diocesan Missionary Festival and 27 June 1930 was a Red Letter day in the life of the College when six choristers and all the adult choir members went up to London to take part in the Festival of English Church Music, held at the Royal Albert Hall. Early in the morning, the party set off for Worcester in taxis and took the train to London, arriving shortly after 11 am. The rehearsal started at 1 pm and ended at 5 pm. At 7-30 pm, everyone assembled for half an hour's hymn singing, conducted by Walford Davies, and the Service began at 8 pm, with the choirs of the affiliated cathedrals and collegiate churches (including St Michael's of course) entered in procession, followed by the boys of parish church choirs. There followed a feast of music lasting more than two hours, conducted by Sydney Nicholson, and including music which was representative of every style and period. Beginning with plainsong and ending with Stanford's *Te Deum* in Bb, it included Orlando Gibbons and Purcell, Walmisley and Wesley, Sterndale Bennett and Parry, Balfour Gardiner, Elgar, Holst, Geoffrey and Martin Shaw, Vaughan Williams, Basil Harwood and Walford Davies. 182 choirs took part and listeners were struck with the marvellous way in which Dr Nicholson controlled so large a body of singers (some 1200) and kept them together. Dr Ernest Bullock was an inspiring accompanist on the organ and the singing was interspersed with organ solos by Dr Henry Ley.

After some time chasing round the endless corridors of the Albert Hall, the choirs at last found some refreshment and then were conveyed by bus to Southampton Row, where they were put up for the remainder of the night in various hotels, everyone finally getting to bed by 1 am. After a sumptious hotel breakfast the next morning, most of the boys spent the morning at Madame Tussaud's with Mr Thorne, the St. Michael's Organist, before meeting back at Paddington with a packed lunch in time to catch the 12-45 pm train back to Worcester, arriving back at St Michael's at 4 pm. Despite the two heavy days, the choir had still sufficient energy to sing the Sunday services. Those of the boys who did

Commemoration 1930's

not go to London listened in to the first part of the Festival, which was broadcast.

On 6 December, the Headmaster represented St Michael's at the College of St Nicholas at Chislehurst, celebrating its second birthday. 'We hope that our College will always show the keenest interest in the growth of this young and vigorous foundation, which, under the energetic guidance of Dr. Nicholson, is pursuing the aims of our Founder, namely, the study and improvement of English Church Music.'(13)

The year 1931 saw a number of changes at the College. Mr Thorne, the Organist, left at Easter to take over as organist and choirmaster of a large boys' school, near Buenos Aires in Argentina. He was replaced by Mr. Laurence Crosthwaite, who had been an organ scholar at the Bishop Cotton School at Simla in India.

Many of the boys had been learning some form of musical instrument, usually the piano, but now, a number of boys were learning orchestral instruments. Although it was only in its initial stages, the formation of an orchestra was now underway with ten boys practising hard to become reasonably proficient in their instrument. However, there was a desperate need of a lst violin player.

Another connection going back to the Founder was broken when the College Sub-Warden, the Reverend A F de Gex died. He had been a member of the Governing Body and Secretary of the St Michael's Society. (His father had been one of Ouseley's fellow curates at St Barnabas, Pimlico). His successor was to be the Reverend Monty Alderson.)

There were a number of changes in the church, with plans to refurbish the lady chapel. A new altar had been provided in memory of a former Headmaster, the Reverend W.A. Renwick and members of the Wareham Guild were asked to make a new white altar frontal which it was hoped would be ready for Commemoration later in the year. Parishioners and local people, Mother's Union members and other associated with the College, including Monty Alderson and Sydney Nicholson all gave donations.

Some concern was expressed at the drop in numbers, from around 50 in 1928 to 35 in July 1931 It was hoped that the drop in numbers would be temporary, but as with many schools, St Michael's was suffering from the general financial depression. Much support was now needed to encourage parents to send their sons to St Michael's. Two advantages were apparent. Firstly, owing to endowments, St Michael's could offer lower fees than those of other first-class schools, with further reductions for the sons of the clergy. Secondly, it was not an exclusive school for musical boys. (This seemed to be a mis-understanding throughout its history and had an obvious affect on recruitment.)

Commemoration on 30 September was very successful, celebrating the seventy-fifty Anniversary of the founding of the College. The new Lady

Chapel Altar and High Altar Frontal being dedicated by the Bishop of Hereford, (Dr Lisle Carr)

Frederick Lowe, a former lay clerk, sacrist and choir librarian died after many years associated with the College and the news was announced that Dr Fellowes had been made a CVO (Companion of the Victorian Order.)

Towards the end of the year, the Brahms *Requiem* was performed in the Church by the College choir and the Tenbury Music Society, conducted by the Warden. George Cole, one of the lay clerks, sang the bass solo at the beginning of what was to be a very long association with the Choir and College. The outstanding event of the Lent Term 1932 was the performance of Purcell's *Dido and Aeneas*. The original manuscript is now lost and the oldest known copy is a full score held in the College Library. There were several concert arrangements, but only a few operatic performances of the work between 1689 and 1895. Helen Swann, the Warden's wife gave an admirable performance as Dido, Queen of Carthage, and among other soloists, Wayland Joyce took the part of Aeneas, a Trojan Prince, with the boys and masters of the College playing the various choruses of Courtiers, People, Witches and Sailors. 'The whole production was 'home-made' and all who shared the enormous labours deserve the highest praise, with a tribute of appreciation paid to the orchestra. Special congratulations are due to Mr Laurence Crosthwaite, nothing so ambitious has ever been attempted before at St Michael's, and it may safely be said, nothing has ever achieved a greater triumph. (14)

At the height of the Summer term, on 21 June, the College went on one of their longest half-term outings. This included a visit to Hereford and the Cathedral, another stop at Monmouth, and then a journey along the Wye Valley to Tintern, where all had a picnic lunch in a garden near the Abbey. The party was taken round the Abbey by one of the most amusing guides they had ever seen or heard; he had evidently taken great pains to prepare a full and accurate account of the history and architecture of the Abbey and his word of command 'Right Ho' invariably gave the sign to proceed to the next station of his tour. The following poem was produced as a result of this experience!

THE LEARNED GUIDE OF TINTERN

Now gather round, you red-cap boys, I have a lot to tell,
And if you'll take a tip from me, you'll find it pays you well,
When anyone's a telling anything as you don't know,
To pay your best attention, like I always do – Right Ho!

Now this is the *sacrarium* where once the altar stood,
(I've always picked up bits of Latin everywhere I could,)
And I'd advise you youngsters if your head ain't made of dough,
To do the same as I do, Come along, this way – Right Ho!

This place is called a *transept* (that's a bit of Latin too)
Trans means across, you know, and *sept* just signifies included
(Yankee dictionaries ain't reliable, and so
I recommend the native British article) – Right Ho!

You see these Latin words *HIC IACET* carved on these 'ere stones
That means "'ere lies," and underneath is *ossa*, that is 'bones,'
This shepherd's crook it signifies a bishop lies below,
Now't isn't right that bishops should be liars, eh! – Right Ho!

This part down 'ere is call the *nave*, and on each side the 'aisle'
Now *nave* mean 'ship and *ala* 'wing' – you gents, you needn't smile,
I knows I'm right because an Eton Scholar told me so –
I meets all ranks of scholars and professors 'ere – Right Ho!

This 'ere is meant to be a fish – why did the old monks choose
To carve so queer a hobject? – well, now 'fish' in Greek's *icthus*,
A sort of 'crostic puzzle – no, not crossword – I can show
You how it works as we go on through that there door – Right Ho!

And now we go outside the Church. Up there upon the right
You see the *dormitorium* where the old monks slept at night;
(In French they call it *dortoir*) Sorry, sir, 'you have to go
yes! very interesting. Thank you, sir. Good-bye. Right – Ho!

(15)

D. O. GRELL

By the summer of 1933, the numbers had risen to 40. Throughout the Lent and Summer Terms, the boys' attention had been focused on the imminent provision of an outdoor swimming bath. A long-felt want had now been supplied, thanks to the initiative and inspiring efforts of Mr. Joyce, who had been nobly supported by other members of staff and the boys. During the whole of the Lent term, the school worked with a will at the excavation, which was nearly completed by the Easter holidays. This term, the work was resumed and the concreting done with the help of a couple of labourers and the result reflected the greatest possible credit on all concerned. Although the bath was put into use in June, it was not formerly opened until 15 July (St Swithin's Day) when the Sub-Warden, Canon Alderson, (who generously contributed almost a third of the cost), performed the opening ceremony.

With over £ 104 raised in donations, it was also possible to provide a dressing shed, planting shrubs and providing all the necessary maintenance equipment. Mrs. Braithwaite provided a diving board, and the Reverend A.S. Commeline a Silver Cup, which he had won for the high dive when he was a pupil at St., Michael's some sixty years ago.

The Sub-Warden then cut the scarlet ribbon which was stretched across the steps at the shallow end of the pool and declared it open.

Scarcely had the words been uttered when there was a loud splash and a dainty young 'lady'was seen struggling in the water, her large picture hat and parasol drifting away from her. Everyone's fears and alarms for her 'safety' were soon allayed by a gallant rescue being effected by Mr. Widdecombe, who plunged in and brought her 'safely' to land. (16)

Other news included the renovation of the large portrait of the Founder when he was a boy of seven years of age, which hangs in the Dining Hall. (Now at RSCM headquarters.) The pigment had all but perished and was just saved in time. The cost of renovation was considerable, but the result fully justified the expense, as the work could not have been done better and the portrait was now a thing of real beauty.

Instead of the College choir, a new departure from the usual routine took place when the Commoners sang the anthem at a service, giving a very creditable performance of Dunhill's *Pilgrim Song*, with words by Bunyan. During this term, the boys performed Mozart's *The Magic Flute* at the Tenbury Drill Hall. This was a departure from the usual musical activities of the College and the opera was staged on modern lines with a minimum of décor and effective lighting. There was one 'hitch', however, when one of the principals' voice broke and his part was taken at very short notice by E W Dann, a boy from Marlborough House School near Reading! For many boys, it was the first time that they had sung with an orchestra. 'Not a hitch anywhere. Scene followed immediately upon scene without any waiting, no cues were missed, no performer lost. It was obvious that the boys knew every note of their parts. The whole performance was absolutely in the spirit of the music, and what could be lovelier than that.'(17)

A choral festival took place on 9 November, with 220 voices singing in Tenbury church, when the Bishop of Hereford preached, and on 13 December, the Tenbury Music Society sang Mozart's *Requiem* with what remained of the College choir, mainly probationers, as the choristers had gone home.

During the term the College had been saddened to hear of the death of William Claxton, in his eightieth year. A Former student, in the very early years of the College, he was College organist from 1866 to 1886 and a Fellow from 1894 to 1921 when he resigned. He had been ordained in 1887 and Vicar of Navestock from1897 to 1921.

During 1934, there were a number of changes in the organisation of the College. At the Governors' request, the Warden agreed to combine the role of Warden and Headmaster, and a new appointment, that of Second Master, was created. As a result of these changes, Mr Crosthwaite, formerly organist, was appointed to the combined post of organist and choirmaster. Mr Crosthwaite was due to give a broadcast organ recital on 30 July, from the College, via the BBC Midland Studio in Birmingham and using a GPO land line. Unfortunately, a day or two before the event, he was rushed to hospital with appendicitis and which necessitated an operation. However, the Recital did take place when Dr Percy Hull, organist at Hereford Cathedral, kindly agreed to take his place and it was broadcast at the original time. Mr Crosthwaite finally broadcast his own organ recital with a few choral items from the choir on 18 October. At the end of the year, the Tenbury Music Society again joined forces with the College choir to sing Mendelssohn's *Hymn of Praise* and Parry's *Blest Pair of Sirens.*

The deaths were announced of two members of the Joyce family. James Barclay Joyce had been a boy at St Michael's in 1864, before leaving to go to Haileybury. He became Rector of Coreley for 40 years, Rural Dean of Burford and Prebendary of Hereford Cathedral. Frederick Wayland Joyce was also at St Michael's in 1864, both of them the sons of one of Ouseley's greatest friends. For fourteen years, he was Rector of Boraston and Rural Dean of Burford, before becoming Vicar of Harrow and a Prebendary of St Paul's Cathedral. He had moved to Lion's Farm at St Michael's a few months previously. He had written the Life of his Godfather, Sir Frederick Ouseley, and he and his brother, now lay within a few yards of the Founder's Grave at the East End of St Michael's Church. Within some months, Mr Wayland Joyce was able to have the small lancet windows in the South aisle corridor leading to the Cloisters glazed with fragments of very old, possibly medieval glass in memory of the his father, F.W. Joyce.

THE CATALOGUING OF THE MUSIC LIBRARY

In Ouseley's time, nothing was ever done to sort out his collection of printed music and manuscripts. Subsequently, J S Bumpus took on the task and two huge volumes represent his work. Sadly, his work was valueless as there was no reference system to connect the entries in his catalogue with the works on the shelves, manuscripts and printed books being mixed together, and other manuscripts and compositions left ignored. It was only after the sudden death of his successor, the Reverend Surtees Talbot in 1917, that Dr Fellowes was appointed and took on the mammoth task in 1918. He first attempted to build on the catalogue of Bumpus but found it impossible. The books, printed and manuscript alike, were crowded into a small room, known as the Music Library, in complete disorder, in shelves round the walls, and supplemented by two large book-cases standing in the middle of the room, while every nook and cranny in the passages and various rooms of the College yielded up its treasures hidden in small bookcases. There was no music then held in the main College Library. It was decided that the music books should be set in order in the main Library, and a large number of volumes, consisting mainly of theological works of the Victorian era and magazines of no value were removed to make room for the music.

The cataloguing was finally completed in 1923, with all the printed music books indexed in a large card index and the manuscripts catalogued in the Librarian's own hand. The desire was to seek publication of the catalogue, but it was only some eleven years later, and by the public spirit and generosity of Louise B M.Dyer (Mrs J B Hanson), that the Lyre-Bird Press of Paris, (Editions de l'Oiseau – Lyre) published a limited edition of 220 copies. (NB. Fifty years later, this catalogue was reprinted on microflm, with various corrections and information not previously available, together with supplements of further manuscripts that had been acquired since then, but limited to academic use only.)

In December 1935, the appointment was announced of Maxwell Menzies as organist and choirmaster. A former chorister at St Michael's, he was an RSCM student before going to university.

During the holidays, more renovations were carried out to the main building. Some months before, all the partitions in the Big Dormitory had been removed, creating much more space and light. Now three small rooms at the east end of the same dormitory were also removed, creating additional light and ventilation as well as more accommodation. A new stone staircase was being added, which led up to the big dormitory, being an extension of that already in existence from ground level in the main corridor to the gallery in the Dining Hall. This gave access to the centre of the dormitory, so that the spiral staircase at one end need not be used so regularly and kept as an emergency exit. Also during 1935, there was extensive repair work done on the roof of the church. All the slates, (which had been originally fixed with iron nails and which had rusted through), were refixed with copper nails. The lead work and several downpipes and drains were repaired with the hope that further work would not be necessary for many years.

There was a surprise announcement at the Commemoration Luncheon in October, when the Reverend E H Swann announced his resignation as Warden, after over eighteen years. The Bishop of Hereford appointed him to the living of Bridstow near Ross-on-Wye, together with an appointment as Rural Dean, and he planned to take up his post in January 1936. The Warden felt that the time was right to make a move, while he still had the health to do useful work for the church and diocese. He had become Warden at a very difficult time and had immediately seen that much in the way of modernisation and other changes needed to be done for the school to prosper and attract boys in the future. He had done a splendid job and everyone in the College was sad to see him and his wife leave. Mrs Swann had also made a very valuable contribution to the life of the school and supported her husband in many ways. Many people in the College felt that

> Nowhere more than in the daily services of the College will his loss be so much felt. The reverent and musical way he conducted the

offices could not be other than an inspiration to the successive generations of masters and boys who came under his influence. With meticulous care he provided for every detail and yet one felt how naturally and devotionally the services were being performed... We thank him for all the work he has done for us; the patience and perseverance he has shown in days of adversity, and for the confidence that our many difficulties would be overcome...We cannot but feel that to the end of his days, the love of the College and its continuing welfare will hold the foremost spot in his heart and whenever he revisits it, he and Mrs Swann will be assured of the warmest of welcomes. (18)

THE TOULOUSE-PHILIDOR COLLECTION

The College accounts for 31 March 1936 show the purchase of a substantial addition to the College Music Library. This was the famous Toulouse-Philidor Collection and was to become one of the greatest features of the Music Library. It consisted of over 400 volumes, bound uniformly in their original calf binding, stamped on both covers with the coat-of-arms of the Comte de Toulouse. The Collection was originally brought together for the use of the Count (Son of Louis XIV and Madame de Montespan) at his Palace in Rambouillet. Most of the music is in manuscript form, in the hand of Andre Philidor, music librarian to Louis XIV at Versailles, supplemented by some 70 printed volumes. The whole collection eventually passed through inheritance to the Duke of Orleans and on to his son, King Louis-Philippe and reached the Palais Royal in Paris. After the death of Louis Philippe, the whole collection was dispersed through a Parish saleroom in 1853. The greater part of the Collection, some 290 volumes and 67 printed volumes, were bought by a rather eccentric Englishman, Williams-Hope, who lived in Paris. Shortly afterwards, these volumes were acquired by Ouseley, who had not known their long history. The remainder of the Collection, some sixty volumes, had been bought by a Frenchman named Cretain. His collection, fortunately, was never dispersed and in 1935,, came into the hands of an English book-dealer, Arthur Rau, living in Paris. At this time, St Michael's College did not have the funds to be able to purchase the rest of the Collection, but Canon Ryley generously made the funds available to the College. (£550 which was repaid some months later), so that they could be re-united with the rest of the Collection at the College. Donations towards this purchase are shown as follows:–

Canon G C E Ryley	£ 50 (apart from the temporary loan)
Mr (later Sir) Adrian Boult	£ 10
Rushout Fund	£ 35
College Buildings and Improvement Account	£ 450

REMINISCENCES

CYRIL WARD (1916 – 1921)

The war was in full swing, the epoch of Hampton and Renwick (Headmaster) was at its close, staff were difficult to come by and it was very inefficient. I realise how low the standard of discipline and work was in those days, but that of the music never flagged, though three organists came and went in as many years. Yet there was always an air of graciousness.

School would begin at 7-15 am with two oil lamps hanging high in the ceiling of the big schoolroom and in freezing cold. Having previously broken the ice on the in the enamel jugs, each in its own cubicle, we small boys were in no mood for work and I am sure it was a pure waste of time.

Then came great changes for the better with the new Warden, Rev E H Swann and Rev R H Freeman as Headmaster. I was a Commoner in those days and we sat up in the chancel. My job was to lead out as we sang the last verse of the hymn, but in my keenness to get some music, I had a Church Hymnal and not Hymns A & M. We stood singing two verses in the vestry. It happened on a Sunday evening unfortunately. After that, I was put on to the large low-pressure bellows of the organ, which was quite fun.

But then, with promotion to the Company of oddjobbers, I later had to take the small bellows. This was really hard work for a twelve year old, but I think a good beginning for my rowing days at Henley. As an oddjobber, we were a very select group. We made six-seater desks, cut a tree out of the forbidden quarry with its bottomless lake. I remember we also broke up several pianos, one apparently in error because my father asked why there was an item under piano on the bill.

Other Chapel memories include the Sunday of the Great Hail. We had just finished the anthem when there was a great roar and some of the glass in the top windows began to break. It was all over in five minutes; afterwards we rushed out and played with hailstones as big as golfballs.

'Organ pumping' ended on 26 June 1919, when the electric blower was first used and I think that it was also in that year that red cassocks and ruffs first came into use.

We always knew when it was time to go in for Chapel on a summer's evening as Mr Cox started up his engine. Incidentally, it was in that same coachhouse years before that I also had my first biology lesson, a gory one too. They used to slaughter and quarter the school pigs in there! (19)

HARRY ROOKE (1920 – 1924)

At the time, the choir was quite good and I think it became even better later on. One really good thing about the choir was that, when you became what is called a probationer, nearly half your fees were paid. I was not very musical, but became a chorister in my third year (1923) and from then my education was free. This was particularly helpful because my father had become what they now call 'terminally ill' and had to leave his parish and was never able to work again. The fact that I had become a chorister eased the financial situation, at least for a time.

I think that the general situation for us little boys is best expressed by one word FEAR – fear of the masters, one of whom, long since dead, was undoubtedly a sadist. The cane, in one form or another, was always at hand. It was used not only for misdemeanours but also for simple mistakes in class or prep. It may be that others of my age took it better but I only had one happy term and that was my last when there was a new Headmaster. Sadly, he didn't do very well, and I am told, didn't stay long.

As for the older boys, I was terrified of them during my first two years. You never knew who was going to be selected next for what was called a 'biffing'. One notorious bully left, mercifully at the end of my first term, but the other one didn't leave until a year later. After that, 1921, things became somewhat quieter, and when I reached the soccer and Cricket XIs, I no longer had any fear of the boys.

About sixty years later, I saw the name of one of the bullies on one of the SMC lists. I had heard from someone that he had become a very pleasant man and the thought suddenly came to me to write to him, which I did. He remembered me and I received a very friendly letter in reply. Three weeks later, he died very unexpectedly. You can imagine how glad I was that I had obeyed the thought to write to him.

During my first term, we younger boys were subjected to a delightful experience know as 'Kid Rush.' This appeared to have been a common event for a number of years, although certain boys, being less obnoxious than the rest of us, were exempted!

The remainder, including myself, were pushed, dragged, or thrown into a heap in a corner of a classroom. Then the bigger boys rushed forward in a body and jumped on us. I don't think that I personally was hurt very much, but a good many were in tears and may have been quite badly injured. Fortunately, no bones were ever broken. I could give you many more instances of bullying, but perhaps they are better left in the past. After I left in 1924, I was told that there was some kind of 'rebellion' against the new Headmaster. What exactly happened I don't know, but I was told that even the old butler joined in and wouldn't refill the Head's heating stove. No wonder he didn't stay very long!

To summarise my own memories of St Michael's would be to say that 'every day for 2 to 3 years, I longed for the holidays and then dreaded going back for the next term.'(20)

CHRISTOPHER HARE (1920 – 1924)

I was undeniably nervous and shy, when I was ushered that day into the cool seclusion of Sir Frederick's Library, a place I soon learned to love – and was put through my paces by the Warden (Reverend Swann.) Apparently I passed muster and in due course arrived at the College for my first term as a probationer. But my first evening at College, after a tearful goodbye to my parents, was distinguished by an encounter never to be forgotten.

The 'Boot-hole' was often a refuge for small fry from the barbarities of older members of the College – though itself was sometimes the scene of bloody conflicts. Here it was that I met another boy as diminutive as myself, (Kemp-Welch), later to become Warden many years later) We asked each other's names and then two small and grubby hands were clasped and Kemp-Welch pronounced the simple words, 'Let's be friends.' (At the time of writing this in 1956, we still are!)

The College had its fair share of the barbarity and rigour, notorious amongst small boys' establishments at the time. To come under the lash of Freeman or Hayter, to receive from Huddy the 'Block' (the broken half of a pair of blackboard compasses), or to be penalised by Moody or Denton was no kindly experience. But we were none the worse, and perhaps a deal better in the long run.

But it was, of course, the unique character of St Michael's as a cathedral-type choir school, set in the glorious Worcestershire countryside, that created the deepest and most lasting impression. There, the daily round of services in a Chapel of surprising beauty…this above all, set the tone of the whole foundation, and imbued it with the highest religious, educational, and musical ideals, which have never been lost sight of, and give it an incomparable position in the whole pattern of English church life. There, many of us had our first glimpses of 'the beauty of holiness,' without any affectation or 'humbug', but naturally linked somehow with the rough and tumble of normal school life. A good Catholic tradition has grown up there over the years, of which the Church of England may well be proud, and the music of the daily service was an abiding enrichment. Here the glories of English church music at its best first began to dawn upon our youthful minds and hearts, and I am sure, for many of us played an outstanding part in shaping our future lives. Those who pretend that choristers are apt to be more poorly educated than those who are kept exclusively at the 'Three Rs' are themselves apt to be seriously misled. What better education could you have than a daily acquaintance with the superb English of the Book of Common Prayer, especially the incomparable Psalms, and the whole 'corpus' of music which has grown up through the years to enrich it, and give it wings to rise to heaven! And with it came the privilege of meeting the great musical figures of the day – Atkins of Worcester, Hull of Hereford, Nicholson, Harris, Ley and Colles – to name but a few of them. But perhaps my most treasured memories of St Michael's centre round Dr Statham, organist during all the time I was there, to whom I owe an incalculable debt as an inspiring teacher, and Dr Fellowes, who for most of my time was still engaged in his great work of cataloguing the Library, and unearthing a wealth of music often performed by us almost 'hot' from the library shelves. We were rehearsing, one day in the Library, some awkward passage of Tudor music, in which the phrasing would not come right, after repeated efforts. Dr Fellowes was quietly working at the top of an enormous pair of steps close by, and I can still remember my flush of pride when (by what I can only regard now as a 'fluke), I sang it right, and Dr Fellowes suddenly turned round, nearly falling off the steps in his excitement, and, pointing to me, called out: 'He's got it! He's got it!'

Looking back at the kaleidoscope of school days at Tenbury, there is much to be thankful for – many joys, and some sorrows which are better buried in the limbo of the past. But certainly, no boy could have wished for a better start in life than to have been nurtured in those beloved precincts. (21)

REFERENCES

1. Watkins Shaw p 60
2. College Magazine   July 1918
3. College Magazine   April 1919
4. College Magazine   December 1919
5. College Magazine   December 1919
6. College Magazine   December 1921
7. College Magazine   December 1922
8. College Magazine   July 1924
9. College Magazine   December 1924
10. College Magazine   July 1925
11. College Magazine   December 1925
12. HCL D863
13. College Magazine   December 1930
14. College Magazine   July 1932
15. College Magazine   December 1932
16. College Magazine   July 1933
17. College Magazine   December 1934
18. College Magazine   December 1935
19. College Magazine   October 1968
20. Personal reminiscences given to author
21. College Magazine 1956

Staff and pupils, c. 1938
Photo courtesy of Ouseley Trustees

CHAPTER TWELVE
THE WAR YEARS AND AFTER
1937-1955

The Reverend Cuthbert Harold Septimus Buckmaster was installed as the fifth Warden of St Michael's College on 28 May 1936 by the Sub-Warden, Bishop Frere, a Fellow of the College and a former Bishop of Truro. Previously, he had been Chaplain of Denstone College, Staffordshire. It has already been mentioned that the Warden now also took over the responsibilities of the post of Headmaster, as well as carrying overall responsibility for the music of the College, although for practical purposes, much of this had always been delegated to the organist. With the appointment of Maxwell Menzies as Organist in 1935, a former chorister of St Michael's with very relevant experience, having previously been organ Exhibitioner of St John's College, Cambridge and later, organist of Birmingham Cathedral. He was therefore ideally qualified to take on the joint post of organist and choirmaster. The choir appeared to be having a very busy time and under the new organist, there was a change of policy with regard to the singing the various services and settings. It was decided to reduce the number of services and settings and to do a few really well. Commemoration again included an organ recital by Dr Ernest Bullock, who gladly returned to play once again at St Michael's, as Westminster Abbey was without an organ at the time!

On 6 December, Evensong was broadcast on the BBC Midlands programme and good reception and satisfactory reports were received from all over the country, although one writer felt that the microphone had been placed too near to the basses and it had been promised to change this on a future occasion. The following Sunday, the College choir were augmented by the Tenbury Music Society for a performance of Haydn's *Creation.* This was conducted by Mr Menzies and accompanied by a string orchestra from Birmingham, which was deemed a great improvement on a solo organ accompaniment.

June 1937 was notable for the Coronation of King George VI. It does not appear that any boys from St Michael's were invited to sing at the Coronation this time; nevertheless the whole College listened to the service on the radio and then went on a picnic. A full day's holiday was given for the Coronation, there was a second one given for the Eastnor Scout Jamboree, where many boys met the Chief Scout, and thirdly the half-term outing. On 27 July 1937, the Choir did a further broadcast, this time a recital of music, rather than a service and including music from a wide variety of composers such as Blow, Purcell, Schutz, Bach, Ouseley, Hunt, Stanford, Bullock, Vaughan Williams and Howells.

The new Warden was beginning to make plans to enlarge the accommodation, with a view to increasing the numbers to 55, although in July 1937, the actual numbers were only 41. Suitable plans for this scheme failed to materialise however, apart from the creation of a small extra dormitory. One plan which did go ahead, was the creation of a new junior library from what was presently the reading room. This room would be completely refurbished and re-decorated, with the provision of window seats, new tables and chairs, bookshelves and current newspapers. To facilitate this development and to raise money towards the cost of around £ 200, parents, friends and Old Boys of the College were asked to give donations. This was completed during the next year and proved to be a great asset, much appreciated by the boys. The total cost for equipment and alterations was actually £ 125 of which £109 had been raised by donations.

(NB. This was the room previously divided and called the Boot Room and now used by the present owners of the College as a Student Coffee bar and T.V. room.)

The choir again started to make a special study of the music of particular composers, this year concentrating on the music of Orlando Gibbons, Heinrich Schutz and English composers from 1887 to 1937. Commemoration in September included an organ recital, by Gerald Knight, organist of Canterbury Cathedral, given on Michaelmas Day, 29 September and on 4 October, the Archbishop of York (William Temple), visited the College. Later in the month, Sir Sydney Nicholson came to Leominster to conduct massed choirs in the Priory Church, including the St Michael's Choir. The term ended with a performance of Handel's *Messiah.* Despite efforts at recruitment, the number of boys had fallen slightly, to 39, and with the approach of War, the College was likely to endure a time of considerable difficulty.

On 16 May, a small number of St Michael's Choristers appeared at a Massed Choirs Festival, held at the Albert Hall, singing in a choir of 1000 voices. On 29 May, the BBC broadcast a 'Hikers' Talk' from the College cloisters with a further broadcast talk about some of the music in the College Library on 13 July.

During the early years of the War, it was not possible to produce a College Magazine owing to paper shortages, staff shortages and a lack of time. The College soon felt the effect of the War, when Mr Menzies, the Organist, was called up to serve his country, soon to be followed by the Warden himself, Reverend Buckmaster, who left later the same year. In the spring of 1940, the Governors were delighted to accept the offer of Sir Sydney Nicholson, who volunteered to take over the direction of music as a war service. His own College of St Nicholas at Chislehurst had been closed at the start of the war since it was not a boys' school but a college for adults studying church music. Sir Sydney came to St Michael's, living in a cottage in the grounds. He also established the headquarters of the School of English Church Music in the vicinity of the College.

When the Warden left for war service, the Governors held an emergency meeting at Oxford to appoint a replacement. The Reverend A V Billen was appointed as acting Warden late in 1940. He tells of the continuing life of the College in those days.

The double change of personnel probably made no sudden or considerable change in the College, which has been pursuing its normal course of life quietly in a quiet corner of England while the whole world is ablaze with war. The school curriculum changed but little, and while some members of the teaching staff were called upon for war service, others remained at their equally important posts at the College. Probably owing to its very safe position, the College throughout 1941 was quite full.

The games continued as in peace time, with football being particularly successful. During the same winter, it was also found possible to revive the Cubs and Scouts, thus adding to the recreative life of the boys, an interest which experience shows to be much appreciated and enjoyed. At the same time, occasional help with potato-picking proved of great service to some of farmers around, who already booked the help of the boys in advance for fruit and potato-picking in the autumn of 1943 if the war had not finished by then. Woodcutting has introduced the senior boys to a form of physical labour which, though rather strenuous, calls our perseverance and assists in keeping down the coal consumption of the College. The Dining Hall and kitchen continue to function well, and in fact, apart from the limitation of the supply of jam and fresh fruit, the boys have not suffered at all from the system of rationing; and they have evidently not found wartime food detrimental too their well-being, since 1941 has throughout been remarkably fresh from illness.

The domestic staff proved even more difficult to maintain at a peacetime standard than most departments of school life, but up to January 1942, it has not been necessary to call on the boys to make their own beds, or wait on one another in the Dining Hall, as has been necessary in many public and preparatory schools. If the war continues many more terms, it is doubtful whether this immunity from domestic service for the boys can continue, and it may be that in the end the boys would be non the worse off by their experience in performing such duties.

Weekday Evensong, however, has taken the boys further away from peacetime routine. The blacking-out of the Church, though considered, proved impossible, and Sunday Evensong during the dark months was sung at 3 pm. An afternoon Evensong was tried in the first winter of the war, but it caused considerable interference with afternoon games and early evening activities as well as proving a difficult time for the attendance of lay clerks, and for the winter of 1940–41, the Dining Hall was used for a 6-15 Evensong, necessitating a quick double transformation of the Hall between tea and supper. Though outward signs of the normal use of the Hall were duly removed each day, the same success was not always achieved in removing the atmosphere and odour of a dining room, and for the third winter of the war, the corridor on the first floor was turned into a temporary Chapel. Those who knew this corridor in ordinary times would be astonished at the satisfactory appearance it presented in the evenings with temporary altar (at the east end too), choir stalls (curtained off during the daytime) and seats arranged in rows of three, with a commodious passage-way, and the whole well lit, warm and comfortable. The corridor turned out to be rather less good for sound, but it is doubtless the best arrangement possible, and if the war continues, will be our usage again for Evensong for the winter of 1942 – 43.(1)

During his time at the College during the war years, Sir Sydney Nicholson spent some time in hospital, but fortunately he was able to call on the services of a friend and fellow church composer, C E S Littlejohn to help out. Sir Sydney also wrote about the depleted choir and other associated activities during his time at the College.

The bringing of the School of English Church Music to Tenbury has meant a good many fresh and perhaps strange activities at the College. During the holiday courses, each lasting a week or more, choirboys from parish churches all over the country, as many as fifty at a time, lived in the College and sang the services both morning and evening. This was later followed by a mixed course for adults and children.

Another new development has been the 'village choir.' I found that there was little or no music at the church during the holidays, so that the services were very dreary. So I managed to collect a few boys from the village to form a choir, and they were soon able to sing fairly simple settings of the Eucharist in the mornings during the holidays and also an evensong each Sunday. This innovation was greatly appreciated by the parishioners and I very much hope that the village choir will become a permanent institution.

It is a great pleasure to work here and to feel that one is able to do something for St Michael's and to help preserve the Founder's intentions in these difficult times, and it is interesting to think that in his church, we are actually singing more 'full cathedral services' than at any cathedral in the land. (2)

As a Fellow of the College, Sir Sydney expressed his admiration and gratitude for the help given by Dr and Mrs. Billen. As music director, he could say that no one could have asked for better backing than they have given. On 25 August 1942, Dr Fellowes broadcast on the Forces Programme with a talk about the Music Library, illustrated with examples. It was a fascinating account and made one realise how important the College was. The College magazine reported that the programme was widely appreciated.

The previous year, at Commemoration, Canon Alderson suggested that it may be possible to prepare a little 'brochure', giving the history of how Sir Frederick came to found his College and began to collect information. From the amount of material which soon appeared, including reminiscences form old students, it was decided that there was enough material to form a book, and including articles by Fellowes, Buckmaster, Billen, Nicholson, Pine on various aspects of the College. H C Colles assisted Alderson with the editing and also contributed two chapters himself. He died suddenly before the book was published and Alderson finished the editing on his own.

The Bishop of Hereford wrote a foreword and the Book was published by SPCK in 1943. It represented the only account of the College, however brief, until Watkins Shaw's book was published after the closure in 1985.

The 1942 edition of the College Magazine represented a summary of College life from 1939 to 1942. The edition for 1943 reported that the number of boys at the College was higher than for many terms past. Mr Buckmaster was working in Liverpool and Mr Menzies was in Africa.

During the year the choir worked hard. On 24 March, the first Confirmation for some years was held, when 13 boys and 5 local candidates were confirmed. Sir Sydney Nicholson gave four broadcast talks on 'Quire and Places where they sing', with musical examples by the Tenbury boys, illustrating some of Sir Sydney's points on breathing, voice production, enunciation and practical performance. The second broadcast was especially interesting as boys from the newly-formed 'village choir' sang the musical examples, although not being able to tackle such difficult music as are fully trained choristers. These talks were later expanded and published in book form under the same title. The choir also became involved with the war effort and gave a concert in aid of the local Red Cross effort, but sadly this was to be Sir Sydney's last effort at the College as the School of English Church Music decided that Tenbury was too far away to be the 'centre of operations' and their offices and headquarters moved to Leamington Spa, where they remained until peacetime conditions returned and they were able to go back to Canterbury. The College was deeply appreciative of Sir Sydney's work during the three years he spent at the College, expressed by Mr Littlejohn.

We owe a great debt to Sir Sydney. It is of course the music which has especially benefited and his wide knowledge and experience have had a lasting effect on many of our Choristers. His enthusiasm is almost contagious and he has drawn St Michael's into the general national currents of musical work and thought in a way which would scarcely have been possible without him.(3)

The College was fortunate that Mr Littlejohn was able to take charge of the Choir and Miss Blackall, the piano pupils.

Just as St Michael fought the dragon, the school endeavoured to repel the dragon 'Luftwaffe' by joining the 'WINGS FOR VICTORY' Week Campaign. The target was 200 guineas. After many enquiries the College found someone who had in their possession an almost intact German incendiary bomb, taken from a battle area. The school invited people to stick saving stamps onto the bomb, there was a display of armaments, an auction and several competitions, with many willing contributors. St Michael's flaming sword once more struck the dragon, more than gaining its 'wings' by raising the magnificent total of £ 307-5s-6d.

Although during 1944, the number of boys at the College was exceptionally high, the numbers were greatly reduced by the end of the Summer Term when 15 boys left. In fact 14 boys were confirmed at Easter 1944, an exceptionally high number. This left a very young school, but with very few likely leavers over the next two years, the school faced a period of consolidation rather than spectacular achievements, with the Choir Probationers taking on much more responsibility than usual and managing to cope very well. Over Easter 1944, Sir Sydney held another SECM choral course for ten days, enabling the large choir of experienced boys to sing the Services on Easter Sunday, with a final Service on Low Sunday with a well-known broadcaster as preacher. This Service was also attended by the Bishop of Hereford and the Dean of Worcester. War service had severely handicapped the performances of the choir, especially the underparts, but the daily round of services was able to continue, under conditions which the Founder little thought would ever exist. The lay clerks were most assiduous in their attendance, very often under considerable difficulties and at no little inconvenience. Despite all this, the choir managed to enlarge the repertoire, reviving a number of Stanford, Harwood and Ouseley service settings. Efforts were very successful in increasing the interest of the Commoners, with a weekly choir practice taken by Mr Littlejohn.

A new interest for the boys was developed with the creation of a Music Club. Twelve programmes included an opening competition, talks on various subjects from the Bayreuth Festival to the History of Carols, a review of the coming week's broadcast music and either listening to a gramophone record or an actual performance of music.

On several occasions, different boys played either solos or duets and on one occasion, never repeated, the adults in the College formed a 'Musical Brains Trust.'

At this time, the Vicar of Tenbury, the Reverend Chesterton, was anxious to go as an RAF Chaplain, and with two ordained priests on the staff of St Michael's, it was thought it might be possible for St Michael's to be responsible for St Mary's, Tenbury, in addition to the College and parish at St Michael's. As both Mr Bennett and Mr Billen were working full-time at St Michael's, it was not possible to promise anything more than the maintenance of Sunday Services at Tenbury, together with emergency pastoral cover as required. At least the College had the satisfaction of knowing that it was helping to maintain the continuity of church life in the two parishes. An abbreviated version of Commemoration took place in September 1943, when the Bishop of Peterborough preached.

Once again, the College helped the war effort through a Savings Week, when everybody made a big effort to spend less and save more. Preparations were made for a SALUTE THE SOLDIER WEEK, held from 3-10 June, the target amount being fixed at £ 150, with Tenbury supplying a large number of posters. A target indicator was placed on a wall in the main corridor, like a large thermometer, graduated up to £ 200 and a pointer being driven up as the amount collected increased. The train room was turned into an Exhibition Room for a display of War Weapons, including many old weapons such as a Mauser rifle, some Zulu spears and two wicked-looking Ghazi swords and many from the current war. With the help of the Governors, and the added stimulus of the Invasion, the incredible total of £ 2044-16s-6d was achieved.

In the King's Honours Lists, many associated with St Michael's were honoured, including Percy Buck, who was knighted, with Edmund Fellowes being made a Companion of Honour. Other Old Boys serving in the Forces receiving a number of decorations including CMG, CIE, DSC, DFC, and others the following year receiving the Military Cross, Croix de Guerre, DSC and MBE.

By 1945, with the end of the War in sight, it was reported that the College was fuller than it had even been throughout its existence. At Easter 1945, there was the remarkable experience of nine new boys arriving, without a single leaver, which raised the numbers to a record high of 56 boys. Due to shortages of staff, it was felt than when Old Boys renewed their personal contact with the College, they would see very little difference in the outward appearance of the College, even the same paintwork and decoration could be seen everywhere which was there in 1939. However, a sum of money, which would normally have been spent on repairs and renewals, had been put aside each year in anticipation of the end of the War, when the whole place would be brightened up for victory celebrations as soon as labour and materials became plentiful again. Staff difficulties remained, though this would diminish as men returned from service in the Forces, and the College was extremely grateful for the help given by retired priests and teachers living in the locality. The Governors hoped that Mr Buckmaster would soon be able to give up his wartime duties and return to St Michael's, so that the post-war development of the school could be planned in the changing world of education. This was likely to take some considerable time to plan and require a lot of thought so that St Michael's could continue to hold a worthy place among the schools of the future.

> Everyone who leaves St Michael's seems to feel sorry to depart and there is no doubt that it is a happy place for boys and staff alike – but we all give up our work here with confidence that St Michael's, with its particular history and traditions, has an important place to take in the education of the future and with our best wishes that the College may continue to fulfil its part gloriously.(4)

Monday 12 April 1945 saw the death of A S Miles at the age of 92. He was an intimate friend of Sir Frederick, a Fellow of the College and was appointed Bursar on the death of his partner in the firm of Tenbury solicitors, William Norris. He had lived at the Homestead, close to the College and for many years, played the organ for the Sunday morning service.

The Music Club continued with great success, topics heard including, *Music at St Michael's at the time of the Founder, how Beethoven composed* and Mr Littlejohn on *the organ*. The last meeting of the term taking the form of a musical party, with Mr Wright's trombone being much enjoyed.

In one of the half-term outings during 1945, the school visited Worcester Cathedral, being shown round by the organist, Sir Ivor Atkins. The boys learnt a great deal about the history of the Cathedral, visiting the Chapter House and going onto the roof to see the magnificent view of Worcestershire and further afield. Later in the year, the College celebrations for VE Day took place amid great rejoicing everywhere.

> We were told the night before the Mr Churchill would announce the end of the War the next day at 3 pm. The dormitory was arrayed with flags of every description and it was nearly ten before anyone fell asleep. The next day, prayers and breakfast went quietly. After breakfast, Dr Billen announced the programme for the day. We had morning service and lessons as usual, during which it rained and thundered. During lunch, everyone talked about the afternoon's proceedings. After a short rest, some of the boys collected wood for the bonfire and some made a 'guy' of Hitler. Mr Littlejohn gave us a pair of trousers, and the cook, some sacks and straw. When all the wood that was needed had been collected, we went indoors to listen to Mr Churchill's speech on the wireless. After the speech, the bonfire was lighted with the guy on top, sitting by a Swastika flag which Mr Bennett had found. It was not long before the guy was alight, but the Swastika took much longer as it was soaking wet. When the guy and the flag went up,

there were terrific cheers. People blew whistles, shouted, cheered and even screamed. The heat from the fire was so intense that nobody could get very near. when the bonfire had died down, all the boys assembled on the cricket pitch for a march round the village. We went through the bottom gate, down to the Cadmore stream, past the College and walked part of the round the Common, Colonel Frost taking the salute by his house. After that, we went back to College, singing as we marched. For a VE Day treat we had a special tea and iced cakes the following Sunday. There was a Thanksgiving Service instead of the usual Evensong, with a very large congregation and appropriate music including Psalms 124 *If the Lord had not been on our side* and Psalm 126 *When the Lord turned again the captivity of Zion*. The service setting was Moeran in D and instead of the anthem, Stanford's *Te Deum* in Bb was sung in thanksgiving. When we were in bed the wireless was brought up and we listened to the King's speech.(5)

Mr Wright, one of the teachers at the College, wrote the following account of a problem which occurred towards the end of the War but is still a recurring problem!

Recently, furtive figures armed with snares and nets have been seen lurking in the College grounds, conducting indescriminate warfare upon the defenceless rabbits. But whatever success St Michael himself may have had with the dragon, St Michael's campaign against the rabbit has proved a dismal failure. And I am glad...Do not misunderstand me – I hold no brief for rabbits generally. They are very unheroic and mainly destructive. There is however, a special case to be put for the St Michael's rabbits, for they help, together with the Virginia creeper, to give the College much of its charm. For one thing, they and the Commoners are the two factors which distinguish us from all other Choir Schools. Moreover, there is something very peculiar about our rabbits, which may account for their large numbers. THEY ARE MUSICAL RABBITS. And because cathedrals stand in the middle of towns, such gifted rabbits are precluded from hearing services sung in the best tradition. So they all migrate to St Michael's. If you do not believe this, just look at the lawns near the Church at 6-15pm – for Evensong is their favourite service. Of course, not much is known of their musical tastes, although I fancy their attendance is smaller when Tudor works are sung. But tests have shown that their ears are very sensitive; a sudden fortissimo sends the more timid ones scampering away for dear life. The singing of a verse by the Commoners, for example, decimates their ranks.

I have come to the conclusion that the day the rabbits disappear, our choral tradition will with them. So long as they are with us, we may be sure that we are proving worthy custodians of our

Aerofilms photograph of St. Michael's, 1946
Photo courtesy of Aerofilms

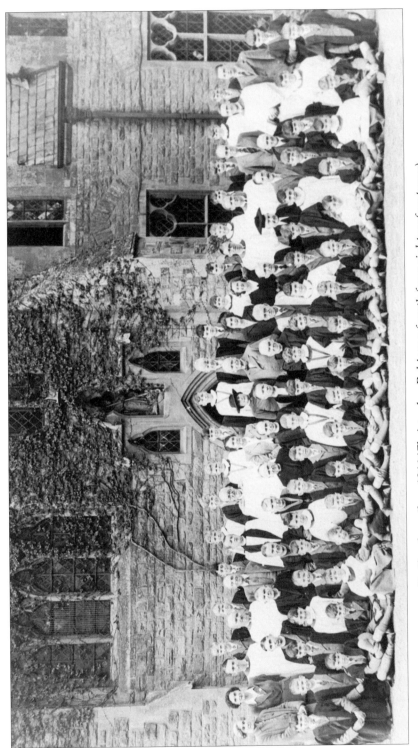

Staff and pupils, c. 1946 (Christopher Robinson fourth from right on front row)

great heritage. Is not a ravaged cabbage a small price to pay for such a guarantee? Anyway, to destroy rabbits because they damage our food shows greater concern for the material things of life than befits residents of such a College as ours. Coming away from the service, I paused to look at the rabbits. They seemed to give me a knowing look. (6)

When Mr Buckmaster returned to the College, he received a very warm welcome from friends old and new. He said it felt strange to be writing the Introduction to the School Magazine after an absence of seven years. He paid tribute to Dr. and Mrs. Billen and those who had worked with them during the difficult days of War. Theirs had been an extremely difficult task and the flourishing state of the school today is witness to the success of their work. Food rationing and domestic problems were difficult enough, but the maintenance of an efficient teaching staff was a high priority and had continued throughout the War. Mr Menzies had now returned to take charge of the Choir, and Mr Pine was demobbed from the RAF shortly after term started in September 1945. Other staff re-joined the school and some new appointments were made, including Mr Brian Demaus, an Old Boy who joined the staff as a master and also as an Alto lay clerk.

There were now 57 boys in the school, with 60 the next term. To meet this record number, there were some alterations to the buildings. The old original classroom, now the Train room, was divided horizontally to provide two new rooms above, which could accommodate at least six students. Until more permanent accommodation was possible, a hut was erected near the classrooms, half to provide an additional classroom and the other half an additional changing room. The present school was very 'young' as far as the boys went. Only seven boys would leave at the end of the year and only seven throughout the whole of the following year. All these spaces were filled, but in 1948 there would be a record seventeen boys leaving. There was a great demand for places, and it became essential that they were booked well in advance.

The day the Warden returned to St Michael's, it was a very hard frost, followed by a thaw when the boys returned. They came back to a school without electricity and without water (at least not in the right places), for the College was flooded, yet they seemed to enjoy it. Shortly after his return, the Warden surprised everyone by his announcement that his stay in the College would be a short one as he had resigned the Wardenship from September 1946. He felt that it was not an easy decision to make, but the right one and that it should be the job of another to build up the St Michael's of the future in this new world, which it was hoped, would be a better one. The Warden had decided to return to the Royal Navy, where he has been so happy the last five years and where there is an acute shortage of Chaplains.

In the choir, the average of the boys was under 12, but was hoped that they would soon be up to the St Michael's standard in a year or so. The lay clerks have now come nearer to their ideal of six members than in times past, two of each voice, and it is hoped that this will give great support to the younger boys.

The Fellows announced that the new Warden was to be the Reverend Noel Kemp-Welch, a former Old Boy of the College (1919 –1924). The Sub-Warden acted as Warden until the end of the Michaelmas Term and the new Warden was installed on 30 January 1947.

During the year, the deaths occurred of Sir Sydney Nicholson and Canon Ryley, who had been Fellows for many years. Canon Ryley had been appointed as Warden after the retirement of John Hampton, but resigned after soon afterwards through ill health.

Sir Sydney Nicholson's contribution to English Church Music can never be overestimated and Dr. Billen gave a moving tribute to him.

> His whole life was indeed given to the cause of good church music, whether in the village church or the cathedral, he recognised quite clearly that the needs and possibilities of the one are not those of the other, but on both he gave to all and especially to the choirboys, a personal interest which called out a strong and deep affection and respect. His death occurred just before a meeting of the Governing Body of St Michael's, of which he had been a member for many years. The opportunity provided by the assembling of the whole Governing Body was used to have a Memorial Service that evening at St Michael's, at which we could remember and think of all we owe to him. (7)

The choir had a busy year, doing much 'outside' work. The BBC recorded the boys singing Gordon Jacob's *Brother James' Air*, which the author John Moore used in a programme about the River Teme. During the year, the choir took part in RSCM Festival Services at Leominster and Gloucester and four choristers sang in the Choirboys' Festival held in Westminster Abbey in July 1947. In March 1947, the College performed Purcell's *Dido and Aeneas*. The performances took place in the dining Room, using a raised platform at one end of the room and the usual doors as entrances and exits. A fine balance was achieved between the singers and the orchestra with an ensemble closer to the original than any since the performance of 1689. The cast were formed of choristers, lay clerks and other members of the school The Warden's wife, Mrs Kemp-Welch, managed to play the violin in the orchestra, as well as singing the part of the Third Witch, owing to the indisposition of Michael Woodward. Christopher Robinson was in excellent form as the Second Witch and his duet with Mrs Kemp-Welch sounded beautifully spirited and was one of the highlights of two wonderful performances.

At Commemoration, there were many visitors, especially Old Boys returning after their absence during the war. Canon L W Grenstead, Nolloth Professor of the Philosophy of the Christian Religion at Oxford University, preached and Gerald Knight, organist of Canterbury Cathedral, gave an Organ Recital.

The boys always looked forward to their half-day holidays, and a 'merit-half' occurred when the school was granted an extra half-day's holiday and as soon as the bell went, a master would say 'Walk.' Here are one boy's memories of such a holiday.

> Everyone groans, as it is a bore. When we come back from the walk, we can't go in the quarry – too wet; we can't have boxing – the master wants to go out; can't have football – too wet; can't toboggan – only one sled. Some people think that a 'merit' is a big treat, but for one boy, the half-day, usually a Monday afternoon, contained two of his favourite lessons, Maths and English. It's the same in the Summer Term. They give the punishment – no bathing. Even if there were bathing, the swimming bath would be empty, as they empty it twice a week and it takes three days to fill. If you play cricket you are out first ball and have to spend the rest of the afternoon sitting on the bank admiring the other players. Then you go to bed – no reading; you can't get to sleep – too hot; you can't fool about – you'll get the slipper. So if you can't play games, and you can't fool about, and you can't toboggan, all's that left is lessons, and if lessons are the only thing left, what's the use of a merit half?(11)

At the 1948 Annual General Meeting of the St Michael's Society, it was reported that a great strain had been put on the College finances by the drop of nearly half the value of its endowments. An Appeal to friends of St Michael's College was launched, to help rebuild the Endowment Fund, with sums large or small, by donation or covenanted subscription or by legacy, to enable the College to help future generations of boys at the lowest possible cost to their parents. The College was registered as a Charity and was a non-profit making institution.

During the year, the music went from strength to strength. Two performances of *Messiah* during the Michaelmas Term and in the Lent Term, the choir sang two performances of Brahms' *Requiem*, with the Tenbury Music Society. In the Summer Term, there were also two performances of Haydn's *Creation*, sung in Ludlow parish church with the Ludlow Choral Society. A Meditation for Holy Week was broadcast from the church on Palm Sunday, an anthology of poetry, prose and music, put together by Mr Pine, and which resulted in many appreciative letters being received afterwards. Dr Fellowes gave a talk on the programme *Midlands Miscellany* on the Philidor Collection of Manuscripts in the College Library. H Watkins Shaw, Music Adviser to Hertfordshire

County Council, was appointed as a Fellow, and Mr. Pine left to go to Westminster Abbey Choir School.

The engagement of Miss Williams, the College Matron was announced to Mr Demaus, one of the masters. They were married at Easter and made their home near the College. Miss Strong took over as Matron from Mrs Demaus.

During the next year, two people retired, whose contribution to the College had totalled over fifty-five years. One was Miss Ashley, who had given devoted service on the staff for twenty-five years and Dr Fellowes, who had retired as Honorary Librarian after thirty years' service. He would ever be remembered for not only transforming Sir Frederick's wonderful collection of musical books into a true Library, but had also made the Library known to Scholars all over the world. The presentation to him took the form of a display case for the Library, with a suitably inscribed plate. After this ceremony, Dr Heathcote Statham gave an organ recital.

Both the Reverend and Mrs. Swann were present, and he so obviously enjoyed meeting his old friends that it was a great shock to hear of his death only two months later, closely followed by the death of the College Visitor, the Bishop of Hereford. After the death of Reverend Swann, his wife kindly donated a Swann Prize for the best all-round chorister and he would have rejoiced to know that the first holder of the award, Christopher Robinson, had won a Music Scholarship to Rugby.

The School Magazine for 1949 listed the following as 'schoolboy Howlers.'

The Albert Hall – a place where many fine corsets are held!

In America, murderers are put to death by Elocution!

St Michael's College was found in the reign of Queen Elizabeth!

A Gondola is a make of car! (9)

Despite the expected large number of leavers, by 1950, there were 62 boys in total, the school again being a distinctly 'young' one. There were 11 leavers in July 1949 including three scholarships, 5 leavers in December (including the now famous explorer, John Blashford-Snell (see Reminiscences) and 10 leavers, (including one scholarship) in April 1950. During the year, there were considerable changes in the church, with it being re-decorated, and becoming much lighter in appearance. New gifts included curtains for the reredos behind the altar and two piano stools, one for the Library and one for the church. The choir did their usual concert with the Tenbury Music Society, performing Mozart's *Requiem* in the church just before Christmas.

Throughout the Summer term, the school watched almost unbelievingly as mains electricity slowly made its way via a series of poles across the Common. Wires have been strung on them, cables have been laid and electricians are working in the buildings. It seems that only

Benjamin Britten's opera 'The Little Sweep'

one thing is lacking, the electric current itself. Perhaps it may arrive before the end of term.

There was more news about the Appeal to re-endow the College after its income from investments had fallen, with nationalisation being another factor. One Fellow, recently deceased, left the residue of his estate to the College, while one Old Boy, despite sending yearly donations to the Organ Fund, also contributed to the Endowment Fund, in the hope that his example would encourage others to do so. The Organ Fund had been set up in order to restore the organ in time for the 1956 Centenary Celebrations and Old Boys were again asked for donations as it was a very heavy expense for a small country parish.

There were rumours going around that there was to be a Festival of Britain in 1951, but at St Michael's it was rather going to be a Festival of <u>Britten</u>, or in other words, *Let's Make an Opera*. Very soon a little town of tents sprang up on the Cloister Lawn and to some it looked like an American G I Camp. The urge to do the opera was given further impetus when Benjamin Britten himself visited the College in order to do some research in the Library, and the intention hardened into determination.

> Never have we worked so hard! From early morning until bedtime she has untiringly rehearsed us, alone, in ensembles and all together. The weekends when she came down were wonderful experiences for all the cast, including the admirable and hard

working understudies. Our other problem was to find an opera house. What about the Big Dormitory? It seemed rather an undertaking at first to get it cleared during term, but people co-operated with a will. At this moment, 'Operaville' is springing up, with tents for half the inhabitants of the Big Dormitory. The other half are migrating to passages and odd corners and so making room for the 600 or so people expected to attend the four performances. The Tenbury Operatic Society have lent us their stage. 'Props' have appeared from all over the neighbourhood. Miss Ashley has almost finished the dresses. Only the dress rehearsals now remain. (10)

The opera was a resounding success, and possibly one of the reasons was the arrival of mains electricity at long last. This had an effect on all areas of College life, with the kitchen staff welcoming the provision of a refrigerator, although it was late being delivered due to a fall of snow.

The Choir improved steadily through the year and at Commemoration, David Willcocks, then organist of Worcester Cathedral, gave an organ recital.The Commoners' choir had now been revived and had been in action over the past three years, singing Evensong once a term and 'Merbecke' on some Sunday mornings. Perhaps the greatest difference in the church was the provision of mains electricity and the best quote was the following one. 'It is a joy to be able to use the organ and still to be able to see one's Psalter.'(11)

For Festival of Britain, many of the College's 'treasures' were required for displays and exhibitions, the *Messiah* manuscript being loaned to the British Museum, while Benjamin Britten studied the College copy of *Dido and Aeneas* for his new version of the opera, and the Mermaid Theatre planned a performance based on the Tenbury manuscript.

Dr Fellowes played an important part in a series of English historical concerts and the College Library received some valuable new items, including two autographed copies of Ouseley compositions, the String Quartet in C and a beautifully bound copy of *The Martyrdom of St Polycarp*. Other gifts included more books for the boys' library, a prayer book for the crucifer, a pair of hymnboards for the choir and two cricket cups. Christopher Robinson founded a prize for the best junior pianist.

On 19 June, four boys set out with Mr Menzies and Mr Bennett to take part in the RSCM Festival in the Albert Hall, conducted by Dr Dykes Bower, with over a thousand singers. Some time for sightseeing was possible the morning following their arrival in London, with visits to Westminster Abbey, and the South Bank Exhibition, before meeting at the Albert Hall after lunch for a three hour rehearsal. Princess Elizabeth listened to the rehearsal and the Festival Service itself was a glorious spectacle of sight and sound, with the singing of Walmsley's setting in D minor and many anthems, before ending with Vaughan Williams setting of the *Te Deum* in G.

Towards the end of 1951, everyone connected with the College was saddened to hear of the death of Dr Fellowes His death, just before Christmas in his eighty-first year, brought to an end an association with the College lasting from 1919 to 1951. After 30 years of his devoted work in the College Library, he had relinquished his post in 1948, to be succeeded by Watkins Shaw. To get an idea of the effort that Fellowes put into the Library, one must realise that all his work in sorting, repairing and classifiying thousands and thousands of musical manuscripts and books, was carried out during his 'holidays' from his full-time post. In 1900, he moved to St George's Chapel, Windsor to a post as Minor Canon, which he was to hold for the rest of his life. When Sir Walter Parratt retired as Organist in 1924, Fellowes then took on the post of Master of the Choir from 1924–27, while Malcolm Boyle acted as organist during the same period, before Walford Davies took up the joint post in 1927. There could be no more suitable or eminently qualified person to undertake the difficult task in the Library at St Michael's and Fellowes succeeded beyond all expectations. Christopher Hare, a St Michael's Old Boy (1919 – 1923), and a colleague of Dr Fellowes at Windsor, wrote a moving tribute.

He often recalled the intense interest and excitement he experienced when scarcely a day went by without some new and thrilling discovery. Often the clock would reach the small hours of the morning before he could tear himself away from the shelves. The chapter he wrote on the Library, in Alderson and Colles' *History of the College*, gives a vivid account of some of the musical and other treasures, which he was in the process of rediscovering...But it was not only as Librarian that Dr Fellowes has left his mark at Tenbury. The whole life of the College, and the ideals which inspired its Founder, were matters of constant interest and concern to him, and although he was not the person to wear his heart on his sleeve, his presence at all College functions – especially the annual Michaelmas Celebrations – showed how greatly he valued his Fellowship of the Foundation, and how deeply he loved the place and cared for its welfare.

There is another memory of him which I shall always treasure. He was a skilled performer on the violin, and the proud possessor of a priceless *Amati* which he carried about in an old-fashioned wooden case. School audiences were frequently charmed by his performances at Michaelmas concerts and 'sing-songs', and little did I think in those days, that when I joined him at Windsor some 20 years later, I should have the privilege and joy of being able to accompany him occasionally, in the latter days of his life, when he rejoiced to play once again the Sonatas he loved so well. These he placed, if not always with the accuracy and skill of his younger days, yet with a sensitive musicianship which never left him, and which showed his deep understanding and love of the classical masterpieces. And who that ever heard him will ever forget his curious and amusing 'tour de force' with Tallis's Canon, whistling one part, and singing the other at the same time. it was a feat which was always the delight of any musical company.

A man of manifold activity, and singular abilities, Dr Fellowes will be greatly missed at St Michael's. But the ideals which animated him will abide, and be an inspiration and challenge to future generations. (12)

Mr. Maxwell Menzies had been appointed to the post of organist at St Michael's when Mr Swann was still Warden. After 17 years, somewhat interrupted by war service, he resigned to become the organist of Maidstone parish church. Generations of St Michael's boys will remember his single-minded work for the choir, the very high standard he set in the choice of music and the care he put into teaching individual boys. The music scholarships won during those years are ample testimony to that. It was felt that his new post would offer him scope in other directions that were not possible at St Michael's. His replacement was Mr Kenneth Beard, BA, B Mus, FRCO, ARMCM, who came highly recommended from Cambridge where he had been Organ Scholar at Emmanuel College. He took over mid way through the Summer Term, so that he had time to settle in before Commemoration in September.

The outstanding musical event of the year 1952 was the performance of Britten's cantata *St Nicholas*, with string quintet, percussion, piano duet and organ. The Chorus included all the College choir, directed by Mr Menzies, the Commoners' choir (their first appearance at such a large event), the Tenbury Music Society and music students from the City of Worcester Training College. At the very last minute, Andrew Gold sang the solo part due to Robert Ellis suffering a bout of severe laryngitis. The performance turned out to be a most stimulating experience for both the singers and the congregation.

The Organ Appeal became ever more urgent as it was hoped to begin the repairs and restoration in the following year. Everyone in the parish pulled their weight, but it desperately needed the help of all well-wishers of St Michael's to reach its target. £1000 being raised so far.

During the year 1953, there was considerable news of Fellows. William McKie was given a knighthood and Sir Ernest Bullock now became Director of the Royal School of Church Music. Cyril Taylor left the BBC to become Warden of the RSCM at Addington Palace. New Fellows elected by the College included, David Willcocks, Edgar Broadhurst, Gerald Knight and Colin Dunlop (Dean of Lincoln.) It was also announced that Mr. Broadhurst had married Mrs Stokes, a daughter of the late Reverend John Hampton, Ouseley's successor as Warden.

Towards the end of the Michaelmas Term, the choir gave a performance of Haydn's *Creation* and during the Easter Term, a performance of Handel's oratorio, *Samson*, augmented by the Tenbury

Boy's choir, July 1953 and choir procession

Music Society. At the end of the Summer Term, the choir presented a programme of Madrigals and part-songs in the Cloisters. Through the year, the choir concentrated on a policy of enlarging the repertoire, involving a great deal of work on the part of both boys and men. The number of new or 'revived' services sung during the year was 27, that of anthems 36. The total number of different services sung during the year was 95, and just over 200 anthems

At present the organ had been dismantled for two months. Every day, however, a little less was seen in the aisles of the church as a little more returned to its appointed place in the loft.

> We have missed the old Willis, yet we have discovered that some of our music sounds better with piano accompaniment, and we have become aware of our faults while lacking the sustaining power of the organ to hide them from our ears. We are hoping to hear the 'playing of the merry organ' before we break up for the summer holidays, and meanwhile, we are doing our utmost to preserve the tradition of 'sweet singing in the choir' at St Michael's (13)

The work now neared completion and the College had to face payment. Thanks to the generous help of Old Boys and parents, as well as the joint efforts of both College and parish, the gap had been narrowed to about £800, which was still a formidable amount to raise for a small College and parish.

Being Coronation Year, it was a great honour for the College to receive an invitation for one of the boys to sing at the Coronation and the present head chorister, Michael Hartley, was an excellent choice. He had also been awarded a Choral Scholarship to Hurstpierpoint College. This is part of his account of his experiences at the Coronation.

> On 8 May, I set off, feeling excited as could be, the journey to London taking three hours. Addington Palace, near Croydon, where stayed while we were being trained, is a very beautiful building. We had a practice everyday, followed by rehearsals at St Margaret's Westminster. The last but one rehearsal was attended by all the Peers and Peeresses, though not in full dress. The last rehearsal was on 29 Friday May. The two most exciting mornings for us were when one Thursday morning, after we had been at Addington a fortnight, a battery of press photographers form all sorts of papers came and photographed us and interviewed us. The other very exciting morning was on Thursday 28 May, when two BBC Television Newsreel cameramen arrived and spent a long time taking many different shots, resulting in a two minute television appearance the day before the Coronation.
> The boys staying at Addington Palace were a cheery group. Besides myself there were 31 other boys. We were woken up at 4 am on the Morning of Tuesday 2 June. We breakfasted at 4-30 am and then

went by coach to Croydon Station, train to Waterloo and then walked up to the Abbey. We robed in the Westminster Choir School's gymnasium and we were all in our places in the Abbey by 8 am. We sat down and waited for two and a half hours until the orchestra started playing. At precisely 11 am, we had our first glimpse of the Queen as she came through the screen with the procession into the Chancel. Beneath us on the north side, Cantoris side, were representatives from other countries. Just before the procession, four people with carpet sweepers and brushes came to sweep the Chancel carpet. At the moment of crowning we looked over the Choir loft and could just see the Archbishop place the Crown on the Queen's head. We also saw the Duke of Edinburgh pay homage to the Queen. We had our best glimpse of the Queen when she came out in the processions at the end. the Queen Mother, Princess Margaret, the Duke of Edinburgh and the Queen all smiled at us as they reached the screen. The Choir started disappearing at 3-30 pm. As soon as we had changed, we all rushed for the Cloisters where a buffet lunch was being served. When we had finished, we waited for Mr Kidd to call us together. When we got outside, we saw some of the troops march off and then we started for Victoria Station. When at last we arrived at Addington Palace, we all lay on our beds for an hour, totally exhausted, before having a slap-up supper. Later on, we watched the firework display from the South Bank on television. At 6-30 am the next morning, a boy from Leeds and I were woken up by the Matron and after breakfast, we travelled together as far as Victoria Underground Station, where we separated, each taking our own way home. Back at St Michael's, I had to tell everyone about the Coronation, so that I had quite an exhausting time at first. I shall remember Addington Palace, the boys, and the staff, and of course the Coronation, as long as I live. A vivid memory indeed. (14)

Jonathan Harvey, later to become a famous composer, left for Repton and his parents presented a cup for the Junior Victor Ludorum Prize. Another of St Michael's Old Boys, Christopher Robinson, passed his ARCO with flying colours at the age of 16 years. He was also awarded the Christopher Tatton Organ Scholarship at Christ Church, Oxford, but was not able to take it up for at least a year on account of his age.

During the year, a visiting organist, Robert Beckett, of Sutton Coldfield, brought his choir, and spoke of the delight in hearing St Michael's choir, especially singing an anthem of S S Wesley. 'The singing of your own choir yesterday amply justified my opinion and my own boys were enthralled. The fact that the organ was not in use rather helped us to appreciate the beautiful tone of your boys.'(15) 'A few weeks later, he was able to compare the singing of the St Michael's boys with the Vienna Boys' Choir on a visit to Vienna. 'Good as the Vienna boys were, the tone of the English cathedral boys nevertheless eludes them.'(16)

For some time, the beautiful Processional Cross given in memory of boys killed in the 1914-18 War had been in need of repair. On hearing of this, Canon Alderson very generously volunteered to bear this expense and also paid for am small engraved plate to be put on the bust of Sir Frederick, which was kept in the College Library. (This is now in Hereford Cathedral.) These were carried out in time for Commemoration in September and the College expressed their appreciation for all that Canon Alderson did for them.

At the end of 1953, the College lost two of its Fellows, with the deaths of Colonel Frost and Sir Ivor Atkins, Organist of Worcester Cathedral. The College had always enjoyed the visits of Sir Ivor, who took a keen interest in the Choir and the College owed much to him for his advice on the reconditioning of the organ. Two more Fellows were appointed, Meredith Davies, organist of Hereford Cathedral and D J Walters, lately Headmaster of Bromsgrove School.

During the Lent Term, a memorable performance of Bach's *St John's Passion* was given with the College choir, the Commoners' choir and the Tenbury Music Society, conducted by Heathcote Statham. Mr Beard conducted the choir at a concert in aid of the Organ Fund. He was also awarded the Choir Training Diploma of the Royal College of Organists. Two more choristers won Music Scholarships to public schools, Michael Hart winning the new Music Scholarship at Shrewsbury School and Julian Dams, winning both a Music and an Academic Scholarship at Cranleigh School. Consequently, the choir lost both head choristers at the end of the Summer Term. They continued to expand their repertoire, although comment was passed on the 'dearth' of modern settings available at that time. Something which is not a problem today.

> Few modern composers appear to consider this need of cathedral music and of those who do, their music is often unsuitable for church use, sometimes too demanding in technical difficulty and sometimes (as in the Walton *Coronation Te Deum*), on too large a scale for a small choir. has no modern composer either the desire or the capacity to add to the heritage of his predecessors in church music? (17)

One of the choir's long standing members, George Coles, was asked to sing in the choir at the official opening of the RSCM at Addington Palace during the summer and all old choristers, lay clerks and present members of the College were delighted for him.

The organ was back in use at Michaelmas. The College was justifiably proud of its fine instrument, now in restored condition. The lowering of the pitch had in no way affected the characteristic tone of the old organ and the action remained quite reliable. Congratulations were expressed to Messrs Willis & Sons on their fine workmanship. By extensive fundraising, the outstanding debt on the organ was now only £ 160 and it was hoped to clear this by Michaelmas.

The following year, 1955, was a year of extensive building and re-building. The very tall chimneys on the main College building were considerably shortened and re-built. Damage had been caused by the weathering of the sandstone, caused by the level of heat given off by modern boilers. There was also the building of the new music strongroom, which was opened in 1956, and plans to build a new playroom for the boys, though this was delayed by a rail strike.

The choir excelled themselves during the year, performing Parry's *Blest Pair of Sirens* at the end of the Michaelmas Term, showing off the newly restored organ. They also performed Haydn's *Imperial Mass* and Handel's *Cantata on Psalm 89,* the College and Commoners' choirs being joined by the Tenbury Music Society and the Wolverhampton String Ensemble. 'Kenneth Beard's work at the Father Willis organ was, as usual, superb. (18)

The winter of 1955 was very severe and after a heavy blizzard on 17 May, snow was still lying on Clee Hill some days later. One of the boys is reported to have said, possibly open to misinterpretation, that 'this school is terribly like a home.'(19)

Further news arrived about Christopher Robinson, who, after gaining his ARCO in 1953 and an Organ Scholarship, was also awarded his FRCO before he took up his studies at Hertford College, Oxford. 'An achievement unique in the school and probably in any other public school.(20)

REMINISCENCES

RICHARD HULL (1934 – 1939)

Most of my time at St Michael's was spent as a choirboy, and my biggest impression was that we choristers had very little time off for play. We despised the Commoners as worker bees and drones, while envying their leisure. Considering our tender years, I still think we worked too many hours in the week at our vocation without enough concrete privileges in return. Our day of real exaltation was Commemoration, when we joined Governors and Fellows to eat in Hall. As a choir, our greatest thrill was to broadcast, for which a boy received five shillings. I dropped one of my half-crowns down the grating in Chapel, but this was of little value compared with what he knew we had achieved. Young as we were, I believe that the smallest Probationer had an inkling that he served the College as the Founder had wished.

After Chapel, next in importance was work. And yet I cannot honestly say that any particular subject stands out in my memory! I was neither dunce or scholarship-candidate. The practice scholarship papers that we tried in our last year for Dartmouth, Wellington and other Public schools seemed impossibly hard. As new boys, we entered Form 2, the lowest, where I can remember no teacher but Miss Ashley. Perhaps the greatest compliment that I can pay that most faithful staff member was that she was immediately, naturally and without reserve 'accepted' by the shyest and smallest boy. She was also respected and obeyed by the largest. Perhaps she realised that she was the yeast in an all male batch of loaves, the bridge between our over-fearful mothers and our homes, and the callous masculine outside world in which we should soon be roaming.

We played the usual games, football in the winter, with new football boots crunching down the cinder path, the smell of Colonel Frost's apples in the nearby orchard, and the chestnut tree laded with promises of future conker battles. Apart from school outings and the compulsory Sunday afternoon walks, the Scout movement was our only regular chance to see the world outside the College during term time. The other occasions only happened if you had managed to persuade your father he could afford horse-riding lessons, or if you were chosen to play in an away match, or if you were taken out by your own or someone else's parents. To be chosen for the latter was a real honour and a sure sign of friendship. Tea in the 'Feathers' at Ludlow would fill you up with boiled eggs and crumpets.

Summer gave us the delights of the swimming pool and cricket. In their annual match, the fathers played with pick-axe handles, but a six into the quarry sent them back into the pavilion. It was the Summer term, with all its outdoor possibilities, that hit the Choristers hardest and made us jealous of the Commoners. So many of the long evenings seemed consigned to choir practice, or piano practice in a dreary dim-lit corridor. The winter evenings were likely top be dim-lit too, as the College was not then on mains electricity. Hour after hour, the engine would chug-chug its exhaust into nearby bushes, but when the organ was switched on, every light in the place reduced its strength by half. To save power, and as a punishment for eating sweets in Church, I was made to hand-pump the organ for another boy who was learning to play. Of course we tried to pump the bellows up over the safety mark, but this was nearly impossible as they were too full of holes.

Another lasting impression that stays with me was the coldness of our living quarters. The Dormitory was a great barn of a place with uneven splintery floors, the hideous blocks of hot-water pipes down the centre and the ones that ran along the wall behind the beds fought a constant losing battle against icy draughts that rattled the diamond-leaded panes. In winter, the twice-weekly bath night was a real luxury of warmth. On the ground floor, the one never-ending passage sported the same hot-water pipes, which were too hot to sit on, but could never combat the ever-opening doors leading to the cold outside. You were much frowned upon for visiting the outside lavatories in a surplice, although I never did discover whether the reason was theological, in that the surplice should not visit such a place, or whether the wind and rain would take out the starch. Only on Sundays did the Church feel warm, probably because the viiage turned out in force to do our services honour, and for Evensong, every light in the place was burning.

Harvest Festival was a great occasion as well as a source of many and varied temptations. you were a poor specimen if you came away from Church that day without an edible souvenir. Funerals, happily, were rare. I was petrified with fear at having to pass near the bier.

Sunday Evensong was always followed by an organ voluntary, one of the rare and valued voluntary events in our life. My own love of Bach and Cesar Franck stem from those Sunday evenings, when most of the Church was dark, the weekend had gone too quickly, the week was before; the choir could relax in the nave for once, and listen to their master wrestling with couplers, the squeaky swell-box and an over-eager page turner. (Only the leading choristers were allowed the privilege of going up into the organ-loft during a recital.) To me this was the climax of each week, our long day's efforts were over. The solo notes prattled round the roof, the pedal sounds boomed seemingly along the floor gratings, round the font and echoed back from behind the reredos. After the Sunday voluntary, another boy and I were slipped a bar of chocolate by Miss Tombs, a wonderful old lady who dispensed sweets, stamps, bottles of sweet lemonade, and doses of dry humour to everyone in her village shop. She allowed no-one to get the better of her in that she tolerated no rowdyism or cheek from the boys, and yet she had no authority over us. 'Master Jones, please to take that bottle outside afore we all 'as a bath.' She never failed us, never 'split' on us, never complained, although at times we must have tried her patience sorely.

Ernest Henry Swann was Warden when I went to St Michael's College. He resembled the type of vicar often seen in pipe tobacco advertisements, except that his straight briar burnt a heavy herbal mixture, his eyes seemed to twinkle in a very shrewd look.

Not very long after my arrival as a new boy, Mr Swann retired and the Reverend C H S Buckmaster took over. His arrival coincided with an extensive programme of re-decoration and internal alterations. A new concrete staircase led up to the main dormitory, which was painted in blue and cream. Soon we had new wooden-ended and comfortable beds. A new recreation room was made for the boys and window seats put in the long downstairs corridor. Eton collars on Sundays were done away with while we wore sandals during the summer months.

The new Warden made plenty of changes in the grounds of the College; flower beds sported climbing roses, hedges were planted, a rockery built, a small aviary appeared, the playground enlarged, a tennis court constructed, the cricket pitch enlarged, and the vegetable garden made to produce more for the kitchen; the latter boasted a new colour, and our meals improved.

'Bucky' was extremely popular with the boys in the best possible way. He had done other things besides teaching; I believe he had been in the Navy – he certainly knew how to sail a boat – and I seemed to remember he had also worked down a coal-mine. He was confident and enjoyed life, and imparted a gaiety to our self-contained world. At the same time, he demanded strict discipline and beat us with gay abandon that scarred our behinds but not our minds. Perhaps one of his pleasantest innovations was to invite a few of the senior boys down to his room of an evening. We were soon at ease listening to music or music-hall, playing some parlour game, hearing him read, or just enjoying ourselves in his company. In return, he would frequently drop in to our recreation room and have a game of chess or billiards in the long winter evenings.

Looking back now, it seems as though he taught us to discard outworn customs and ideas if they were meaningless, to behave ourselves, to work hard, and above all to enjoy civilised everyday pleasures as a matter of course. (21)

JOHN STANSBY (1939 – 1944)

I was nine years old when I arrived at St Michael's in September 1939. Something big and very serious and just happened to the world outside. We were at war. This was not as frightening as arriving at St Michael's for one's first term, nor was it quite so exciting, but it was not long before both seemed a normal condition of schoolboy life. The War became blackout curtains, and steel helmets, and BBC news bulletins. It meant margarine and spam, sweet coupons and uniforms. it sometimes became very thrilling but, even when I left in 1945, extremely knowledgeable about every detail of a Vickers machine gun and performance of a Messerschmitt, the War remained an intrusion, and St Michael's was ordinary life. Looking back now, it is easier to see. St Michael's was the beauty of the Teme valley, it was the spinney in autumn, the Clee Hills looking down on the Common, and the Nunc Dimittis sung every evening. It was the orchards full of fruit, and the noise of insects in the quarry on a warm summer's evening. It was the villagers taking Communion in squeaky shoes and tight blue suits and plainsong chanted in the quiet of a Sunday evening.

St Michael's was, as it still is no doubt, a little world of its own, but it was never an island; and on all the normal rhythms of preparatory school life, – even the crazes and hobbies, the excursions and outings, the pre-occupation with petty finance, – the war impinged. To start with it all seemed a question of gas masks fitting properly, (this was done in the dormitory), and of evacuees, who started to appear in the village. The turret windows were painted black and acres of black-out material were hung up in the corridors. A rather vivid magazine called *War* was collected and cut up for scrapbooks and souvenir collections assumed the appearance of small arsenals. Old cartridge cases, bayonets, revolvers, trenching tools, steel helmets, shell heads, grenades, piles of shrapnel collected form the street during the holidays, badges and scraps of uniforms, even a working Verrey pistol and an intact German incendiary bomb appeared at one Train room exhibition. And after a visit to a destroyed German bomber on display in Tenbury, the amount of scrap hoarded in lockers nearly doubled. There was a big craze for Dinky Toy tanks and army vehicles, and on one occasion at lunch, the entire end of High Table was covered by a miniature mass parade of our orders from Ludlow. But all this, like communiques from the Western Front and leaflet raids over Germany, did not last. There was silence at meals as the wireless gave us the news bulletins, and there was a grim look on the Warden's face when the surrender of France was announced. The war had become serious and, if it never quite ceased to be a sort of monster wide game, St Michael's did its best for the War Effort. Mr Buckmaster joined the Navy and Dr Billen replaced him. he was a large, restless figure, full of energy, who was to remain an indelible portrait to his pupils. We all got to work with raffles and auctions to help buy Spitfires, and books of National Saving Stamps. We were shown how to use stirrup pumps and what to do with incendiary bombs. We all started knitting scarves for the Forces in all shapes and sizes, with Mrs Billen in constant demand for retrieving dropped stitches! We read eagerly about Molotov Cocktails and stripping the tracks from German tanks; how to deal with paratroopers and how to block roads. Colonel Frost led the local Home Guard and our Scout Troop marched proudly at Savings Week processions in Tenbury.

We picked and planted potatoes, and helped with the harvesting, and dug for victory in the College gardens. The Scout truck was out collecting, salvage paper and cardboard, scrap iron and pots and pans. Once, sorting out old papers from a musty attic of Miss Tombs, I searched hopefully for a Penny Black amongst bundles of Victorian stamped envelopes. We kept our bath water to the regulation 2 inch mark, and above all, we sawed. Dr Billen at one end of the cross-cut, and relays of boys at the other, we sawed our way through fuel for the winters, And they were bitter winters too. There appears frequently in a diary I have just found (among huge gaps marked 'forgotten), 'snowed', or 'lavatories frozen', or 'thawed'. Dr Billen, however, kept us reasonably warm.

And as important as fuel was food. Fuel, food and the blackout was the War as we felt it. The Home Front and rationing meant the appearance of strange new foods like *Pom* and *Spam,* and dehydrated eggs. it gave a high market value to tuck boxes with units of Army composite rations, the block of powdered bacon in particular. It meant queuing for emergency cards at holidays. Bananas disappeared for the duration, and eggs became luxuries. Sweet coupons appeared and visits to Miss Tombs became restricted by more than personal finance; and orange juice concentrate, and the odd packet of chewing gum, only compensated a little. The blackout meant black paint (very chipped), on the corridor windows and shutters in the train room. It meant cramped, rather atonal Evening Services in the long corridor instead of Church. But we survived, and even when the Dormitories were packed with Chickenpox and

Cubs with Miss Ashley, 1956-57

At Scout camp, 1956-57

German Measles, and the news bulletins and newspaper headlines gave us nothing to cheer, nobody worried or, at least, we didn't.

We missed nothing, and, travelling back from blitz-scarred London on crowded trains running hours late, away from the sirens and ARP wardens, and the galaxy of strange uniforms in the streets, – we gained at once, a special sort of peace. Hectic, purposeful, very busy, it was above all durable. As durable as the portraits that looked down on us each meal time; Sir F A G Ouseley and his companions in gilt frames from other centuries and times so different. As durable as their Foundation, alive and remembered in the excitement of Commemoration each year – always the biggest event in our school calendar. The beautiful and greater durability of the services we sung each day; conceived in a simple beauty of life, they were part of our life; the creaky raising of the font head for baptism, the banns of marriage read of a Sunday, the fresh mound of earth and clay in the churchyard, the prayer and response of a litany on a Friday morning, the exultation of our evening anthem with the sun a pool of dappled light by the altar. And with this durable, peaceful fullness, everything else had its place. (22)

COLONEL JOHN BLASHFORD-SNELL OBE (1947-49)
(GIVEN IN NOTE FORM AND EXPANDED BY AUTHOR)

One of his abiding memories was of the Cubs and Scouts, organised by Miss Ashley. She was large and fierce, but kindly to small boys. Another member of staff remembered was the Reverend Buster Bennett, who was very hearty and jolly.

Colonel Blashford-Snell could not sing, but he reports that he played a fair hand of poker in the back stalls in College Chapel.

Even at a such a tender age, his exploration activities were already well established and these included mapping the school. However, his great adventure was being caught by Miss Ashley when out rabbiting with his .410 shotgun – after lights out. On being captured, he spun some awful yarn about being homesick and Miss Ashley took him back to school for a cup of cocoa and a gentle talking to! Amazingly the good lady thought that his .410 gun (which was rather compact), was a toy gun...so it was not confiscated! Other memories included races over the beds in Long Dorm. – He remembers breaking someone's bed – being, as ever, overweight.(23)

REFERENCES

1. Alderson & Colles pages 67 – 69
2. Sydney Nicholson, College Magazine 1942
3. C.E.S. Littlejohn, College Magazine 1943
4. A.V. Billen, College Magazine 1945
5. C.A.R. Irby, College Magazine 1945
6. E. Wright, College Magazine 1945

7. College Magazine July 1947
8. College Magazine July 1947
9. College Magazine July 1949
10. College Magazine July 1951
11. College Magazine July 1951
12. College Magazine July 1952
13. Kenneth Beard, College Magazine July 1953
14. College Magazine July 1953
15. College Magazine July 1953
16. College Magazine July 1954
17. College Magazine July 1954
18. College Magazine July 1955
19. College Magazine July 1955
20. College Magazine July 1955
21. College Magazine July 1956
22. College Magazine July 1956
23. Colonel Blashford-Snell to author – 22 October 1999

CHAPTER THIRTEEN
THE CENTENARY
1956

The year 1956 was a memorable one in many ways in the life of the College. The main event was the celebration of the Centenary of the Foundation of the College in 1856, with a week of Commemoration services and events taking place in September.

Other major events included the Opening of the new Music Library and the celebration of the Mozart Bi-Centenary.

COLLEGE LIFE.

Despite the financial constraints which had always been present throughout its existence, it was always the aim of the modern-day Governors to try and improve the facilities available to the boys at the school. By 1956, the building of the new playroom had been completed, (later to become the theatre), and after its temporary use for an exhibition of Library treasures, it was now available for its proper use. It was also hoped to equip it with chairs and gymnastic equipment at a later date.

In June 1956, Canon 'Monty' Alderson resigned both as a Governor and Sub-Warden of the College. Tributes were paid to the long and faithful service which he had given to the College. He continued however to be involved in the affairs of the College, retaining his Fellowship.

THE MOZART BI-CENTENARY.

On 16 March 1956, in honour of Mozart's Bi-Centenary year, a performance took place of his *Requiem* and other items, performed by the combined forces of the College choir, the Commoners' choir and the Tenbury Music Society. It turned out to be an unusual performance as the newly restored Father Willis organ in the church developed a temporary technical fault, resulting in only two flute stops being available for accompanying the Mozart. As a result, it was decided to use the piano instead and Kenneth Beard's virtuosity compensated for the deficiency, ably assisted by the Wolverhampton String Ensemble. 'A packed Church testified to the growing appreciation in which St Michael's efforts are held. Their music commands an appeal far beyond local interest and the performance was given with the support of the Arts Council of Great Britain.'(1)

THE CHOIR

The choir returned early at the start of the Michaelmas term to begin preparations for the Centenary Commemoration, and also broadcast two Choral Evensongs in October 1956. Writing in the College Magazine, Kenneth Beard spoke of the Centenary.

> A time not only for looking back over a hundred years with all the feelings of pride and admiration which such a record inspires, not only for taking stock of the present, but perhaps most important of all, a time when we should look to the future. The probationers are nowadays selected in one of two ways, either by a Public Voice Trial, or by examination after entry into the College as Commoners. It is probably still true that the best voices go elsewhere, though the standard of entry is quite high, and the quality of the boys' singing in church remains very good. Choristerships are eagerly sought after, the announcement of the result of a chorister's trial causing great and universal excitement. The two head choristers are appointed by merit rather than by seniority, again producing keen competition and hard work.
>
> The men of the choir comprise a small number of official lay clerks, singing Masters and helpers. At present, this works extremely well, and the College is fortunate indeed to have the services of so many good men. No choir notes on this occasion would be complete without a tribute to the work of the choir men in the last hundred years. Certainly, none of my predecessors can have had more willing or able help than is my fortune today.(2)

Kenneth Beard then went on to compare the present choice of choir music with the view expressed by Sir Sydney Nicholson many years before, that it should be 'limited.' In Mr Beard's time, it had been the policy to widen the repertoire as much and as often as possible. There were times when this was not possible, due to a sudden epidemic of colds or flu, but then there can be the return to more well-known music, which can be re-vitalised after a period of absence. He also makes an important general point in choir training, that it is easier to correct any fundamental weakness when learning some new music, rather than to correct a similar fault in a well-known piece such as Stanford in Bb. This principle also avoids the danger of a limited repertoire reflecting too greatly the individual preferences of any choirmaster. He believed that the music sung at St Michael's is at least as large as any comparable institution. A hundred years ago, the first Statute of the College stated that 'The College has been founded and dedicated to the service of God and the Church of Christ in these realms.'(3) Mr Beard then pointed out that it was our first obligation to remember this, which could easily be forgotten in the rush of everyday activities. Ouseley's College is above all else, a religious foundation. The second Statute spoke of the object of the Foundation. 'To form a model for the Choral Services of the church.'(4)

It was an obligation on those in the College to maintain the highest possible standards in the conduct of the daily services and a third obligation, reflecting the spirit of adventure in which the College was founded, was to be adventurous in their turn.

> We must be willing to accept new ideas, particularly new music. At the least, we must give any such music a fair trial, and welcome it if offered as a sincere contribution to church music. The test of time largely determines what we consider good and fitting in music of earlier periods; the only test we can give modern music is one of practice and performance.(5)

Many years before, Sir Sydney Nicholson had expressed the hope that St. Michael's might become the 'Mecca of English Cathedral Music.' It is now clear that the musical standards in our cathedrals have improved greatly since those words were written, but despite this, Kenneth Beard implores us to remain true to the Founder's ideal in establishing the College, not only by maintaining it, but wherever possible, by enriching it as well. 'Let us preserve a spirit of adventure. Let us seek to improve our standards. Let us widen our influence through personal contacts and visitors. Let us spread the knowledge of the continued existence of St. Michael's College and its objects.'(6) As a statement of these intentions, it was felt that the music at the Centenary services should represent as many styles as possible and that musicians particularly associated with St Michael's should be represented. It was therefore appropriate for some of the best music from the 16th Century to the present day to be included.

BYRD	Sing Joyfully
BYRD	Justorum Animae
DERING	Factum est silentium
DI LASSO	Jubilate Deo
PURCELL	O Sing unto the Lord
BULLOCK	Give us the Wings of Faith
OUSELEY	Jerusalem on High
OUSELEY	From the rising of the sun
MORLEY)	
NICHOLSON)	Settings of Evensong and Holy Communion
SUMSION)	
STANFORD	Setting of Psalm 150

The music also included special commissions by

HEATHCOTE STATHAM – Festival Te Deum

BRITTEN   Antiphon

and a chant for Psalm 122, written by Christopher Robinson

Some of the Founder's hymns were sung including *They come, God's messengers of love* (written especially for the Consecration Service in 1856), and his glorious tune to the hymn *When all the mercies O My God.*

THE OPENING OF THE NEW MUSIC LIBRARY

St Michael's possessed one of the most valuable and extensive private collections of music and books on music in the whole of Europe and concern had been expressed for many years about the safety and conservation of such a collection. As a result, a special fire-proof strongroom was built, leading off the main library and using what had been the old recreation room. This had been made possible by the generosity of the Pilgrim Trust, which had donated £ 5000 towards the project and the balance of £ 1500 had been given by Miss F Hascall of New York, in admiration for the work of the late Dr E H Fellowes. The architect was Mr E A Roiser of Cheltenham and the Library was officially opened by Professor Jack Westrup, Heather Professor of Music at Oxford. He spoke of the library's value and importance to scholars and the necessity of keeping the collection together.

THE CENTENARY COMMEMORATIONS AND CELEBRATIONS

The week of special services included a Saturday Sung Eucharist at St Michael's, at which the Dean of York, Dr Milner-White preached. In his sermon, the Dean referred to the College as 'a powerhouse of English Church Music.' At this service, there were present in an official capacity, representatives of the organisations with which the Founder had been associated. The Bishop of Hereford represented the Dean and Chapter, Mr H G Pitt, an Old Boy, represented the University of Oxford, Dr. Statham represented the Royal College of Organists, and Mr Frank Howes, MBE, the Royal Musical Association. At the luncheon held afterwards on the Cloister lawn, Canon Alderson, together with Edgar Broadhurst and his wife, Mary (the daughter of John Hampton), represented the older generation of the College and especially the Wardenship of her father, while Reverend and Mrs. Stride represented the future of the College after his appointment as Warden. At the Sunday Evensong, the preacher was the Bishop of Hereford.

The Honorary Librarian of the College, Watkins Shaw, wrote a summary of what the College had achieved during its hundred year existence. In its early days, the College had stuck closely to the ideals of its Founder and John Hampton, Ouseley's successor as Warden, continued this from the Founder's death until 1917. Afterwards, under the guidance of Warden Swann,

A progressive educational policy was launched, whereby a small school for choristers with a handful of non-singing boys was developed into an excellent preparatory school in which the choristers, though increasingly in the minority, had the advantage of better graduated academic teaching and of fuller community life in a better equipped school. At the same time, 'commoners', or non-singing boys, have enjoyed a corresponding advantage in receiving a normal preparatory school education in a permanent non-profit-making institution inspired by a religious ideal. A modern classroom block was built to take the place of the old schoolroom, the number of staff was increased and an open-air swimming bath added. (7)

At Commemoration, it was announced that the present Warden, the Reverend Noel Kemp-Welch, the first old boy of the College to be appointed as Warden, would be leaving at the end of the Michaelmas term after ten years as Warden and moving to St Peter's School, York, as Chaplain. The College was thus placed to begin its second century with a new Warden.

RETIREMENT OF THE REVEREND N H KEMP-WELCH

BY KENNETH BEARD

On 30 September 1956, at the close of the Centenary celebrations, Reverend N H Kemp-Welch retired from the Wardenship of the College, after holding office for ten years. He had brought many gifts and a wide experience to his work as Warden of St Michael's. His early training as a chorister at the College, followed by a Choral Scholarship at King's College, Cambridge, ensured a deep understanding of the nature of the music at St Michael's. His call to the priesthood and previous experience as a parish priest ensured a standard of Churchmanship and a concern for the needs of his parishioners, which, together, enabled him to preserve the claims of College and parish in a right proportion.

Facing the future of a Preparatory School in 1947 can have been no light matter, for problems of maintenance and staffing were acute in the immediate post-war period. That St Michael's carried on its work, the number of boys in the School actually increasing during this difficult period, is entirely due to the work of Mr Kemp-Welch and those who helped him. Many of his boys have achieved great success in various fields of activity.

Among individual memories one will always associate with Mr. Kemp-Welch, one of the most vivid was his singing of the priest's part in the Daily Offices in Church. Surely few men have brought greater gifts of musicianship, combined with a sensitive understanding of the majesty of the Prayer Book language, to this important function. Herein was established and preserved at St Michael's a 'model' for the Church of England! We shall also remember his energy and enthusiasm in promoting several large-scale musical performances, both religious and secular. In these we recall with pleasure and delight, the singing of Mrs

Kemp-Welch. We remember too, his ready humour and kindness to staff and boys; and we value the example he set of gentlemanly and thought for other people. A particular debt St Michael's owes him is the raising of funds to make the re-building of the organ not merely a distant hope but a reality. A figure of almost £3,000 was no small sum to raise in a small country town. This project was realised well before the Centenary Day itself and its completion was a result of patient hard work. No appreciation of his work would pretend to be complete, as parents, boys, staff and Fellows, continued to recall different reasons for personal gratitude.

Christopher Hassall, an old boy of the College (1921 –1925), wrote a poem to celebrate the Centenary of the College and this was published in the College Magazine of 1956.

POEM FOR MICHAELMAS DAY

Variation on a theme of Thomas Hood

I remember, I remember, grey stone, a spiral stair to bed,
A long dormitory, like the creaking hold of a galleon,
With slit windows, too high for gazing out,
Where clouds went by and the moon came searching
Through shafts of uninvited silver:
A library, august and serious-coloured, remote as night itself,
Where the still air was tinged with sandal-wood,
Mysterious with motets and Latin titles embossed
On leather bindings brown as conkers, all waiting,
Mute, compacted spine to spine, and out of reach of hand or
Understanding.

I remember, I remember, the windy cloister-walk,
The bellows, gasping and shuddering in the effort to let
Bach breathe, or it might have been Widor
Demanding full-blown lungs for a dogmatic statement on the pedals;
St Michael painted in his triumph round the pipes.
A choir screen of wrought iron supporting candlesticks,
A row of little ornamental dishes like top notes hoisted and sustained;
The English language lying open on an eagle's wings,
Music, unfolding like a fair, untravelled, promised land,
With meadows of flowering chords and sinuous, contrapuntal streams;
Merbecke, William Byrd of Lincoln, S S Wesley, Walmisley in
(Was it D minor?), and Stanford (which was certainly in C),
And another bird, a robin that had lost its way, flickering against a
Stained-glass patch of Galilean sky,
Unable to regain its own, contemporary, blue;
A flutter and hedgerow chirrup just audible in the timeless pause after
The Benediction.

I remember, I remember, coming upon an amiable, shy, grass-snake in
The tangles beyond the boundary-six line during cricket;
Watching a golden-crested wren managing to get on all right without
Geography in a fir-tree during prep:
Biting a windfall of excruciating sourness on the way
To football, never suspecting it was a foretaste of so much;
Filling a cap with damsons in the time of damsons,
A foretaste of so little, had one but known,
But one never thought. There was no need.
The world was innocent and singing.

I remember, I remember, the tuck-shop down the road where
Marshmallow fish were three a penny;
Enormous mole-hills on the Common where for an instant
The linnets would perch and survey
The prospect as from an 'eminence';
Six-spot burnet moths and the low-flying, vivid cinnabar
Whose underwing was the colour of the school magazine;
Clee Hill, away to the north, huge and consoling as a psalm,
A lot of sky, and almost too many yellowhammers;
An old gypsy woman who frightened me by asking the time in
A bass voice, so deep she could have sung the
Bass part in Purcell's anthem *Jehovah quam multi*
And taken the bottom E in her stride;
An attack on a wasp's nest when we were badly outnumbered;
The thought of a letter in my pocket, the foreign stamps
She had sent me with news of my chrysalis;
Everywhere happiness, like the summer haze that hovered
Over the yellow-burning gorse and even seemed
To be spreading far, far across the border
Into Shropshire;
And all the while, from every aspect, wherever you were,
The grey roof of the Chapel exalted above the elm-tops,
St Michael's Chapel, reassuring, bearing witness, saying
To workers in the cider orchard, young boys
Mooching on the Sunday walk, and old ones
Coming in from Tenbury for Evensong,
Saying to earth and to the heavens where the clouds from
Ludlow and Clee will for ever eve holding to the
Course of their serene, dissolving journeys,
Night after night whispering gravely to the radiant constellations –
*God is a spirit..........God is a spirit..........and we must worship him
........must worship him.........in spirit and in truth* (8)

IMPRESSIONS OF THE CENTENARY BY CHRISTOPHER THOMPSON

The procession passed up the aisle, the youngest boys concentrating on keeping in line. The older boys walked straight without effort, and their eyes moved to take in the size of the congregation. The choir passed, self-possessed, singing, each individual voice becoming distinct for an instant before merging into general harmony again. The familiar pattern of the sung Eucharist was especially moving because the singing had never seemed purer or more freed from sentimentality. The Nicholson *Kyries,* Mr Cole singing the *Agnus Dei* – half-forgotten echoes of Michaelmas sprang to life again and inspired me with a feeling of personal joy and gratitude to add to the communal thanks for one hundred safe and fruitful years.

The undertone of excitement among musicians apparent throughout the weekend became more marked during the pause before lunch. Many Old Boys gathered in the main corridor. Some praised, a few criticised, for praise is not freely given by those whose memories may be tinged with gold already. All were eager to hear the new works composed for the Centenary and to congratulate Mr Beard. Discussion passed from the present to the past in easy stages. After a photograph on the lawn, when no ill-timed urge for perfect grouping was allowed to spoil the friendliest occasion of the day, it was now lunch time. There need have been no fears that lunch in a marquee on the cloister lawn would lose anything of the traditional atmosphere. The Founder's Grace both blessed the meal and broke the ice completely.

The afternoon was the time for reminiscences. Groups became smaller, scattered in every corner of the college. It was also time to see what was newly built. Outstanding was the addition to the Library. We peered through the new gateway into a low compact room that was once the train-room (and before that the original schoolroom). The gate was locked, but we could see where the precious books lay, safe in a honeycomb of metal shelves.

We wandered slowly, attracted from place to place by the same peculiar fascination that led a few a far as the Poet's Stone. We met others, and each time, stopped to talk. The memories evoked by those once familiar scenes reminded us of those who had shared our early years. Contemporaries drew together to speak of common experiences and of the intervening years, as travellers having started from the same point and reached a resting place by different routes, might gather to compare the journey. Inseparable from the scenes and incidents remembered were the personalities of those who taught us. Many found that all but one had left. That one person was Miss Ashley, too well known and respected for me to add any tribute. The continuous stream of visitors she received during the weekend was ample proof of the place she holds in the affection of her pupils.

Sunday was a quiet day and for me passed very quickly. I went to Matins, but it seemed that I had scarcely reached the College after walking back from lunch in Tenbury before it was time for the last Centenary Service. When Evensong had ended, many of the congregation paused outside the Church to say goodbye. Before leaving, I spoke with Canon Alderson. He told me that he was learning by heart the music he used to play, so that the risk of failing eyesight should not deprive him of the pleasure of using his piano. Those who struggle now with the gallery piano and think it invincible should take courage. Those who fought and lost should blush with me!

With the chastening example in my mind I left. The Church and College are as we remember them, for St Michael's has a quality that has endured a hundred years of outward alteration. I am sure that the permanence we feel springs from a happy union of Worship, Music and the Countryside, and that it will never be lost as long as they remain. (9)

REFERENCES

1. College Magazine July 1956
2. College Magazine July 1956
3. HCL D483
4. HCL D483
5. College Magazine July 1956
6. College Magazine July 1956
7. College Magazine July 1956
8. Centenary Brochure 1956
9. College Magazine 1957

CHAPTER FOURTEEN
COLLEGE LIFE
1956-1976

Following the resignation of Warden Kemp-Welch and his departure in December 1956, The new Warden, the Reverend Desmond Stride, moved into residence on 1 January 1957. The school opened on 15 January and he was officially installed as Warden on 18 January. Mr Stride came from a post at Dover College and was well qualified for the task ahead. There were more changes to follow as Miss Ashley, who had been a member of the teaching staff since the early 1920's, was retiring and would be missed by many boys and Canon Alderson's retirement from the Governing Body was already known. In an introduction to his time as Warden, Mr Stride spoke of his aims for the future.

> In these days, everyone is agreed that only the highest academic standards will suffice. But the successful schoolmaster is one who is willing, not only to maintain these, but also to spend much spare time in doing the numerous odd jobs that mean so much in the running of a school. St Michael's is most fortunate in this respect and I am happy to end these notes by expressing my real thanks to all the teaching staff for their most loyal support. St Michael's has now started on its second century and I believe the prospects for carrying on our Founder's intentions are as bright as they have ever been (1)

Musically, as well as in every other aspect of College life, it had been perhaps the busiest period for the choir in the history of the College, and both the men and boys were to be congratulated for all their splendid work. After all their excellent efforts for the Centenary celebrations, life went on and at the end of the Lent term, the choir sang Faure's *Requiem* and other works, ably assisted as usual by the Tenbury Music Society. Another Madrigal programme was presented in the Cloisters at the start of the Summer Term and the BBC were busy making recordings of the choir to broadcast in September. The normal service repertoire was maintained, despite all these extra commitments. In this connection, the choir was fortunate in having several top boys of long experience. As more boys than usual left by the summer of 1957 (17), the average age of the school dropped a year. This inevitably meant a longish period of training and consolidation at the beginning of the next year, but the silver lining was that only one boy was destined to leave the choir over the next two years.

One happy event was a party for Mr George Coles, to celebrate his 'Twenty-fifth' anniversary as a lay clerk. He has been in the choir for almost 27 years, singing in both the daily services and in oratorio performances. Kenneth Beard spoke of the College's appreciation.

> We delight in the richness of his voice and in his musicianship, fully realising how fortunate we are to have him. For myself, I record gratitude not only for his singing, but also for his constant help and encouragement. I can only imagine what restraint may be required if a young man comes along trying to make changes, when you have been doing the job since he was a babe in arms. We wish him many more years of singing at St Michael's. (2)

One very sad event for those at the College was the sudden death of Anthony Peter Smith, aged 13. He became a chorister in 1954 and was Head Chorister at the Centenary. He was always keen on games and outdoor activities, he played in all the first teams, and was vice-captain of both football and rugger during 1956 –57. The moving obituary, again written by Kenneth Beard, tells of the tragic loss felt by all at the College.

> At St Michael's, he will be remembered as one of the best of choristers. By his own enthusiasm and obvious enjoyment of singing, he had set so good an example that by the time his voice began to change, the remaining boys were able to carry on in a splendid way during one of our most important and busy periods. This was the kind of leadership which we knew and valued in him. 'Smithy' had achieved much in his short but happy life. He had already passed Grade VI in piano playing in 1956, and without doubt would have gone on to his Public School with a major music scholarship. He was a boy of many interests, full of energy and enthusiasm for everyday life and fun. But this does not say all, for together with a certain outspoken quality of expression, was a real regard and concern for other people. This was notably obvious in the pride and delight he took in his family and friends.
>
> It seems strangely fitting that his passing, if it had to be, came in the fullness of his life at St Michael's, after a morning spent mostly in music-making, and during the course of a game which he so well liked to play. We are grateful to think that he did not suffer pain or prolonged illness, and we believe he has entered into the nearer presence of our Lord, who was no stranger to him on earth. (3)

One piece of welcome news received by the College during the year came from the Ecclesiastical Music Trust of The English Hymnal Ltd, who generously undertook to endow the sum of £ 90 for six years to help meet the cost of one of the choristerships. This did not add to the number of choristers, but relieved the College of a large part of the maintenance of one of them, who would be known as the English Hymnal Scholar. St Michael's was once again in the news when the BBC broadcast a programme, entitled *In Service High and Anthems Clear,* an account of the Centenary Year, with Mr Stride and Kenneth Beard being interviewed by Maurice Dean. They spoke of Ouseley's aims in founding the College, the history of the organ, the choir and its repertoire and the necessary changes that have made the school develop into an attractive preparatory school with a long-standing musical tradition. The interviews were illustrated by the St. Michael's boys singing Bullock's *Give us the wings of faith* and Stanford's *Magnificat in C.*

The following year, the College made the relationship between themselves and the local community even stronger by holding a Grand Gala at the end of the Summer Term to raise funds for the re-building of the Village Hall. It was heartwarming to see what could be achieved through co-operation between those living inside and outside the College. The College and the Church together formed the centre of the life of the Parish of St Michael's and in order for all to benefit from the Founder's great work, all must share in the responsibility of giving a lead.

The Commemoration of July 1957, the first for Warden Stride, was marked by most members of the College being stricken with influenza. Commemoration was observed only in ferial form. Despite this, the College was honoured to have Dr Francis Jackson, Organist of York Minster to give the Organ Recital.

In September 1957, Mr Stride appointed a new Art Master, John Gray, who was destined to become part of the life of the College and church for more than forty years. One of his first innovations was to introduce a monthly 'Boys' Paper', recording school activities and enabling boys to express themselves. This appeared on a monthly basis throughout the year and was duplicated and circulated around the school.

The Carol service in December attracted a full church and was held in candlelight and in the following June, the BBC again visited the College for a short live broadcast and the choir sang a number of anthems, including Howell's *Like as the Hart,* Blow's *O pray for the peace of Jerusalem* and Farrant's *Call to Remembrance.*

Three new Fellows were appointed in 1958 – 59. They were Herbert Sumsion, organist of Gloucester Cathedral, the Dean of Gloucester and Dr J H H Oliver, who lived in St Michael's. The Governing Body also awarded the title of Sub-Warden Emeritus to Canon Alderson in recognition of his service to the College. He would be 90 in July 1959.

Early in 1959, it was announced that Kenneth Beard had been appointed Organist and Rector Chori of Southwell Minster. Over a

The library from prospectus 1960

period of seven years as Organist, he had raised the standard of the choir considerably and taken a full part in those many other areas of school life. He would be greatly missed, but fully deserved his promotion. Shortly afterwards, Kenneth's replacement was announced and everyone at the College was soon able to welcome Lucian Nethsingha, FRCO, BA, to the staff, having previously attended the Royal College of Music and King's College, Cambridge. He was able to settle in at the beginning of September and prepare for his first Commemoration.

In connection with the Purcell-Handel Commemorations, the Honorary Librarian arranged a two-day exhibition of manuscripts and printed music. This created a great deal of interest and resulted in many visitors to the College. It was featured briefly on a Midlands ITV programme.

For some time the Warden had felt that, owing to the larger number of boys, he was unable to spend as much time on parish affairs as he would like. As the College now had the use of the Vicarage again, it seemed a timely opportunity to try and solve this difficulty and this resulted in the appointment of a Curate for the Parish the following September.

> He will have no duties connected with the College and will immensely relieve the Warden of responsibility which he has to feel towards the Parish. The close connection between the College and parish has been valuable, but as time has gone on, the College has demanded more and more time to the detriment of the parish. The parishioners for their part have supported the activities of St Michael's church very loyally and it is only fair that they should have a clergyman who will regard them as his major concern. (4)

During the Academic Year 1959 – 60, there were 10 boys leaving the school and 16 new boys arriving. One of the longest serving Masters, Mr Demaus, was appointed as Senior Master. He had been at the school as a Master since 1946 and before the War, attended the school as a boy.

Mr F S Miles, from the Tenbury firm of Solicitors, retired from the post of Bursar of the College. He had served the College for over 46 years, handling the often difficult financial and legal affairs of the College throughout this time and giving excellent advice to the Governing Body. George Coles, one of the College lay clerks and Mr Miles' assistant, now took over as Bursar.

In a small guide available to visitors to the church, the church services were listed as follows:–

Weekdays 8-45 am   MATINS   (Monday – Thursday and Saturday)
          8-45 am   LITANY   (Friday)
          6-15 pm   EVENSONG   (Monday – Friday)
                                     (Wednesday – boys' voices only)

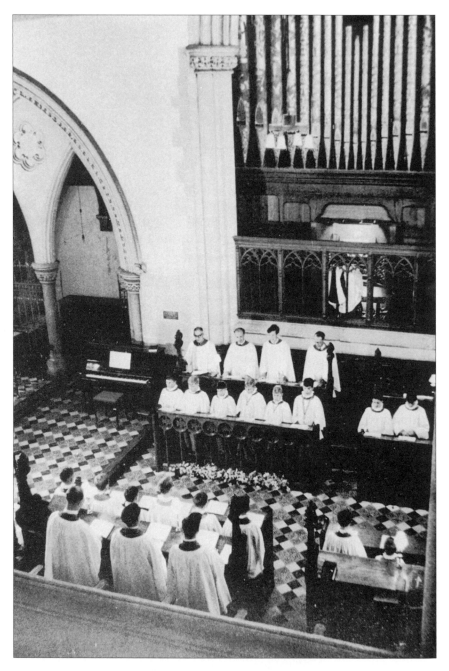

The choir from prospectus 1960

Sunday   11-00 am   CHORAL EUCHARIST

             6-30 pm   Evensong and Sermon

The College and church continued to receive many gifts. Sir Percy Hull endowed a prize to be awarded annually to the best performer on a musical instrument other than the piano; new cushions were given for the altar rail; a new gold curtain behind the organ; a new gong for the Dining Hall, and small silver reproductions of the head choristers' medallions to be worn by choristers.

One very memorable event for many of the boys was the visit of John Betjeman to the College. He took the boys on a tour of the College, and brought the buildings to life as only he can, as well as telling the boys a great deal about the architect, Henry Woodyer. He noted particularly the patterns of his hinges and ironwork, the patterns of tiles on the floor of the church, the span and symmetry of arch upon arch of windows and woodwork and boys tramped all over the College, looking at the usual from unusual angles! Mr Betjeman very generously awarded a prize for the boy who did the best drawing of some feature, typical of Woodyer's detail work. Accompanying Mr Betjeman was the poet, Christopher Hassall, an Old Boy who had written his famous poem on St Michael's for the Centenary Celebrations, and the boys were thrilled by this visit.

> These two eminent literary figures did us a great honour by spending the night with us and we all, from the youngest to the oldest, were thrilled by their wisdom, humour and friendliness. To have poets of such standing reading their own works to 35 boys in the Dormitory at night is an experience few preparatory schools can have enjoyed, while their talks on Verse Speaking and Architecture were a great inspiration. (5)

It was announced soon after that Christopher Hassall had been made a Fellow of the College and in the recent Birthday honours, another Fellow, Herbert Sumsion was made a CBE.

The Warden spoke in the magazine about the College finances. He compared the fees paid by parents whose sons go to other preparatory schools of equal quality will show that, even for Commoners, the fees are low. It was the Governors intention that this should remain so in the future, but there were problems.

> Despite the endowment laid down by the Founder for the provision of bursaries, etc, the present value of endowment income has greatly decreased in recent years and it is hoped to re-endow the College in the next year or two with new benefactors. This being a preliminary notice for the launch of an Appeal connected with the College, essential to maintain the high standard of the choir and music as well as the general improvement of facilities in the College. (6)

Chapel dormitory from prospectus 1960

Two deaths occurred during the year of people connected with the College. Dr Billen, who as Acting Warden, had guided so well the affairs of the College through the dark and difficult years of the second World War, died at his home in Banbury on 3 June and earlier in the year, the death of Mrs Hampton, wife of the second Warden, brought back memories of the College of almost sixty years ago.

> St Michael's was then rather monastic, and the softer side of life lay at the Vicarage. To me, Mrs Hampton is a delightful memory – most charming both in face and character and hospitable in the extreme. She entertained two boys to supper every Sunday night throughout each term, and what welcome feasts they were. She always made us feel at home, which perhaps was not easy because of the Warden's presence. I am sure that she exercised a mellowing influence on the whole College, which will always be remembered with gratitude by those who so much benefited by it. (7)

During the year, the choir continued with its outside work, recording for a BBC programme, while Mr Nethsingha recorded two organ recitals, also for the BBC.

The following poem appeared in the July 1962 edition of the College Magazine and in view of the boys' (and Masters') interest in railways, was a sad reflection on the 'axe' wielded by Doctor Beeching!

LAMENT FOR A CENTENARIAN

(The Bewdley – Tenbury railway of the Western Region was to close in the immediate future, after 101 years of service)

Alas, Dr Beeching, so remote and so smug,
That you erase from the map the 'Tenbury Slug'
With a slash of the pen in a distant city,
Deaf to the pleas of the Transport Committee.

But to hundreds of boys who wore caps of bright red
The poor smoky old 'Slug' will not ever be dead;
Gas-lit and clerestoried, cobwebb'd, dingy and slow,
Panting up from Bewdley with chimney all a-glow!

Or daisy-picking idly in cuttings full of May,
Uncaring when you get there – it *may* be today?
But written of by Houseman, trav'ling down by Wyre
Through Francis Young's 'Far Forest' autumnally afire.

Stations where you waited were know to us scholars;
One I well remember was known as 'Clean Collars.'
For we, who were Eton-suited ev'ry Sunday,
Looked forward more to the coming of a Monday!

The one tunnel on the line was dank and musty,
The button'd leather seats were brittle and dusty;
The smoke rose in columns to overtop the Clee
Or smother the banks of the winding River Rea.

On chill December mornings, hedges white with rhyme,
Small cold faces peered through windows grey with grime;
Waited – the window being lowered – for a chance
To hurl a packed lunch at Severn's icy glance.

When the train swayed like a reed on the high-spanned curve
Above old Bewdley's river; or plucked up the nerve
To throw hard-boiled eggs at an innocent porter
Watching at Cleobury while the engine took water!

But how, Dr Beeching, so remote and so smug,
Can you hope to remove the old 'Tenbury Slug'
From the lines of a Houseman or Francis Brett Young,
Or from the tales of those who its praises have sung?

(8)

'S. M. L. R.'

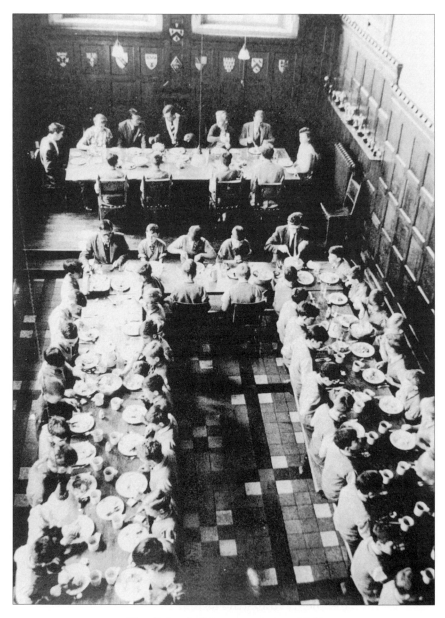

The dining hall from prospectus 1960

Over the academic year 1961 – 62, a large number of boys left the school (15), but the school was fortunate in receiving 20 new boys. The school was literally bursting at the seams and during the year, they had to turn away a number of prospective new boys because of a lack of space. Future entries were very good but the College was desperate for more space.

The College Visitor, the Right Reverend Tom Longworth, Bishop of Hereford since 1949, announced his retirement and his successor was to be Bishop Mark Hodson.

Another important announcement for anyone connected with the College was the appointment of Christopher Robinson as Music Master at the King's School, Worcester and Assistant Organist at the Cathedral from September 1962. Within two years, he was appointed Cathedral Organist when Douglas Guest left to take over as Organist of Westminster Abbey. Both Christopher Robinson and John Hampton, (son of the second Warden), were appointed as Fellows of the College.

The BBC were hard at work with the choir, recording a Service of Meditation for radio on Good Friday, and a great many encouraging letters were received after the broadcast. Before the end of the Summer term, two more recordings were made, one to be heard on the BBC Home Service on 28 July and another on 13 August. During the Summer Term, the Choir rehearsed a great deal of secular music which they planned to perform at the end of term, including a 15 minute recording for a BBC Children's Programme, singing folk-songs, rounds, a madrigal, etc.

Just as the College Magazine went to press in July 1962, the College was deeply saddened to hear of the death of Canon Alderson, shortly before his ninety-third birthday. He had been perhaps the College's strongest remaining link with the Founder. One of that now tiny band of Old Boys who were boys in the school before Sir Frederick's death. Alderson came to St Michael's as a boy in 1878, leaving in 1883 to go to Winchester. He was elected a Fellow in 1922 and remained one until his death. Most of his life was spent in faithful service as parochial clergyman, in Hatfield, Chesterton, Lutterworth and finally, Rector of Fugglestone with Bemerton in Salisbury Diocese. In 1943, he was appointed as a non-residentiary Canon and Prebend of Durnford in Salisbury Cathedral. His father had been a Canon of Peterborough Cathedral and a Chaplain both to Queen Victoria and Edward VII. At the Michaelmas meeting of the Fellows, Watkins Shaw spoke of the tremendous debt of gratitude owed to Canon Alderson by the College.

No-one could exceed Alderson in his devotion to the College and it is not too strong to describe his love for it as intense. His association with it as a Fellow meant a great deal to him and his visits gave him keen pleasure. Alderson's loyalty to Ouseley is an impressive tribute to that remarkable personality, with whom he was such a vivid link. We respect the memory of Alderson's venerable figure, concealing an enthusiastic boyishness, and inspiring loyalty to the College. (9)

The BBC continued to use St Michael's extensively throughout the next year, with choir and organ being recorded for a number of programmes and a recording of the programme *Meeting Point* for BBC Television, introduced by John Betjeman. Choral Evensong was recorded on 13 and 20 November and also a Christmas children's programme for radio.

An Endowment Appeal was now well under way, with 5000 copies of an Appeal Leaflet being printed. Its two-fold aim was to raise £12,000 for a Building Fund (over £6,300 already being raised), together with the much larger sum of £ 60,000, in order to re-endow the College. The Appeal drew people's attention to the need to maintain the choir, the provision of scholarships for the choristers and the upkeep of the noble Father Willis four-manual organ. It was also noticed that the necessary nature of its buildings made them expensive and difficult to repair. Moreover, the school in which the choristers were educated was also an up-to-date preparatory school for non-choristers as well, and the Governors always tried to keep the fees as low as possible for all boys.

In a school prospectus of the early 1950's, the fees for boys (per term), were listed as follows:–

Commoners £ 70

Brothers who are Commoners (while at school together) £ 55

Sons of Clergy £ 45

Probationers £ 35

Choristers £ 25

All members of the Choir receive free tuition in piano or organ.

Extras: piano, organ, violin, flute, cello, etc.

Although these fees were somewhat higher by 1963, it will be seen that the Governors offered very generous concessions to the sons of clergy as well as choristers and probationers. In the Appeal Leaflet, the Patron, Lord Harewood, wrote of the unique place of St Michael's.

This is no ordinary or routine Appeal for an increase in funds in order to expand, but a plea for survival, addressed from a small institution, which, after a century of service, had qualified to be regarded as part of our national heritage...It would be a poor reflection on our day and age if this College and all it stands for were allowed to fall by the wayside for want of funds.(10)

As the Appeal gathered momentum, members of the College were deeply saddened to hear of the sudden death of Christopher Hassall. Four days previously, he had attended the St Michael's Society Luncheon and had made great efforts to further the Appeal among many influential people. He was particularly remembered for the poem he had written

ST MICHAEL'S COLLEGE

TENBURY, WORCESTERSHIRE

First Report on Re-Endowment Appeal

29th September, 1964

Endowment appeal leaflet 1964

Dear Subscriber,

It gives me pleasure to send you this interim report on the progress of the Appeal and to inform you that up to 31st August, 1964 we have received the following sums, either in cash or in the grossed-up values of Covenants:—

	£
Re-Endowment Fund (for Choristers' Endowments and Sons of Clergy Bursaries)	18,766
General Purposes (to augment our Endowment Income)	4,084
Building Extension Fund	7,357
551 donors have subscribed or covenanted for a total of:	£30,207

The Re-Endowment Fund figure includes four gifts of £2,000 each, specifically given for the endowment of Choral Scholarships, and in respect of which plaques are being attached to Choristers' Stalls, namely:—

The English Hymnal Scholarship, endowed by the Proprietors of The English Hymnal.

The Marion Packer Memorial Scholarship, endowed by The Triangle Trust 1949 Fund.

The Olsen Scholarship, endowed by an anonymous donor.

The Christopher Hassall Memorial Scholarship, endowed by the Schroder Charity Trust.

Old Boys and parents in particular will be pleased to know that the Governing Body has decided to proceed as quickly as practicable with the ambitious building extension programme. This will provide three new classrooms (including a science room), completely new changing rooms and improved accommodation for resident masters. Plans have been approved and specifications have gone out to tender and we hope that it will be possible to make a start on the work early next year. The final cost is expected to be in the region of £15,000; but we are able to proceed by using (in accordance with a Governing Body resolution), in addition to the Building

Appeal cash so far available, the generous bequest (amounting to some £8,000) of the late Canon M. F. Alderson, who was a Fellow of the College and one of its most revered Old Boys.

It should also be mentioned that included in the Building Fund is some £327 raised in St. Michael's Parish and earmarked for furnishing and equipping a new boys' library which will be provided by the new building programme.

From what I have said it will be seen that while much has been achieved, nevertheless much remains to be done and a considerable sum has still to be raised before our re-endowment target of £60,000 is reached. The Appeal therefore is still open, but we feel that some account of our progress is due to those who have so far subscribed. If you know of anyone to whom we might profitably send an Appeal brochure, we shall be very grateful to know his or her name and address.

There follows a Summary of Contributions and a List of Donors. We are more than grateful to you and all who have helped us.

Yours sincerely,

D. W. A. STRIDE

Warden.

SUMMARY OF CONTRIBUTIONS

(to 31st August, 1964)

DONATIONS

5 @ £2000 or over; 1 @ £1500; 2 @ £1000; 1 @ £790; 1 @ £500; 1 @ £400; 1 @ £350 approx. (Shares); 2 @ £200; 15 @ £100 or over; 1 @ £60; 14 @ £50 or over; 2 @ £30 or over; 16 @ £20 or over; 49 @ £10 or over; 91 @ £5 or over; 171 @ £1 or over; 30 @ under £1.

GIFTS UNDER COVENANT

(Amounts per annum)

2 @ £50; 1 @ £30; 2 @ £25; 1 @ £22·10s.; 2 @ £20; 5 @ £15; 3 @ £12; 21 @ £10; 1 @ £8; 1 @ £7; 3 @ £6; 39 @ £5; 6 @ £3; 2 @ £2; 5 @ £1; 1 @ £10 10s.; 1 @ £7 7s.; 10 @ £5 5s.; 6 @ £3 3s.; 7 @ £2 2s.; 7 @ £1 1s.

The Chapel from prospectus 1960

for the College Centenary – Poem for Michaelmas Day, and this was reprinted in the Appeal Leaflet. A year later, the First Annual Report of the Appeal was produced and reported that a total of 551 donors had subscribed or covenanted a total of £30, 207. This included four gifts of £ 2,000 for the endowment of Choral Scholarships from the following.

1. English Hymnal Scholarship from the Proprietors of hymns A. & M.

2. Maria Parker Music Scholarship (Triangle Trust 1949 Fund)

3. The Olsen Scholarship (Anonymous)

4. The Christopher Hassell Music Scholarship (Schroder Charity Trust.)

The past year was noticeable for the great publicity the College had received through television, sound broadcasting, the cinema and the press. Thousands of people who had never heard of St Michael's College were now aware of its existence and this was reflected in the large numbers of visitors, both singly and in parties. The superb musicanship of Mr Nethsingha and the Choir, the Meeting Point TV programme, visits by Field Marshall Montgomery, Sir Arthur Bliss, John Betjeman and many more. A long-playing record was produced by ARGO and was released after Christmas.

The visit by Field Marshall Montgomery took place on Sunday 12 July. He had tea with the Warden, signed autographs and talked to senior boys, had a grand tour of the school and then read the lessons at Evensong.

During 1965, Warden Stride announced his resignation to take up the post of Chaplain of Heathfield School, Ascot and an appreciation of his time as Warden was given by Dr Oliver in the College Magazine (October 1965.)

> Anyone who was a frequent visitor to the College could never feel that he was other than in control; not only of the day to day routine, but also of the future planning of the direction in which the school should move. Now that his term of office has closed, he as left behind not merely a memory, but a viable, active and happy school. A school which has become far more nationally known for what it is and what it does than before he came. This dissemination of the image of the school he relentlessly pursued through every personal contact he could make; persuasion of the BBC to record far more broadcasts than ever before, the first television programme and the production of a long-playing record.
>
> He himself is on record as saying that it has always been his resolve to instil into boys the three Cs, Christianity, Classics and Cricket – and with conviction of the first, an understanding of the second, and a love of the third to send them forth into the world with a firm base on which to build.
>
> Out of his sincere Christian beliefs sprang a great love and affection for the boys, a love tempered with a strict, but fair, discipline.

'The Singing Dolphin' – A rollicking story of the high seas of Christmas 1760. Performed at St. Michael's in December 1963

Because it was so transparently honest and fair, it was a love returned by the boys with respect and the desire to give of their best at all times. Indeed more than one stranger coming into the school left remarking what a happy place it was.

An account of what Dick Stride did for St Michael's would be totally incomplete without mentioning his wife, for she gave herself to the College every bit as much as he did. She mothered the little boys in their first terms at the College, she solved the insolvable as far as getting domestic staff was concerned and keeping them contented, and did the impossible in running the housekeeping on a shoestring. Indeed she worked for the College until her health would allow her to work no longer.

We wish them both every success in their new life and a speedy return to good health for Mrs Stride. For those of us who are still associated with the College, surely the greatest compliment we can pay them both is to maintain and uphold the high standards set before us. (11)

By 1965, the Appeal had generated £36,631, which included a bequest of £8,000 from the Estate of the late Canon Alderson. This bequest was earmarked for a new building, providing for four classrooms, including a Science room. This was built on land near the swimming pool and included a boiler room and filtration plant for the pool. it was named the ALDERSON building in recognition of his magnificent bequest. The previous 'new' building, opposite the tennis courts, was now modernised and extended and named the SWANN building after Warden Swann (1917–1936). Both buildings were opened by his widow in January 1966. These extra classrooms meant that the school was adopting many of the latest educational requirements, in that many classrooms were now specialist rooms, with provision for French audio-visual teaching, a Science laboratory, a Mathematics room and a boys' library.

The Christmas services a few days previously were unique in that for the first time since 1889, the College had choral services on Christmas Day. A successful experiment which was much appreciated by the parishioners who came in large numbers, both for the Midnight Mass and the Family Service on Christmas morning. Services were sung by a small part of the choir, five boys and five men, who also sang a daily Matins and Evensong between the end of term and Christmas Day, with the boys being looked after outside the College by a number of local residents. The boys were then free to go home to their parents after the Family Service.

After being elected as Warden in April 1965, the Reverend Denis Paxman was installed as the eighth Warden of the College during the first Evensong of Commemoration on 29 September 1965. 'The church was filled with the academic robes and hoods of the Fellows who took part in the processions and ceremonial, adding a brilliant splash of colour. The music, too, was colourful, the Canticles being sung to the setting of

Gibbon's *Short Service,* and the anthem, Byrd's sparkling and joyous *Laudibus in sanctis.'*(12)

That year, the Warden's Report also voiced concern that 'these are uncertain days for preparatory schools. The fastnesses of Tenbury seem infinitely remote from the crowded cities in which national policies are formed.'(13) There was also concern for the effect of the new Selective Employment Tax. Many independent schools suffered, but St Michael's managed to escape its full impact because of its legal status as a Charitable Trust.

Other news included Watkins Shaw being elected as a Fellow of RSCM, and Heathcote Statham, a former Old Boy and former organist of the College, retiring as organist of Norwich Cathedral after being there for 34 years. Shortly afterwards, he was awarded the CBE, in recognition of his long and distinguished service to Church Music.

During the year 1966-67, 12 boys left and 20 new boys arrived, again causing the school to be full to capacity. The new facilities provided by the Alderson building were greatly welcomed. Again the choir returned to sing the services on Christmas Eve and Christmas morning and during the Summer Term, for the first time for many years, the choir went to Tewkesbury Abbey to sing in different surroundings, giving a recital of unaccompanied anthems and motets. It was a memorable occasion for the choir and the large crowd of people who came to hear them. During the same term, Christopher Robinson brought the choristers of Worcester Cathedral to sing a very splendid Evensong in the St Michael's church. The BBC were again at work, recording a programme in the series *Choirs and Places where they sing* and then returned in the Summer term to record a half hour programme of Byrd motets. The choir also released another record on the ARGO label, entitled *Sing Joyfully.*

The next year was notable for many events connected with members of the College. George Coles, the College Bursar, was elected as a Fellow. Lucian Nethsingha was pleased to announce the birth of his son Andrew. (Andrew Nethsingha is now organist of Truro Cathedral.) Undoubtedly the saddest news of the year came with the death of Sir Percy Hull, Fellow and former organist of Hereford Cathedral. Born in Hereford in 1878, he was first rejected by Ouseley at a voice trial in his capacity as Precentor of Hereford Cathedral when he was ten years' old, but he was successful at a later one in March 1889, shortly before Ouseley's death. Long afterwards, he recalled his disappointment at not being allowed to come to St Michael's with the Hereford Choir to sing at Ouseley's funeral. As a cathedral chorister, he was first under Langdon Colbourne, who had been organist at St Michael's, and then under G R Sinclair, an Old Boy and Fellow of the College, who occasionally sent him across to St Michael's to play in an emergency. With his death, the College lost its last living link with its Founder.

During the year, there were more changes in the College, with the screen and entrance doors being taken down and entrance to the Dining Hall being made through two new glass doors in the main corridor, enabling all present boys to eat together, instead of having an overflow in another room. This did not involve any change to the Minstrels' Gallery, but a new South door was opened next to the little oriel window of the former boot room.

Over the years, there had been many attempts to start an orchestra and with the enthusiasm of Mr Coleman and the generosity of various friends and benefactors who had made possible the purchase of necessary instruments, and not least, the enthusiastic support of the boys themselves, this was soon a popular activity. What caused some astonishment during the Lent term was the sudden award of a BBC contract for the recording of secular music. This was quite a landmark in the life of the College. These programmes consisted of eight excerpts from *The Beggar's Opera,* recorded in the Library for broadcast on the Schools Service during the Summer term and the school itself was planning a full stage production of the same during the following year. Other broadcasts during the year included two Choral Evensongs on 1 and 8 November, another programme in the series *In Choirs and Places where they sing,* and a broadcast of part of the newly released long-playing record. All these musical activities have shown the limitations of space available for instrumental practice at St Michael's. Generations of boys have practised on pianos dotted about in dark and unsuitable corners, often in cold and cheerless places such as the vestry. Woodwind players recently practised in the boot room and even in the wash-basin area. Temporary arrangements created two practice rooms and a classroom in the theatre area, which had also been modernised and heated. The orchestra itself functioned in the Library, but this was far from ideal. It was proposed that the next major development at the College must be the building of a proper Music School, with Recital Room, teaching and practice rooms, but this was needed now, not in ten years' time.

The steady expansion of numbers made possible after the erection of the Alderson building in 1965 brought the numbers up to 80 for the first time in the history of the College. It was still small when compared to other prep schools, yet this represented a 20 % growth from its average numbers over the last few years. At their Michaelmas meeting, the Governors gave the go-ahead to ambitious plans for the building of a Music School. Of similar construction to the Alderson building, it would stand across the road from the Theatre and the Swann Building and would be T-shaped, with the Music Studio / Hall at the head of the 'T'. It would become the largest room in the College apart from the church, seating an audience of 120 to 150 for a concert, depending on the space required for the performers. Building was planned to start in the spring of 1970, and it was intended to be in use by the end of the year. It was going

The school orchestra 1968

to cost over £20,000, half the amount being raised by the sale of some silver belonging to the College, as well as money given by recent benefactors for this purpose. Around £6,000 would still be required. Another appeal was launched to make up the shortfall as well as a request for three more pianos in good condition for the new facilities, a grand and two uprights, if possible.

For once, the choir was free from broadcasts and recordings during the year, which enabled them to concentrate on enlarging their repertoire, restoring many works which had been discarded over many years. There was a recital of unaccompanied music in June and the choir sang a few items in the final concert of the Ludlow Festival in July. Some choristers sang in the Music Festival, held yearly at Edington Priory in Wiltshire and directed by Simon Preston. This was a festival of church music, lasting a full week, with boys attending from the various choral foundations up and down the country, including a number from Cambridge.

During the year 1969, *The Beggar's Opera* was performed in the College with resounding success, the opera being a glorious vehicle for the voices of choristers, and so it proved. 'The damsels were delightful and a credit to their sex, and the male characters were natural rogues, and obviously revelled in it...The presentation afforded real delight to the audiences on all three nights of its performances, and obviously to the cast.' (14)

The year 1970 was notable for a number of important anniversaries involving past and present members of the College. The first of these, Heathcote Statham, had succeeded Ernest Bullock as Organist of St Michael's 50 years ago. Now retired from his post as Organist at

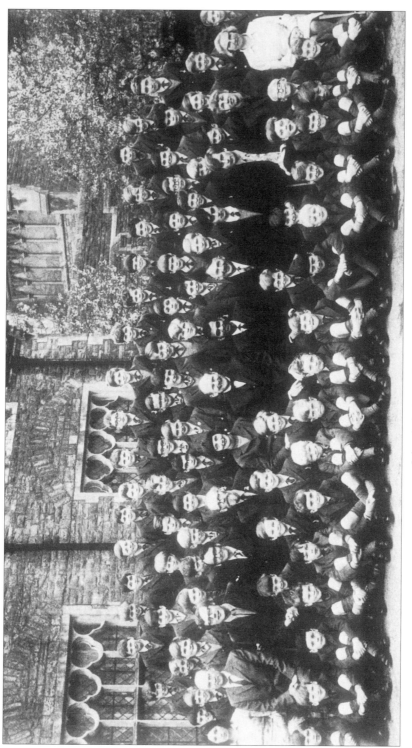

School photograph, summer 1970

Norwich, he still lived in the Cathedral Close there and recently celebrated his eighty-first birthday. Another notable anniversary was that of George Cole, a member of the College administrative staff, who celebrated forty years as a member of the College choir. He was the longest serving members and still possessed a fine melodious bass voice.

Building work on the College continued with the new Music School nearing completion. It was able to be used, but work had still to be done to get the acoustics of the main recital room exactly right. More improvement work was done in the Big Dormitory during the summer holidays and a complete new fire alarm system was installed. Instead of a hand-cranked bell which kept falling off the wall in the main corridor and which only very rarely disturbed the slumbers of the boys, the new electric bells were a great improvement, creating such 'aural havoc' at the mere press of a switch that the boys were only too keen to get across to the Swann Building to enjoy a little peace.

On the music side, twelve boys entered Associated Board Music Examinations, not one a pianist, all offering orchestral instruments. Eleven boys passed, including two merits and four distinctions – a credit to the school's visiting instrumental teachers.

On 5 July 1970, the Choir took part in the Festival Service of the Cheltenham Music Festival,which was held in St Matthew's Church. Roger Nichols played works by Ouseley, Leighton and Fricker before the Service and music by Wills afterwards. The music sung included two festival commissions, *Festival Jubilate* by Ian Kellam and *Benediction for the Arts,* composed by Elizabeth Poston.

Later, in August the same year, the Three Choirs Festival was held at Hereford and the Festival Programme carried an article about the Herefordshire/Worcestershire/ Shropshire border country, mentioning Houseman and other poets associated with the area and an article about St Michael's, which pointed out the past and present links between the College and Hereford and Worcester Cathedral organists. It invited visitors to the Festival to visit the College. 'St Michael's has provided a firm first rung on the ladder of musical education for many boys and they sing a greater number of services a week than any other choral foundation except St Paul's.' (15)

The College Magazine for 1971 began with a tribute to Brian Demaus, who had made his first appearance at St Michael's in 1932. Commoner, Probationer and Chorister followed and he returned to the College as a Master in 1946. He had just completed 30 years at St Michael's this year, 25 as a Master and now held the post of Senior Master.

Recently, it had been discovered that the Church needed re-wiring and Sir John Betjeman's recommendations concerning the lighting of ten years ago were re-discovered and put into use. Tony Penn, one of the St Michael's parishioners, took these into account when designing a scheme of lighting which was more efficient and in keeping with the architecture of the Church. With the help of Geoff Bright of the local electrical company in Tenbury, the proposed lighting was made and installed. Instead of the harsh over-lighting of the nave and the really brutal lighting of the altar, coronals of bulbs now hang low down in between the nave pillars and can be controlled by a master 'dimmer' switch. Electric Candles have also been installed on top of the Chancel Screen and Reredos. These avoided the intermittent downpouring of molten wax – which had been a hazard on many previous occasions.

More broadcasts for the Choir were followed by the privilege of singing Evensong in Gloucester Cathedral at the Dean's invitation.

Towards the end of the Summer Term, the Opening of the new Music School took place on 3 July 1971. It was opened by Lord Redcliffe-Maud, a former Government Minister and now Master of University College Oxford. A *Fanfare for Brass Instruments,* composed by Christopher Robinson, signified the official opening. There were numerous public school headmasters present, together with many well-known musicians and friends of the College. This was for many the highlight of the year. The College now had two good teaching rooms, six practice rooms, a storeroom and a fine studio / concert hall. The six practice rooms were shaped as irregular rectangles, presumably for reasons of acoustics. There was an opening concert, together with a special Evensong later in the afternoon, at which Elizabeth Poston's anthem for the Cheltenham Music Festival, *Benediction,* was performed again.

With the tremendous improvement in music-making facilities, music at St Michael's developed rapidly. There were two orchestras meeting every Saturday, a brass consort, a Chamber Music group, a Recorder Consort and the Commoners' choir as well as the College choir. A new innovation was the arranging of three Master Classes for strings, woodwind and brass, giving boys the opportunity to meet experienced professional players and study technique and interpretation to reinforce the teaching by regular staff. An ambitious series of concerts took place throughout the year, ranging from Baroque music to a concert of twentieth century music, and this resulted in attracting people from as far away as Cardiff and Oxford, to visit St Michael's for the first time.

The following year, the College organist, Lucian Nethsingha was appointed as Organist and Choirmaster of Exeter Cathedral, after being at St Michael's for thirteen years. Throughout the College's existence it had always been the policy to choose a young man of the right calibre, who after some years of the unique experience that St Michael's affords, would secure distinguished promotion. Lucian was the latest of a long line of organists who had done just that, starting with the appointment of the College's second organist, John Stainer, to be organist of Magdalen College, Oxford and later, St Paul's Cathedral. His reputation as a solo organist in BBC and other public recitals had brought renown to the

Choir practice with Lucian Nethsingha, 1970

College and the Wednesday broadcast Evensongs from St Michael's had won high praise. Maintaining the high standards of Kenneth Beard cannot have been easy, but from his time at St Michael's, Lucian Nethsingha was able to single out two characteristics which marked out its choir, even with the much higher standard of church music that is heard today. 'Firstly, the high standard of discipline that is maintained at St Michael's and secondly, the sense of worship one gets at the services here is not readily found at choral services at some more well-known institutions elsewhere. This was noted particularly in the letters received after services broadcast from St Michael's.'(16)

Mr Nethsingha's successor was announced as Roger Judd, MA, FRCO, Assistant Organist at Ely Cathedral and Assistant Director of Music at the King's School, Ely, who joined St Michael's in January 1973.

Unusually, the Choir found itself free of extra commitments, and this enabled Mr. Judd to introduce new repertoire such as Howell's *Gloucester Service* and also re-introduce other music that has fallen into disuse. It was also noticeable that some of this new music bore a markedly East Anglian flavour, much of it written by Arthur Wills, Roger Judd's 'mentor' at Ely.

Other musical activities in the school continued to expand with almost 50 boys having individual lessons and almost half learning two instruments, together with the regular series of concerts held in the church and music school. In 1973, these included a performance of Bach's *St John Passion* in the Summer term, with a chamber orchestra and an

236

augmented choir which thrilled a packed church, a concert performance of Purcell's *Dido and Aeneas* and a visit from the percussionist James Blades for a lecture / recital. Later in the year, the choir took on a number of outside engagements, including a recital at Tewkesbury Abbey and services at Great Witley and Hereford Cathedral.

A number of memorable events occurred in September 1973. The Reverend Noel Kemp-Welch, a former Old Boy (1919 – 1924) and Warden (1947 – 1956), preached the sermon at Commemoration and the death was also announced of Mrs. Swann, the second wife of Warden Swann, who had died at the age of 86. She was responsible for the permanent endowment of the Swann Music Prizes. Her will also provided a generous legacy of £5,000 to the College and her ashes were interred in her husband's grave on 4 October. Two week's later, the death of Heathcote Statham took place on 19 October. His distinguished service to church music had been recognised by the award of the CBE in 1967.

There was now some concern about the Father Willis organ in the Church. It was some years since any major work had been done on the organ. A humidifier had been installed, necessary since the improvement in the church heating arrangements some years ago. Harrison and Harrison of Durham spent three weeks doing general cleaning and restoration and fitted wooden covers to enclose the mechanical action.. A second stage during the summer holidays involved one or two tonal changes to give a wider range of sound, eliminating certain duplications which had previously existed. They also fitted a new pedalboard, as the old one is completely worn out and is not of standard size. This had caused some difficulties for visiting recitalists in the past!

Despite the national development of diesel and electric trains, there was a continued interest in steam trains among the boys. The Warden and Mrs Paxman, accompanied by Mr. Judd, took the boys on a number of visits to centres of steam railway activity such as the Severn Valley Railway at Bridgenorth, and a visit to Hereford Station to see the famous Great Western engine, *King George the Fifth.* There was also the time when the same engine, double-headed with *Flying Scotsman,* raced through Leominster, when the boys were otherwise 'employed' at school. However, it should be noted that the College was more than adequately represented by its senior officers!

By 1974, the Warden noted that nationally, there were large question marks, both political and economic, which were over the country and the independent schools, and therefore St Michael's. However, he also noted that morale within the school was high and that numbers were increasing. After the introduction of the 'three-day week' the previous winter, the second stage of work on the organ was delayed and it was hoped to complete it by the summer of 1975.

Announcements concerning Fellows were welcomed at the College, when David Willcocks left King's College, Cambridge to be Director of the Royal College of Music. Christopher Robinson, also a Fellow and former Old Boy, became Organist and Master of the Choristers at St George's Chapel, Windsor.

At Commemoration on 3 October, the new Bishop of Hereford, the Right Reverend John Eastaugh, was present throughout the day, as well as Mr Buckmaster, (Warden 1936–1946). In November 1973, the Choir honoured Benjamin Britten with a concert on his birthday and by performing his one-act opera, *The Golden Vanity.* He was 60 years old on St Cecilia's Day. In December, the traditional end-of-term Carol Service was altered to a more Advent orientated one, and from comments received, the change was appreciated.

The College's adventure organisation, Pioneers continued to go from strength to strength, ably organised by the enthusiasm and effort of John Gray. The Tree House was renovated and repaired, the 'bridge stile' at Cadmore was completely rebuilt using heavy railway sleepers. More entertainingly, the Summer Term and holidays saw the usual programme of weekend camps and rowing on the River Teme. The camping chalet was repainted inside and out and a permanent meal table was built outside. The boys obtained their first two-seater canoe and spent some time repairing and repainting it before testing it in the College Swimming Pool. Summer camps were held at Llangorse in the Brecon Beacons, with many activities taking place on Llangorse Lake.

John Gray's art class, 1972

Taking the plunge

Energetic exercise was too much for one boy

John Gray and his unbeaten rugby team, 1974

There were considerable changes in the 'higher echelons' of the College during the years 1974-75. A number of the Fellows retired, including Dr Herbert Sumsion of Gloucester, owing to ill-health, and the appointment of new ones, including Professor B W Harvey and Roy Massey, who had been appointed Organist of Hereford Cathedral in 1974.

Perhaps the most notable change at St. Michael's at this time was the presence of four girls among the ranks of boys. This was not really a revolutionary development generally as girls' numbers were increasing in many IAPS schools, but for St. Michael's, it was a significant change, although it was clearly stated that there was no intention for the school to have equal numbers of boys and girls and thus become truly co-educational. In order to fulfil its proper and traditional function, St. Michael's needs to be essentially a boys' school. However, this did not preclude the College from admitting a number of girls, and the number of day boys now amounted to a quarter of the total number. They made a very valuable contribution to the life of the school and became fully integrated into every facet of life at St Michael's.

In these days when it is a growing trend to introduce girls' choirs in many cathedrals, it is interesting to note the justification given for the traditional choir of boys' voices as at St Michael's. 'A girl's voice and a boy's voice are two different musical instruments. Most of the repertoire we sing was composed for men and boys' voices. it could not be authentically sung by any other combination of voices.'(17) The school magazine also went on to talk about the role of girls in boys' sports. 'Unlike the boys, the girls will not be *required* to play rugger, though they will not be constrained from doing so if they wish to play. One girl has already astonished her parents by electing to do so, and has astonished them even more by being twice selected to play for the Under 11 XV against other schools.'(18)

The past twelve months were rather unsettling ones for the choir. It had been evident for some time that a large exodus of boys was looming and this has now happened. Roger Judd explained the problem.

> We have said farewell to or lost the services of (through natural causes!) of no less than seven boys. For a choir such as St Michael's, this is quite traumatic, because with so many senior and experienced boys leaving over such a short period, great responsibility falls on boys much younger and less experienced. Having said this, these younger boys have shouldered the burden well and the boys' choir is now well on the road to recovery.'(19)

Despite all these problems, the choir faced a hectic schedule of extra commitments during the year. At Christmas 1974, a carol concert was given in the State Rooms of Hartlebury Castle in front of the Bishop of Worcester and his wife. The paced audience raised a considerable sum for various charitable causes. As well as the usual carols, a number of new carols, more suitable for a secular venue were performed and the centre piece of the concert was a performance of Benjamin Britten's *A Ceremony of Carols.* During the Lent term, the choir made a short but telling contribution to a Radio 4 programme about the College and its music, seen from the boys' point of view. The boys were heard at practice, a voice trial was staged and the full choir was heard singing part of a Byrd motet and a Howells Service, all of this being compressed into twenty minutes. Listeners wrote in and praised the BBC for having captured the spirit and character of St Michael's so well in such a short time. During Holy Week, the gave a performance of Stainer's *Crucifixion.* Perhaps surprisingly, this appears to have been the first performance of the work at St Michael's since the College did not possess any copies. [Despite the closure, this work has been performed at the College in Holy Week during recent years, together with Faure's *Requiem.*] In the Summer term 1975, the choir prepared for various concerts, performing music by Gibbons, Bach, Handel and Britten. A BBC broadcast took place on 25 June when Howells' *Gloucester Service* was performed. it was a very hot day and despite strange things happening to the organ because of the heat, the Service went very well, resulting in many favourable comments.

Despite its age, (built in 1873 – 74), the organ was still going strong (and loud!), being regularly maintained by Harrisons. It was commented that the same firm had previously worked on the organ from 1867 to 1872 for the Founder, but Tom Harrison had failed to do an entirely satisfactory job. However, in present days, the organ is well looked after and will continue to sound to the greater glory of God for many years to come.

One of the St Michael's choristers, James Conybeare-Cross, passed an audition and attended the 1974 IAPS Orchestral Course, held at Brandeston Hall, near Ipswich. 'It was quite different playing in an orchestra of almost 100 players and I was surprised at the sound we produced for our first time together.'(20) The week ended with a full concert performance of works by Elgar, Schubert, Bourgeois, Massenet and Grieg, held at The Maltings at Snape.

In 1976, St Michael's was elected as an Associated School of the Woodard Corporation, which began in 1848, eight years before the Foundation of St Michael's. There were similarity of aims between the two Founders, both of them profoundly influenced by the Oxford Movement, though it is on record that Nathaniel Woodard did not have a high opinion of Ouseley as a church composer. Many St Michael's boys have gone on to one or other of the Woodard Schools, and the familiar and congenial ethos had now been given formal recognition. As an Associated School, St Michael's retained its full independence and full control of its own affairs. There was added security for the small school in those difficult times of the 1970's, knowing that they were part of a larger family. In the Magazine, the Warden pointed out the dangers of being infected with the 'ivory tower mentality.'

> One can come to feel one is serving God and one's generation by a fierce determination to keep everything exactly as it has always been. A degree of conservatism and traditionalism is highly desirable. It saves one from being uncritically carried away by every passing fashion. Equally, one cannot ignore developments that are taking place in the world outside the white gates. (21)

Following this line of argument, one tradition of the College was to disappear after 120 years. This was the daily singing of Matins. Not a decision to be taken lightly, nor fundamentally for reasons that lay within the College. Looking over the white gates and beyond, a steady and continuous rise in musical standards of choirs throughout the country was noted. In cathedral and college choirs, the rise in standards was partly connected with their own reduction in the number of daily services from two to one. The time had come to decide how best to fulfil the Founder's intention to provide a 'model' for the choral services of the church. Would this be better fulfilled in 1976 simply by singing more services than any other choir in the country, or reducing the demands in order to sing as well as we are capable of doing? It was a straight choice between quantity and quality. With the blessing of the Governing Body, quality was the chosen option. St Michael's College can be proud that it was the last choir still to be singing twice a day until this year. As a

School photograph, 1975

consequence of the choir's singing of only one daily service, the boys no longer rehearsed after a strenuous game of rugger or soccer, but in the early morning after breakfast, where the principle hazards were baked beans or fish cakes. The full choir now rehearsed before each service and this change was of enormous benefit. Another innovation was the introduction of the Series III form of the Eucharist, which now replaced Series I and was already familiar with most boys as they used it in their home parishes. The College liked it because it gave greater opportunities for congregational participation, but to date, they had not found a musical setting of the new Service which they liked. They therefore continued to use the Gloria, Sanctus, Benedictus, and Agnus Dei from existing settings in their repertoire, as they were in churches throughout the land.

Some long desired alterations were made to the choir stalls, closing the gaps which had had the effect of dividing each side of the choir into two halves on each side of the chancel. This was now a great improvement and as a result, it was now possible to add a higher music desk to the stalls.

The Commemoration of 1976 was a rainy one, presided over by the Bishop of Hereford. The were some problems in the choir due to the lack of a bass, and later a tenor but this was more than compensated for when Stephen Brown sang his hundredth solo and no one could forget his singing of Allegri's *Miserere* earlier in the term. The choir made a record of secular songs with the recording of these taking place at the end of June at the beginning of a heatwave. Recording had started in the church at 10-30 am, and after breaks for lunch, tea and swimming, it was finished at 7-45 pm after a very hard day's work. the choir also sang Evensong in Worcester Cathedral in June and shortly after the beginning of the Michaelmas term, they were invited to sing Evensong in Coventry Cathedral in 25 September. Other concerts included one by the choir and chamber orchestra of music by J S Bach, singing *Cantata 106* and *Brandenburg Concertos 3 & 4.*

REMINISCENCES

DERRIK JENKYNS (1941 – 44), while at university, acted as Canon Alderson's chauffeur on some of his journeys to Tenbury and Alderson called him his 'charioteer!' He has a journal which Alderson wrote about his visits to Tenbury. The following extract relates a visit to Tenbury from Friday 4 July to Tuesday 8 July 1958.

Friday

When all the preparations had been made, I started from the Close just before 11 am...reached the College soon after 4 and tea, then evensong 6-15.

Saturday

Attended Prayers in Library 7-50. (One of the Masters read the lesson and the Warden said the prayers. Had breakfast in the Warden's quarters 7-55.

In the afternoon, attended a Cricket Match at Moffats, in a house of Childs who still owns it and the estate around. This is near the Wyre Forest and Bewdley. The Warden drove me over via Cleobury Mortimer and after the match and tea, we went back by the Ludlow high road just below the Clee Hills. The boys lost the match. The school had formerly been in Hertfordshire near Hatfield...When I came back I watched the swimming and visited the dormitories, and then had a cup of tea in the drawing room before going upstairs to bed. We arranged together the programme for the services on the morrow.

Sunday

Holy Communion at 8. I vested and read for the Warden (the Celebrant), the Gospel, and there were nearly 20 communicants. I then attended the informal Service at 9-45. The form used was one drawn up by C S Woodward, printed by SPCK, consisting of hymns and responses. The parents sat in the nave pews with their children, and all sang most heartily the hymns, psalms and versicles. – During one of the hymns, 2 youngsters collected and took their bags to the chancel entrance where the Warden received them and proceeded to take them to the altar. I was very much impressed with the reverence and orderliness of the congregation – no staring about or turning round to gaze – showing their interest in the very homely address spoken to them and also singing lustily the music.

This Service was followed at 11 by a Choral Eucharist, which all the school attended and lasted a short hour, (again the Warden celebrated). The music was Charles Macpherson in G...Luncheon followed in Hall at 1 and then I sat in the garden and wandered around. The trees in the front of the spinney have been cut down and the result making the surroundings of the College greatly improved. Also the paths which had been so untidy have been remade and well metalled. Of course, one regrets the loss of the tall chimney stacks which had been a great feature of the building and which the architect Woodyer intended as a glory. I was told they had become dangerous and had for safety's sake to be removed. However I could not help regretting it...Evensong was held at 6-30. We had a setting of the Canticles by ? and an anthem of Ouseley's entitled *O ye that love the Lord*, which I had edited and persuaded Novellos to publish. My sermon was based on St. Matthew's 13th Chapter (the seven parables there contained) and Our Lord's warning to the people and the Disciples in the text 'he that hath ears to hear, let him hear.' My only hope is that it did some good to my audience (boys chiefly and the parishioners). Surely that is what a sermon should attempt to do.

I must say that throughout my visit, I was greatly struck by the friendliness of the staff and the scholars to make me enjoy my visit to the scenes of my youth (1878 – 1882).

Monday

I drove down to Tenbury in my own car to replenish it with petrol, etc. and to make it ready for tomorrow's journey home. I found out that the lack of pulling power which had distressed me when I neared the end of my outward journey was caused by the loosening and slipping of one of the coils which conveyed electricity to one of the four pistons of the engine. In other words, I had been running my car on only three pistons.

I collected the daily papers from the shop. Called at Miles' office in Cross Street. I saw and talked to John Coles who is now working at his office. He has just returned from a week's holiday in Mid-Wales. When Fred (Miles) came in he told me about the satisfactory way the College was working with our new Warden, although of course (he said) it would take some time (with increased expenditure, such as the granting of higher salaries and other everyday expenses), to reach a satisfactory and healthy state. I am so glad he is happy about it all and that he rejoices that the Governing Body did make a wise selection when they appointed Warden Stride and his wife. Then I returned to luncheon. In the afternoon, I watched the games and sport, conducted by the Warden in flannels – tea at 4-30 and then Evensong and Prep. Farrer conducted me over the Scouts' Quarters in the Quarry Spinney, which was most interesting and shows great cleverness on the part of the Scoutmaster (Demaus), and the boys, in planning and executing it. I played on the Library piano to the boys until they were sent to their dormitories, and I took tea with Mrs Stride in the drawing room before going upstairs to bed.

Tuesday

Choral Matins with Wesley in E and his motet *Lead us Lord.* I thanked the Choir as they took off their surplices in the corridor for their good singing and also Mr. Beard for his selection of the music in order to please me during my visit.

I went out of the College to pay some visits in the Parish – Mrs Garman (out shopping in Tenbury. NB. It was Market Day and I ought to have remembered it, but saw and spoke to her housekeeper), Dr Oliver, Mrs Davies and Walls.

After the luncheon, I took final leave of the College boys and Staff and of my good host Warden and Mrs Stride. (How dear it is to me, more and more every visit I take of it, increasingly so!) I drove by Kyrle, Bromyard, Ledbury, Gloucester by-pass, up Birdlip where I foolishly tried to change gear from 4th to 3rd and got stuck at the top of the hill – luckily only momentarily – then drove on to Cirencester where I was greeted by Mrs Swann at her front door and came in to talk and she gave me tea in her garden.

I reached Salisbury at 8, having accomplished the forward and return journeys quite easily of 240 miles with the consumption of about 7 gallons of petrol and a pint of oil. This works out I reckon at nearly 27 miles per gallon. Good old Standard 10!! (22)

REFERENCES

1. College Magazine   July 1957
2. College Magazine   July 1957
3. College Magazine   July 1957
4. College Magazine   July 1960
5. College Magazine   July 1961
6. College Magazine   July 1961
7. College Magazine   July 1961
8. College Magazine   July 1962
9. HCL D863
10. HCL D863
11. College Magazine   October 1965
12. College Magazine   October 1965
13. College Magazine   October 1966
14. College Magazine   December 1969
15. Three Choirs Festival Programme 1970
16. College Magazine   December 1972
17. College Magazine   December 1975
18. College Magazine   December 1975
19. College Magazine   December 1975
20. College Magazine   December 1975
21. College Magazine   December 1976
23. Canon Alderson's Journal

CHAPTER FIFTEEN
THE FINAL YEARS
1977-1985

During the year 1977, 19 pupils left and 15 new pupils arrived. More improvements were undertaken in the College, with the old boot and locker rooms being made into one, creating a games room for the boys and girls. A table-tennis table, some furniture and the television from the College Library were installed and it soon became a popular place to relax. Croquet was also introduced on the Cloister Lawn.

With the support of parents, the playground was surrounded by wire netting to a height of 9 ft and this enabled the area to be used for a variety of sports, including tennis (two courts), hockey, basketball and outdoor badminton.

During the Second World War, pupils from St Michael's had given great help to farmers and other local inhabitants and the school now planned to introduce a Community Services Unit, so that help could now be given around the Parish. The relationship between the College and the parish grew and prefects attended the Village Harvest Supper, where some of the choir, both boys and men, entertained those present after the meal was over.

During this year, Warden Denis Paxman announced his resignation and the Governors met to appoint his successor. They chose Andrew Farrar Walters and for St Michael's, it was an unusual appointment as he was not ordained. Despite the splendid efforts of Warden Paxman, who had improved the College in so many ways, and which had attracted increasing numbers of boys and girls, the Governors were becoming increasingly concerned about finance. They felt that there could be future problems with recruitment as the recession of the late 1970's and early 1980's began to bite and the result of this would affect the efforts of the College, possibly resulting in its eventual closure. Other financial problems resulted from the 'Houghton' Teachers' Pay Award of the early 1970's, which imposed a heavy strain on St Michael's as they tried to give a more realistic salary to their teachers, without ever reaching the levels that Houghton recommended.

With the appointment of Andrew Walters, the Governors had chosen from the widest possible range of both clergy and laymen and it was his brief to increase the recruitment of full fee-paying pupils. He was installed as the ninth Warden of the College at Commemoration on 28

September 1977 and spoke about 'The fine tradition at St Michael's on which we must build. We must be bold in our visions and be firm in maintaining sound standards in all that we set out to do.'(1) This appointment created a further problem, as every previous Warden had been ordained. Indeed, it had been a necessary requirement of the College Statutes and Ouseley's intentions, as the Warden had always been Vicar of the Parish of St Michael's. In order to get round this problem, an amendment of the College Statutes (XIIA) was approved by John Eastaugh, the Bishop of Hereford, in his capacity as the College Visitor. This approved the appointment of a Chaplain if the Warden was not ordained and the Governors appointed the Reverend Graham Atkins as Chaplain to the College and Priest-in-Charge of the Parish.

Watkins Shaw, the Honorary College Librarian, preached at the Installation Service and spoke of younger people looking to the future and older people tending to look back to the past. However, he emphasised that those who are responsible for the College must look forward, never more so than at the Inauguration of a new Warden. Although superficially, Ouseley may seem a Victorian period figure to some, in reality he was a pioneer and his very foundation of the College was an act of commitment to the future.

> On today's birthday, then let us take strength from this pioneer aspect of Sir Frederick Ouseley's work. Is it not therefore right that there should be many things here that he would not recognize – the theatre, our ways of teaching French, the modern classroom block, the music school, the swimming bath, and many other things? So may we always keep abreast (at the very least) of what is best in educational practice – the relations of teacher and taught, the lives and interests of our pupils, their bodily welfare, the subjects and methods of learning. Under new leadership, then, I hope that we shall be inspired, using borrowed words,
>
> To cherish the past,
> Adorn the present,
> Construct for the future. (2)

The choir enjoyed a year of stability and considerable activity, doing rather more outside work than is normally the case. The previous year ended with a concert of seasonal music given for the Redditch Music Society, where the choir sang to a large and appreciative audience. The concert was notable for the fact that it took place on the day Benjamin Britten died, and by a strange coincidence the major work in the concert was his *Ceremony of Carols,* sung by the boys. They gave a moving and fitting tribute to a great musician.

In March 1977, the choir took the road once again to Hereford Cathedral, where they joined with Roy Massey and the Cathedral choir in a recital of music from the major festivals of the Christian year. Mr Massey master-minded the recital, which took the choirs all over the

Cathedral, from the East End down to the bottom of the Nave, under the Tower and in the choir stalls. Roger Judd and Roy Massey shared the direction of what was a thoroughly memorable evening. Plans were made for another recital in 1978.

The Summer term began with a concert for the friends of Great Witley Church, which took place in marvellous weather, enabling everyone to enjoy the grounds of Witley Court. In May, the boys of the College choir gave a recital at which they were joined by Roy Massey playing the organ. They sang works by Purcell, Deering and Byrd, Mendelssohn, Leighton and Britten. Roy Massey played the great B minor Prelude and Fugue by Bach and the Fantasia and Fugue in C major by Parry. Regretfully, the organ decided to misbehave rather dramatically, and the fact that the audience was largely unaware of these difficulties says much for Roy Massey's skill and dexterity. The biggest musical highlight of the Summer term was an invitation to sing for the second time at the Cheltenham International Music Festival – a great honour. The service was Matins and the music honoured Herbert Howells, who was 85 in the October. His *Collegium Regale* setting, one of his finest compositions, was performed. As the anthem *A Sequence for St Michael* was sung, which had been written for St John's College, Cambridge a few years before, a difficult piece which required a great deal of hard work. St Matthew's church was very full and included the Festival's President, Sir Lennox Berkeley.

The life and work of the choir is of course much more than these special events, its main work being the singing of Evensong each day to a very high standard. On Remembrance Sunday, the pattern was changed with the choir singing Faure's *Requiem* in place of Evensong. Special tributes were paid to two members of the choir, George Coles, who had now reached the amazing milestone of 47 years as a bass in the choir, and was now singing under his seventh Warden. Special mention was also made of one of the boys, Stephen Brown, who joined the Choir over four years ago and who, at his voice trial, was described as 'promising', a most happy understatement. He left the school in July after being head chorister for the past year with a music award to Wells Cathedral School and had sang over 200 solos. One remarkable feat was to sing Allegri's *Miserere* four times, including a superb performance at one of the Hereford recitals. Roger Judd spoke of his voice in the following way. 'His was the sort of natural voice that an organist will be lucky to meet more than a few times in his life. St Michael's and I have fortunate that we have had the voice and the service of Stephen Brown for the past four and a half years.'(3)

The school music side continued to develop and the proportion of boys learning an instrument remained remarkably constant, staying at around two thirds of the College. Over the last four years, three boys had won the top music award at Oxford, this being a great reflection on the standard of music teaching at the College.

Hereford Cathedral

A RECITAL

by the Combined Choirs of

HEREFORD CATHEDRAL

and

ST. MICHAEL'S COLLEGE, TENBURY

Organist - ROBERT GREEN

Directed by
ROY MASSEY and ROGER JUDD

Saturday,
May 6th, 1978   7.30 p.m.

During 1978, 15 pupils left and 8 new pupils arrived. No fewer than 34 pupils had left over the previous two years and the College had only managed to recruit 23 new pupils in the same period. In April 1978, the College announced the launching of another major Appeal, with the target of the first phase being £40,000 for a new building. By December 1978, it had raised just over £36,000. The second phase of the Appeal was to provide for further chorister Endowments and a major organ-rebuild, this part of the appeal being mainly directed towards industry and grant-making trusts.

Again, the choir was involved in much outside work, alongside its work in the College. The choir sang right through until Easter and performed some of the wonderful Lent and Holy Week liturgy, the *Tenebrae Responses* by Victoria, motets by Bruckner, Byrd and Morley and a performance of Stainer's *Crucifixion*. This was followed by a visit to Ellesmere College to sing in the splendid Chapel.

The Summer term began with a visit to Southport for the Nine Hundredth Anniversary of the Church of St Cuthbert's, South Meols. A second combined recital at Hereford followed, with both Choirs singing Evensong, accompanied by Roy Massey on the newly-rebuilt Hereford Organ, which performed splendidly in the Finzi anthem, *God is gone up*, Roger Judd directing both choirs. The annual concert at the College took place in early July, followed by visits to recitals in three local churches.

There was a return visit with a coachload of staff and students from Ellesmere College, who descended on the College for Evensong and then entertained the St. Michael's pupils with a widely varied concert, ranging from Barbers' shop singing, to Vivaldi and a Strauss March. Roger Judd gave a last recital on the Schudi / Broadwood harpsichord of 1773, which had been at the College since Ouseley's time and which was shortly afterward sold at auction, achieving a national record sum for an English instrument.

In his Librarian's report of 1977, Watkins Shaw had suggested that the future accessibility and conservation of the Music Library, particularly the manuscripts, had become problematic. In his 1978 Report, he went further and suggested that as his term as Honorary Librarian was coming to an end, the Governing Body should give serious consideration to the matter. After many deliberations, it was decided to ask

---

£20,000 HARPSICHORD

In a sale of musical instruments at Phillips's, a harpsichord made by Shudi and Broadwood in 1773 was sold for £20,000. It was sent for sale by St. Michael's College, Tenbury.

The school was founded in 1856, and the harpsichord was given to it by Messrs Broadwood in that year. It was bought by P. Woolf, a London dealer, acting for an unnamed client, and it is expected that it will stay in Britain. The sale made a total of £86,421 with 4 per cent bought in.

Berrow's Journal of Worcester, 16th March 1978

School music collection makes £120,000

By FRANCES GIBB, Art Sales Correspondent

AN important collection of French classical music, sent for sale by the choral school, St Michael's College, Tenbury Wells, Worcestershire, to meet inflation, was auctioned for £120,000 yesterday.

The price, double that expected, was paid by the Paris dealer, Pierre Beres, who is going to sell some of the items to the Bibliotheque Nationale which already has some 40 volumes from the original collection, and to the Bibliotheque de Versailles, which has some 30.

The collection, known as the Toulouse - Philidor collection, comprised some 96 lots of both printed and manuscript music, mainly of operas and ballets. It was acquired over 100 years ago by the Rev. Sir Frederick Ouseley, a collector of early music and founder of the school.

His music library formed part of the assets of a trust to provide scholarships at the college. Over the years, inflation has eroded the value of the scholarships however and prompted the sale of the collection to lessen the gap between what parents and what the school provide towards fees.

The collection was formed by Louis-Alexandre, Comte de Toulouse, the son of Louis XIV and later owned by King Philippe of France.

*Daily Telegraph
27th June 1978*

the Bodleian Library whether they would accept charge of them on an indefinite deposit.

Accordingly, all but a very few of our manuscripts were transferred to the Keeper of Western Manuscripts in the Bodleian Library early this month (September 1978), the few exceptions being Handel's *Messiah,* the Batten *Organ Book* and Britten's *String Quartet No. 2.* The College retains absolute ownership of all the manuscripts transferred to the Bodleian. They are being kept together, separate from the Bodleian holdings and will be referred to by their internationally known Tenbury MSS numbers. (4)

The Governing Body approved this arrangement and agreed that it would serve four purposes.

1. St Michael's College can fulfil more easily their responsibilities to make the material available for study.
2. It relieves the College of all trouble and administration connected with it.
3. It ensures that it remains properly cared for.
4. It is in the hands of Librarian / Scholars who are equipped to understand it.

As things had developed over the previous twenty-five years, the Music Library could have been a serious distraction to the work of the College and over his thirty year tenure as Honorary Music Librarian, Watkins Shaw had seen his task as to deal with this distraction so that, as far as possible, the College has been unaware of it. Also, his work had been a voluntary service to the general world of musical scholarship rather than to the College itself. There were some voices raised in protest at the removal of most of the manuscripts from the College, but in the eyes of the Governing Body and the Honorary Librarian, they felt that their decision in doing this was the right one for the College at that time in its history.

Michaelmas 1978 was the Sixtieth Anniversary of Fellowes' acceptance of the post of Honorary Music Librarian at the College. At a meeting earlier in the year, the Governing Body had faced another contentious issue in deciding to sell the Toulouse-Philidor Music Collection. These manuscripts and books had been purchased by the College in 1935, for the sum of £ 550 (see details in Chapter 12), in order to add to and complete the related manuscripts and printed books which the College already possessed. As a result, the most publicised event of the year at the College was the auction by Sothebys of a quantity of non-musical books, together with the manuscripts and printed books of the Toulouse-Philidor Collection. Despite previous sales of non-musical books, this was the only occasion on which the integrity of the Music Library had been breached. In his Librarians's report for Michaelmas 1978, Watkins Shaw gave his reasons to justify the sale and the results.

1. The Collection was sufficiently spectacular to raise a considerable sum.
2. It was not related to the majority of holdings and its sale would not impair the remainder as a collection.
3. It was of non-English provenance, its musical contents were not part of the English artistic heritage, like works by Tallis, Purcell, Handel, etc.
4. As acquired by the Founder, the collection was incomplete and hardly understood. A small but very important balance was purchased in 1935 by the College itself out of its own resources.

The results of the sale were as follows.

Non-musical books	£ 19,000
Toulouse-Philidor Collection	£ 120,000
Total	£ 139,000
less commission	£ 16,000
Amount received by the College	£ 123,000

The Collection was sold as a single lot to a Parisian dealer, M. Pierre Beres and as the manuscript portion of the Collection was over 100 years old, an export licence was required and granted.

St. Michael's choir, 1970's

Deep though his devotion to our Library was, I am certain that in the last analysis, the Founder would have placed first the needs of our Choral Foundation. (5)

The 1978 IAPS Orchestral Course again took place at Brandeston Hall in Suffolk, the home of Framlingham College Junior School, with the final concert being held at The Maltings Concert Hall at Snape, near Aldeburgh. The director was John Lubbock, conductor of the orchestra of St John's, Smith Square. Over the course, there were six hours of rehearsals each day, and with an ambitious programme, they were needed, although everyone still found time to enjoy the prep school sports facilities, including mini-golf, swimming pool and tennis courts. The *Daily Telegraph* gave a good review of the final concert. 'The Maltings reverberated with superbly performed modern pieces, Prokofiev's *Romeo and Juliet* ballet suite, Walter Leigh's *Concertino for Piano and String Orchestra,* Berio's *Variations on a Theme by Boccherini,* and finally, Holst's *Mars* and *Jupiter* from *The Planets.'*(6) Kevin Jacot enjoyed the week very much and summed up his experiences.

Performing on the vast stage of The Maltings at Snape was a thrilling experience, and I am sure that many professional musicians would be jealous of us. the atmosphere was tremendous 'on the day' as we played to a capacity audience of eager parents and friends, including Sir Peter Pears and Imogen Holst. What better way to end an orchestral course? Don't miss the chance if you get it! (7)

In December 1978, the College put on an ambitious production of the farce, *The Happiest Days of your Life* and both boys and girls put on a splendid performance of this popular play.

The year 1979 was a very busy year in the life of the College and its reputation continued to be known over an wide area. The on-going Development Appeal was still increasing, though somewhat slowly. The Vicarage, first lived in by John Hampton when he became Warden, was re-purchased by the College and accommodation was provided on the ground floor for three single staff. New junior dormitories and the re-fitting of the chapel dormitory for girls was completed. Later in the year, the second phase of the Appeal was launched, to fund Choral Scholarships and a necessary organ re-build. The College was fortunate to be receiving many donations of equipment, including library books, a television set, cricket stumps, a stop watch, a cheque for games room equipment, a cheque for a music prize (The Holt prize), and strawberries for the whole school!

The deaths of two Fellows were announced during the year, Dr Ernest Bullock, a former organist of the College, Exeter Cathedral and Westminster Abbey, and Gerald Knight, organist of Canterbury Cathedral and later Director of the Royal School of Church Music. At

Commemoration in September 1979, Gerald Knight's ashes were interred outside the Church, near to the north wall of the Chancel in accordance with his wishes. He had no personal roots at St Michael's, though he had been introduced to St Michael's in boyhood by Canon E C Corfe of Truro Cathedral, (one of Ouseley's first Old Boys.)

The choir had a very busy year with a number of outside engagements, including in the Michaelmas Term, a recital at Ludlow parish church (boys) and a full choir concert in Pershore Abbey. Christopher Keyte and Christopher Irby gave a recital in the Music School at Commemoration. The choir recorded a programme of Christmas music for BBC Midlands TV at Great Witley church, and a further concert in Hartlebury Castle. In the Lent Term, there two joint recitals given with the Hereford Cathedral choir in Hereford Cathedral, followed by the turn of the College to welcome Roy Massey and the Cathedral choir to St Michael's. A recital at Belbroughton, a village near Kidderminster, proved to be a very unpleasant journey, due to high winds and drifting snow, but after a very good recital, followed by a party at the Vicarage, the Choir managed to return home safely.

One death which was deeply felt by many St Michael's Old Boys was that of Kate Ashley, who had served the College from 1923 to 1957 without a break. She had been a dedicated French teacher and Cub Mistress to many generations of boys. A lady of deep personal Catholic Faith as received by the best traditions of the Church of England, followed through her worship in St Michael's church. She kept up a busy correspondence with many Old Boys during her long retirement in Malvern and was an inspiration to all who met her.

The Summer term was highlighted by an appearance of the choir at the Malvern Festival, giving one of the major sell-out concerts in the Priory, together with the Cotswold Brass Ensemble and Roy Massey on the organ. Later in the term, the choir spent much time working on a new recording for the Abbey record label, who specialise in recordings of choral music. This was released in November 1979 and offered a selection of music chosen because of its connections with St Michael's. Following a Parochial Church Council decision to allow the use of Latin in the services, the choir was able to add Masses by Byrd (four voices), Palestrina (*Missa Brevis)*, and Schubert (*Mass in G*) to the repertoire.

The Warden, Andrew Walters, was in hospital during the Michaelmas Term 1979 and the Lent Term 1980. Great support was showed to his wife and himself by Fellows, Old Boys, former and present parents and present pupils, staff and friends of the College. St Michael's was a closely knit family in which all were able to share and support each other. During this illness, Mr D M Annett, a former Headmaster of the King's School, Worcester, was appointed as Acting Warden, with the Warden resuming his duties at the start of the Summer Term.

The Tenbury Festival ran throughout the month of May, with an opening service, a Festival Evensong being held at St Michael's on 4 May. The College theatre was used for a drama production by the Tenbury Players, and there was a recital by the Tallismen (!) in the Music School. In June 1980, the Pasadena Boys' Choir from California visited the College for a week. This was a great success and resulted in many new friendships with St Michael's boys and girls.

The year was a problematic one for the choir as it was without a regular tenor voice, with much of the music being re-scored among the available voices. Music performed during the year included Schubert's *Mass in G,* Faure's *Requiem,* and two carol services, given to a full church. The Lent term had no outside engagements, so the opportunity was taken to enlarge the repertoire. In the Summer term, the choir once again joined with the Hereford Cathedral choir, followed by a recital in the cathedral. Further visits to Kidderminster and Great Witley took place and the boys' choir also visited Dudley. The top twelve boys in the choir went to Gloucester during the last week of term, to join with the Cathedral choir at Evensong and to play them at cricket. (SMC lost by 10 runs.) After a concert given by the Galliard Brass Ensemble, the Summer Term ended with a musical feast, Christopher Robinson persuading the great English soprano, Elizabeth Harwood to give a most wonderful recital. 'The audience were spellbound by this international artist, being brilliantly accompanied by Christopher Robinson, who matched her virtuousity at every turn.'(8)

Over the summer holidays, another boy from St Michael's, Francis Acton, attended the Orchestral Course at Brandeston Hall, and the week of rehearsals ended with a fine concert, again in The Maltings at Snape, with works by Rachmaninov, Berlioz, Moussorgsky and Elgar.

At Michaelmas 1980, the College choir travelled to Hereford to join the Cathedral choir for Evensong and for a recital of music by S S Wesley,

St Michael's College, Tenbury

A SONG RECITAL

by

ELIZABETH HARWOOD

with

CHRISTOPHER ROBINSON

1 Bist du bei mir   J.S. Bach

2 Aria : "On Mighty Pens"   Haydn
   (from Creation.)

3 Die Forelle
   Nacht und Träume
   Romanze from Rosamunde   Schubert
   Du bist die Ruh
   Rastlose Liebe

   Alleluja   Mozart

                INTERVAL

4 Blauer Sommer
   Meinen Kinde
   Ich wollt ein Strausslein   R. Strauss
          binden
   Wiegenlied

5 Fish in the unruffled lakes   Britten
   Wagtail and Baby

   Orpheus with his lute   Vaughan Williams

   To Daffodils
   In the garden of the Seraglio   Delius
   The Bird's Story

The College is extremely grateful to these two artists who have given their services for the Re-endowment Appeal.

Rugby team, 1980

part of the celebrations for the opening of the Treasury in the Cathedral. Wesley's anthem, *The Wilderness*, was written at Hereford.   On 18 October 1980, the choir celebrated with a buffet supper for George Coles, who had served as a bass in the College choir for fifty years,- an amazing achievement which was honoured by many of his friends and Old Boys. A new innovation for the choir was the appointment of a Choral Scholar, Martin Turnbull, from Birmingham University, who was able to attend services most weekends and sing as a bass.   In November 1980, the school orchestra and the newly re-formed Commoners' choir, gave a very successful concert, conducted by Stephen Gowland.   Later in the year, Stephen was to leave the College for a teaching post at Hereford Cathedral School and a lay clerkship at the Cathedral.

The choir visited Shrewsbury Abbey church to give a recital and in March 1981, welcomed Roy Massey and the Hereford Cathedral choir to sing a joint Evensong at the College.   The theme was 'Music for Great Occasions' and included Handel's *Zadok the Priest* and Parry's *I was Glad.* The boys' choir gave recitals at Inkberrow near Worcester, Malvern Link, Kidderminster Parish church, St George's Worcester and a concert at the Norman church at Rock.

Some of the boys took part in the Choir Schools 7-a-side rugger tournament at Bristol Cathedral School.   After tea, the boys were transformed in cassock and surplice as they rehearsed and sang Evensong together – 85 choristers – a glorious sound!

During this year, the numbers had increased, with 81 boys and girls attending St Michael's. This was partly due to the introduction of a pre-prep department, which had started the previous September.   The College had been able to gain some very welcome national publicity with six-page article and photographs in *The Countryman* magazine, which was published during the previous year. This long established magazine about country life and work painted an idyllic picture of school life at St Michael's, with the Warden, Andrew Walters, speaking of St Michael's in an interview.

It's a homely size.   There are only 61 pupils.   I think that this is perhaps the greatest virtue of St Michael's, but there is also a certain magic and atmosphere about the place – I certainly felt it the very first time I came here.   As you turn at the gate, you feel you are in a marvellous oasis of peace and quiet, where you can get on with things, without the hurly-burly of town traffic and distractions.   I never have to sell the school to parents – it sells itself.   Parents are profoundly traditional.   – they want their children to have traditional values, so I stick fervently to things like school uniforms and the basic disciplines of life.   you respect those older than yourself and those in need – a caring spirit – I put good manners high upon the list.   One of the great joys of a boarding school is that you have the children for twelve weeks at a time, twenty-four hours a day, and the whole thing can be steadied down. There are no double values – they are not allowed to sit up and watch telly every night – there are strict bedtimes for each age group.

For the non-singing pupils, the school's music often catches them unawares. A lot of children arrive here with supposedly no music in them, but when they find children of their own age singing or playing an instrument, they think it would be nice to try it themselves. 'If he can do it as well as that, I can do better.' – it spirals that way rather than through direction by the staff. (9)

The numbers continued to grow the following year, with 20 pupils leaving during the year and 36 joining the school, making the total of 97 pupils the highest it had ever been. The Lent Term of 1981 was notable for the privilege of being able to welcome Sir John Betjeman to the College once more, accompanied by Mr Jonathan Stedall. Sir John recalled his first visit to the College, when he listened to Christopher Hassall reading his splendid *Poem for Christmas Day* to the boys in bed in the Big Dormitory.

On arrival, it was his first wish to revisit the Big Dormitory, which brought back so many happy memories. Whilst no longer a fit man, Sir John was determined to see as much as possible of the school again. He wrote glowingly of his visit. 'You have humanised Anglican church music for me. Henry Woodyer is very pleased up in heaven and soars with the arches and calls for more spikes against the sky as some of them have fallen off. There is a magic about St Michael's which has not dimmed in any way since its foundation.'(10) Writing to the Warden after his visit, he enclosed a generous cheque to go towards the fabric of the building.

Undoubtedly, the school, as a preparatory school had moved forward and was preparing boys and girls for the present and the future, not the past, an important point made by Watkins Shaw, in his Sermon at the Wardens's Installation, some four years previously.

As in the previous year, two of the 1981 Tenbury Festival events were held at the College – the gap, physically created by the Common, was narrowing! Also, throughout this year, the College received an amazing number of visitors, including St Edward's School Orchestra, two Organists' Associations, Brecon Cathedral choristers, Gloucester Cathedral choristers, the West Midlands branch of the Elgar Society, the Worcester Wind Soloists, Music Master of both Preparatory and Public schools, a group from Bloxham School on a Geography Course, and a group of boys from five preparatory schools in Surrey, Berkshire and Hampshire.

Roger Judd took over the Commoners' choir and as part of the 1981 Summer Concert, they sang excerpts from *Captain Noah and his Floating*

CHELTENHAM INTERNATIONAL FESTIVAL OF MUSIC

FESTIVAL SERVICE
SUNDAY, 5th JULY, 1981 at 11 a.m.

The Festival Service is conducted by
THE REVEREND DAVID C. NYE
VICAR OF THE CHURCH OF ST. PHILIP AND ST. JAMES, CHELTENHAM

Preacher:
THE VENERABLE ERIC EVANS, ARCHDEACON OF CHELTENHAM

THE CHOIR OF ST. MICHAEL'S COLLEGE, TENBURY
under the direction of ROGER L. JUDD, MASTER OF THE MUSIC

Organist: MARTIN STOKES, (Organ Scholar, St. Michael's College)

Organ music before the Service

FANTASIA OF FOUR PARTS	*Orlando Gibbons (1583-1625)*
VOLUNTARY FOR DOUBLE ORGAN	*Henry Purcell (1658-1695)*
PRELUDE AND FUGUE ON A THEME OF VITTORIA	*Benjamin Britten (1913-1976)*

The Offertory will be taken during the singing of the last Hymn
and will be in aid of The Parish Centre (formerly St. James' Church)

Zoo. 5 July saw the Choir again performing at the Festival Service for the 1981 Cheltenham International Festival of Music, the choir's third visit and the second in four years.

There were three evening recording sessions at St Michael's (7 –10 pm), which resulted in the release of a new record, *The Seasons at St. Michael's*, again recorded on the Abbey label. It was the first Abbey record to be nominated as 'Critics Choice.'

On 17 October 1981, there was an inaugural service of the Friends of St Michael's. Sir David Willcocks agreed to act as Patron, and Sir John Betjeman sent a contribution to the brochure.

A number of changes took place in the College buildings during the year. The centre of the big dormitory was carpeted, making it much warmer and more comfortable. New showers and washbasins were fitted in the girls' dormitory and in the boys' bathrooms, the old iron baths were taken out and replaced by showers, and the old washbasins (installed in 1915), replaced by new ones.

The winter of 1981 – 82 was largely indescribable, the whole area being clothed with large quantities of snow at the end of the Michaelmas term. After an early thaw, the Raddle Bank Reservoir pipes, leading from there to the College, were badly damaged by land movement. If the term had started on time, there would have been little heating, no water, no sanitary arrangements and no food deliveries possible.

The second carol service had to be abandoned for the first time in the College's history and there were extreme problems for the College staff in trying to put things right. On Oldwood Common, there was a

Roger Judd explains the making of a recording, c. 1982

A quick game of Swingball

temperature reading of – 30 degress Fahrenheit and the start of the Lent Term was delayed by ten days.

After the 'tenor' problems of the past year, the choir now has some new faces. For much of the Lent Term, most of the services took place in the warmth of the music room, as the church flooded and froze alternately. The choir sang at Belbroughton, Redditch and Broadheath, and broadcast Choral Evensong for the BBC, which was later released on an LP record.

In the Summer Term, the choir joined forces with Hereford Cathedral choir, firstly for an RSCM Service conducted by Lionel Dakers and later, at the Ordination of the College Warden, Andrew Walters. Visits to other cathedrals included Wells (for rugger 'sevens'), Gloucester (for Evensong and cricket), and Bristol, as part of the World Congress of Music Educationalists. Christopher Robinson was elected President of the Royal College of Organists, following in the footsteps of Ouseley himself (their first President), Stainer, Bullock as well as several other of the College Fellows.

The St Michael's Father Willis organ could now be heard on an Abbey record, recorded by Roger Judd and released in the summer of 1982. Entitled *English Organ Music from Tenbury*, it was very well reviewed.

Roy Massey included St Michael's in one of the 'fringe' events of the 1982 Three Choirs Festival, held at Hereford. On 28 and 29 August, there was an Exhibition of Manuscripts and other items in the College Library, arranged by Watkins Shaw, and two Organ Recitals, given on the first day by Andrew Millington, then Assistant Organist at Gloucester. [After some years at Guildford, Andrew has been appointed Organist of Exeter Cathedral, after the retirement of Lucian Nethsingha.] Roger Judd gave two Recitals on the second day. Some 250 visitors attended and were entertained to a buffet lunch on each of the two days.

At the start of the school year 1982–83, the numbers dropped slightly with the number of pre-prep pupils falling from 26 to 15 and the boys and girls in the main school remaining stable at 64, making a total for the whole school of 81.

The Governors announced the appointment Mr C G Syers-Gibson as assistant Headmaster and it was hoped that the warden would now be able to promote the College more widely in the additional time available.

The Friends of St Michael's held their first meeting during the Michaelmas term 1982. After an organ / lecture recital by Roger Judd, members were entertained by the Choristers, with a variety of songs and readings base don the animal kingdom. Since their formation, the Friends have given the College a video recorder, a photocopier, the game of short tennis, and all senior pupils enjoyed an outing to the Wild Fowl Trust at Slimbridge. In February 1983, the choir the College sang Choral Evensong on Radio Three, but the previous day, only seven boys were on their feet and able to sing. Roy Massey not only played the organ for this

Thursday Morning 26th August
at St. Michael's College, Tenbury
10.30 - 13.00
EXHIBITON OF TREASURES
FROM THE MUSIC LIBRARY OF
ST. MICHAEL'S COLLEGE, TENBURY

St.Michael's College lies on the right hand side of B4553 about 5½ miles from its junction with A49 at Stockton Cross, slightly north of Leominster.

The exhibition will display a selection of historic items, many of great rarity and some of them unique, from the remarkable musical library assembled by the founder of St.Michael's College, Sir Frederick Ouseley.

A complete annotated catalogue of the items on show will be available in the library. Among others they will include Handel's own conducting score in manuscript of his great oratorio *Messiah*, an autograph composition of Benjamin Britten, and a famous album of manuscript English cathedral music dating from before the Civil War. There will also be rare early (in some cases, first) printed editions of works by Byrd, Morley, Dowland, Purcell, Handel, Haydn, Mozart, etc., including the important unique form of Thomas Tomkins' *Musica Deo Sacra*. Many examples will be displayed of valuable early books of musical instruction from which knowledge of early musical theory, practice, and instruments are derived, including Morley's *Plaine and Easie Introduction to Practicall Musicke,*

some incunabula, the foundational work on organ-building by Dom Bédos, a copy of Praetorius's notable *Syntagma* which belonged to the composer Telemann, and others.

Though not intended to show the history of music printing, many of the exhibits happen to illustrate various developments over more than 250 years.

Visitors to the exhibition will also have an opportunity at 10.30 a.m. and 11.30 a.m. to hear the organ at St. Michael's, one of 'Father' Willis's notable 4-manual instruments, played by Roger Judd, Master of Music of the College. It is hoped that these alternative programmes will enable everyone to see the exhibition and hear the organ without too much congestion in the limited space of the Library.

10.30 a.m. First Programme: French Music

Variations de Concert	*Joseph Bonnet (1884-1944)*
Fantasie in E flat	*Camille Saint-Saens (1835-1921)*
Pastorale ⎫ 24 pieces	
Berceuse ⎬ in a free	*Louis Vierne (1870-1937)*
Divertissement ⎭ style	
Sonata No. 1 in D minor (3rd movement)	*Alexandre Guilmant (1837-1911)*

11.30 a.m. Second Programme: English Music

Carillon	*Herbert Murrill (1909-52)*
Rhapsody on a ground	*Heathcote Statham (1889-1973)*
Largo, Allegro, Aria and 2 Variations	*Michael Festing (c.1680-1752)*
	arr. George Thalben-Ball (b. 1896)
Fantasia and Fugue in G	*Hubert Parry (1848-1918)*

A buffet lunch will be available in the College Hall from 12.00 to 1.15 p.m. to those holding tickets.

97

Three Choirs Festival, Hereford, 1982 (Fringe event)

broadcast, but brought four of his senior boys from Hereford to help out! They also recorded a Choral Evensong in May, to be broadcast on the Feast of St Michael and all Angels, 29 September. On 16 March, the Choirboys travelled very far afield, to give a recital in Liskeard parish church in Cornwall. The recital was very successful and delicious refreshments were served afterwards. All the boys slept in sleeping bags in Dr Patton's house. The next day, the boys travelled to Dartington Hall, where they gave a lunchtime recital in the Great Hall, and enjoyed the beautiful grounds.

Shortly after the end of term, St Michael's was host to nine other Choir Schools for the Annual Rugby Sevens. Choirs from Grimsby, Hereford, Worcester, Oxford, Bristol, Tewkesbury, Wells, Llandaff and Exeter attended and despite a day of icy drizzle, everything went ahead as planned, with Exeter being the eventual winners. After the presentations, some 110 choristers robed and sang Choral Evensong in the church, such a large choir never having sung in the church before.

During the Summer Term, the choir had several more outside engagements, with recitals at Church Stretton, Fladbury, Great Whitley, and three weddings.

In October 1983, the choir again visited Hereford Cathedral to join the Cathedral choir for Evensong and to give a joint recital afterwards. Also in October, a representative body of choristers and Commoners took part in the Woodard Festival Eucharist held in Westminster Abbey. Schools in all Divisions of the Woodard Corporation were represented, including St Michael's, as an Associated School.

The Christmas carol services were performed as usual, this time with no weather problems!

School improvements included the introduction of the tiny Sinclair ZX 81 computer, which made a triumphal entry into the classroom and became heavily booked. Later in the year, the boys brought their own computers to school and as a result, the school appealed for any black and white televisions to use as monitors.

At the Commemoration Service in September 1983, the Bishop of Wakefield was present as President of the Woodard Corporation, and two days later, the Music Directors of the Woodard Schools (Midland Division), held their Annual Meeting at the College. Three days later, the College welcomed the Friends of Cathedral Music, with around 150 members coming from all over the country, including Christopher Dearnley as their Chairman and Christopher Robinson.

In March, the College choir was busy rehearsing for an EMI recording of a Christmas Carol record, together with the BBC making a film of EMI making a record! This enabled the College to make an appearance on BBC Breakfast Television.

Due to the vaguaries of the Calendar, the College returned for the Summer Term before Easter and this enabled the choir to sing the Holy Week and Easter Services, something which had only occurred at very rare intervals in the recent history of the College.

A Medieval Banquet was held in the Dining Hall on 5 May, and was greatly enjoyed by those who attended, although numbers were somewhat disappointing. Staff and senior boys provided Medieval choral and instrumental music. In many people's eyes, being better than outside music brought in on previous occasions.

Roger Judd conducting the choir, 1980's

Another view of the choir, 1980's

Pupils and staff, 1984

The choir had remained fairly stable throughout the year and good news came when it was announced that Air Canada were to sponsor a record by the College choir. The finished record was broadcast by the choir during Commemoration 1984, having been recorded the previous May. Visits by the choir included, Inkberrow, Monmouth, Belbroughton, Ribbesford near Bewdley, Lugwardine and St Michael's once again hosted a joint Evensong and recital with the Hereford Cathedral choir.

In May, a Promotions Evening, was held at the College, arranged by the Daimler Car Company, with a formal dinner in the Dining Hall and classical music, the choir performing a short recital in the Church.

During the Summer Term of 1984, the school undertook an extensive advertising campaign in an attempt to recruit more boys, with a special effort at the EXPO 1984 Exhibition supported by friends, parents, pupils and staff. there were also a number of Open days at the College, but despite many visitors, there was little effect on future numbers. At the end of the Summer term 1984, three long-serving members of staff left the College. They were Brian Demaus, after a long association with the school as boy, teacher and later as Senior Master; John Gray, after twenty-eight years of total involvement in the life of the school and choir; and Graham Atkins, who as Chaplain, had developed an important pastoral role within the school, and this had endeared him to those in need of help in this way.

What was to become the College's final year of existence developed into an extraordinary year for the choir. Their carol record, entitled *Torches*, which had been released in March 1984 sold over 17,000 copies in the six weeks before Christmas 1984 on the Classics for Pleasure Label. During the year, there were changes (and welcome additions) to the men's voices, with friends such as Neil Page, Michael Gillians, Julian Todd and Michael Antcliff helping to 'cover' the tenor line for recitals, BBC recordings and the like.

At the beginning of the Michaelmas Term, the choir were asked to record an Evensong for BBC Radio 3 (recorded on 10 October and broadcast on the 12th), followed by a recital to a full church in Bromsgrove. A concert in Leominster Priory was not a very satisfactory one as the church had failed to generate any publicity. There was a PCC Meeting going on in the Vestry at the same time and the bells were ringing throughout the concert. There would have been no audience if it had not been for parents and staff, although the boys gave a very professional performance.

On Remembrance Sunday, there was the usual performance of Faure's *Requiem* and at the end of November, the Boys' Choir went up to Liverpool to sing Evensong at the Anglican Cathedral. This was a wonderful experience for the boys and they were entertained lavishly by their hosts. On their return, the boys boarded a coach early the next morning to take the choir on their one and only trip abroad.

269

Early in October 1984 Roger Judd received a telephone call from a Utrecht-based agency, offering the choir a four day, four concert, all expenses paid tour in Holland, to take place a few days before Christmas. Roger had only a day to accept or reject the offer and it was decided to go ahead with the tour. The Monday following the Carol Service, the choir were woken at 4 am, and after a rushed breakfast, both boys and accompanying adults boarded a coach heading for Birmingham International Airport. Apart from the choir and extra adult singers, the party included included Simon Holt as organist, who was an Old Boy of the College, Anne Clegg, the Matron and also the Warden. On arriving at Schipol Airport in Amsterdam, the party were provided with a coach and driver, and courier for the five days of the tour. The first concert was in Aardenburg in Southern Holland, involving a journey of two and a half hours. Rehearsals in the church took some time, a difficult problem being the organ at the other end of the church to the choir, but these were soon overcome and after a rest and a meal the choir returned to the church for the concert, and found an audience of around 400 people present. After a very successful concert with a standing ovation and presentations of tulips, the choir had an early start before travelling to Utrecht. the usual concert preparations followed, but on returning to the church for the concert, the choir were amazed to find a long queue of people outside the church. The concert was given to a full audience of around 850 people. the programme was of Christmas music and included carols, anthems, motets and four organ pieces, and afterwards, the coach took the choir back to Amsterdam, where they were going to spend the next three nights. The third concert took place in the Nieuwe Kerk (New Church) in Dam Square, which dated from 1578 and the concert was given in a 'magical' atmosphere, with lighted brass candelabra and an audience of over 1100 people. After a morning of sightseeing and shopping, the choir were driven to S'Hertogenbosh, where the final concert took place in a fine Dutch Reformed Church, with an early nineteenth century organ. although to a much smaller but very appreciative audience. After a few hours of sleep, the choir departed to Schipol Airport in the early morning. During the flight, the boys visited the cockpit and entertained other passengers by singing carols at 16,000 ft over the North Sea! The plane landed at Birmingham at 8-15 am and a very tired party of boys and adults embarked on the final leg of the return journey to Tenbury. It was a wonderful experience for everyone with the choir achieving great success musically and being received with a great enthusiasm not usually found in England.

During the Lent Term of 1985, there was only one outside engagement, a visit to Pevensey in East Sussex, where Raymond Pugh, the father of one of the boys, was Vicar. The Summer Term proved rather busier, the boys giving a recital for the Friends of St Michael's, another one being given at Ellesmere College, and the full choir travelled to Hereford to sing Matins during the summer meeting of the Cathedral Organists' Association. All the organists present found it a 'most moving and poignant service.' Two further evensongs were recorded for the BBC, one to be broadcast in Michaelmas 1985 and one to be broadcast in January 1986.   Further recitals included one at the College for another Daimler/Jaguar Car Company promotional evening, and a recital at Harborne Parish Church for the father of another chorister who was Vicar there. As the life of the College in its final term drew to a close, Roger Judd summed up the feelings of all who sang at the final Service.

> And then the end of term and our Thanskgiving Service for all that had been done at St Michael's over 129 years. Augmented by many who had either been Choristers or Lay-Clerks, or friends who had sung with us regularly, we gave of our best. No words can describe the feelings of the singers at that service, let alone the feelings of that great congregation. I will simply close this final report on the work and witness of the Choir of St Michael's College by saying two things. Ouseley's vision has been more fully realised than he can ever have hoped for in the general state of church and especially cathedral music. The realisation of that vision will live on far into the future and for that we should all say 'Deo Gracias.' (11)

Before the Closing Service of Thanksgiving, a message was read out from the Archbishop of Canterbury.

> My thoughts are with you as you prepare to hold your Service of Thanksgiving for the work and witness of St Michael's College over more than a century and a quarter.
>
> With its magnificent library, the catalogue of distinguished musicians who have been members of its staff, and its illustrious list of Old Boys, St Michael's needs no help from me to secure its reputation. Thanks to the College, the standard of cathedral music is higher today than it has ever been.
>
> Though I shall be sharing your sadness that this happy and triumphant chapter in the history of the English Church and its music is drawing to a close, I shall also be thanking God for all that has been achieved since St Michael's was founded.
>
> The College has completed its task. But the spirit of Tenbury will live on through all those who learned to love their Church and its music at St Michael's.
>
> + Robert Cantuar (12)

The College closed on Sunday 14 July 1985, when a final Thanksgiving Eucharist was held in the Church, attended by a huge congregation. Both Christopher Robinson and Roy Massey played the organ before the service began. The Warden celebrated, the Bishop of Hereford preached and the Choir were joined by many ex-choristers. The service included

S. MICHAEL'S COLLEGE
Tenbury Wells

1856 — 1985

SERVICE OF THANKSGIVING

Sunday, 14th July, 1985

10.30 a.m.

some of Ouseley's music; *Jerusalem on High* from his oratorio *Hagar* was sung as an introit and his tune *Contemplation* for the hymn *When all Thy mercies.* Communion motets included *Ave Verum Corpus* by Byrd, *Christus Factus Est* by Bruckner and *Bring us O Lord* by Sir William Harris. The Communion setting was the *Missa Sancti Nicolai* by Haydn and very appropriately, the final hymn was that glorious hymn of praise at the end of Stainer's *Crucifixion.*

All for Jesus – all for Jesus
This our song shall ever be;
For we have no hope, nor Saviour
If we have not hope in Thee.

All for Jesus – Thou will give us
Strength to serve Thee, hour by hour;
None can move us from Thy presence,
While we trust Thy love and power.

All for Jesus – at Thine altar
Thou wilt give us sweet content;
There dear lord, we shall receive Thee
In the solemn Sacrament.

All for Jesus – Thou hast loved us;
All for Jesus – Thou hast died;
All for Jesus – Thou art with us;
All for Jesus crucified.

All for Jesus – all for Jesus –
Thus the Church's song must be;
Till, at last, her sons are gathered
One in love and one in Thee. (13)

[Words by J. Sparrow Simpson reproduced by permission of Novello & Co. Ltd.]

All possible assistance was given in finding places at other schools, and nearly every boy holding a choral scholarship was able to obtain a similar or better one elsewhere.

The Head Chorister, Tobias Edwards, became Head Chorister at Worcester Cathedral. Jonathan Snellin also went to Worcester Cathedral, Alistair Todd to Peterborough, Anthony Todd to King's College, Cambridge, Peter Hall to Salisbury, Adam Aiken to Westminster Abbey, Jonathan Wheeler to the Southern Cathedral Singers, while of the adults, Simon Kiln went to Clare College Cambridge and Christopher Chivers to Magdalen College, Oxford, both as Organ Scholars. David Truslove went to sing at Rochester, while Roger Judd became Assistant Organist at St George's Chapel, Windsor, a post he still holds, combined with piano teaching at Eton College.

LET YOUR SOFTNESS BE KNOWN

Imagine for a moment – sunlight. the clear bright sunlight of a May morning. Sunlight flooding through an open doorway and throwing a long gothic pattern over the foreground of red and white and black tiles. Look through the doorway and you see a sunlit field, framed in the darkness of the arch; and in that field, a class of children seated in a half circle singing rounds. Where can it be but Saint Michael's?

deep is the quarry pool: and difficult the search therein. (Psalm CLI)

If you have not seen cricket played on a pasture freely dotted with cowpats you have no idea of the heights the noble art can rise to, especially if the duty master be weak. I have seen two players nearly fall to blows over a little matter of who should keep wicket, settled only after both players agree to keep wicket at the same time, one wearing the gloves and one wearing the pads. I have seen a batsman throw to the winds all that twaddle about standing back to the ball; not for him such cautious talk; he takes three strides up the pitch towards every ball and fetches it the most tremendous wallop. The bowler is a dreamy fellow, and he knows there are other things you can do with a cap besides wearing it – you can catch a ball with it, or butterflies. The game is interrupted by squeaks of excitement from the pavilion. Somebody has caught a grasshopper. ("Don't kill it!"). Back on the field, the bowler has captured a beetle which waves its tail in the air and clicks its back. The beetle is put through its paces so often it grows sulky and refuses to perform any more. The game is resumed and events take an interesting turn. Both batsmen are run out together and there cries of "NEXT TWO BATSMEN!" (Panic in the pavilion.) Have they crossed? That is the question. What says the umpire; The umpire says nothing. He is doubling up as scorer and has his head deep in the scorebook.

I remember Commem, and the whole school at morning service, and the disgust on the face of a probationer as he comes through the door and beholds Girls in the Commoners for the first time. The Bishop raises two fingers to bless the servers and is returned the scout salute. In his sermon, Canon Purcell compares the College to Jacob's ladder and says that Jacob's ladder is in danger of being kicked away by utilitarians. During the Sanctus there is a knocking at the porch door. (Pay no attention; perhaps he'll go away.) Repeated knocking, louder this time. Dr Oliver goes to see who it is. "Please, I'm from Banfields, and I've brought the mops for cleaning the church." Mr Coles fiddles with his music, rubs his neck, hitches up his surplice and sings a solo, all at the same time. The Dean of Gloucester arrives late and stands in the aisle like Banquo's ghost. He looks abstracted and gloomy, pays little heed to the sermon and drops his Series One booklet. It appears he was caught speeding through Leominster at 39 mph in his Daimler Jaguar. He is angry and puzzled. "I told them I was the Dean of Gloucester, but it made no difference."

In the Library afterwards, a distinguished Fellow, recently doctored, is undecided which of his many gowns he should wear to lunch. Should he cut a dash and wear his splendid new Doctor's robes.? or should be play for safety and wear a modest MA gown? He throws them all off and goes to lunch as he is.

Lunch in hall, and laughter as we learn to cope with wooden forms again. First the form is too far out – everybody gets up – heaves – and sits. Then the form is too far in – everybody gets up – heaves – and sits. Mr Gray has a special bottle of orange squash by his plate and asks Mr Parry to taste the trifle in case it has sherry in it.

In the afternoon, Dr Jackson gives an organ Recital. Mr Demaus marches the boys to their pews, where they sit quietly until two pieces from the end, when they rise in a body and walk out. Mousey, nodding, looks up, blinks; no boys! They have been told to leave after six pieces and have counted the trio sonata as three.

Evensong, and the privilege of taking part in the choir, and the discovery that it is no longer possible to process two abreast in the tunnel. A sunbeam momentarily touches each pair of Commoners as they pass the lectern. Fifteen commoners try to squeeze into a pew meant for six. Three luckless little girls are left standing in the central aisle with every prospect of being mown down by the choir, like the chariot race in Ben-Hur. Places are found for them in the nick of time. Colonel Prescott reads the lesson. His long association with the College has made him intimately acquainted with Gibbons in F and his timing is perfect: he has just got his spectacles unfolded and placed on his nose when the canticle ends. Two Commoners exchange half grins when he says Amen and pronounces it 'Ay-men.' The yellow evening sunlight makes coloured patterns on the stonework and on the face of the crossbearer as he stands near the altar. When the sun goes in, the sedilia takes on a little glow of its own, lit by a secret lamp.

There were great preparations for the Warden's enthronement service at which the Mayor of Tenbury and his lady wife were chief guests. Two library chairs (the only pair with a full complement of knobs) had been looked out, and these were placed sideways to the pulpit so that everyone could see when *she* turned east and *he* turned west. The visitors were escorted to their seats with all due pomp, and after service a deputation of top brass came to escort them out. But the Mayor, a little ferret of a man, was too quick for them. With the air of a trapped animal he tried to bolt down the tunnel behind the organ. This would not do at all, for the Mayor was not expected to dinner, and the Warden hared after him to head him off. It turned out that all the little man wanted was to drop a coin in the collection bag..............

"I couldn't get into the room – it was full of angels." The boy in Canon Harbottle's sermon had been upstairs to see his dying father. It was like that when, as the sole human eavesdropper, one attended Matins on a Wednesday morning. Nowhere in England, one reflected, could you hear Matins sung at that moment, not even at Saint Paul's. Ouseley's choir had God's undivided ear.

Ah, Ouseley, where are you now? Perhaps he is walking past matron's bedroom at this very moment (the part where the floorboards creak), wondering where his boys have got to and why they are not celebrating Advent. His eyes are large and sad and he says to himself that saddest verse in all the psalter, *O remember how short my time is: wherefore hast thou made all men for nought?* Was it for this that he travelled third class, and wrapped himself in a shabby blue cloak?

And Monty Alderson, you who died on July 14th, the very day the College died, where are you? Was not the saying most often on your lips *That which has been, can never be again?*

Edward Pine said once that Saint Michael's was the place which put English music back into England. No doubt he meant Fellowes and the music of Elizabeth the First, but was he thinking too of Nicholson and the School of English Church Music? Few know that Nicholson was inspired to found his College of Saint Nicholas by Ouseley's example; a debt that Nicholson himself acknowledges in his manuscript autobiography. It is to Nicholson's foundation, I submit, that we have to look for the continuance of Ouseley's ideals.

In a field near the Teme is a mound called Castle Tump. Some say Caractacus is buried there; others that it is a river fort left stranded by the Teme when it changed its course. Till lately a great oak grew there. That oak has fallen, felled by human hand, though it had life in it still. But there is hope: two young oaks yet remain; and from the bole of the parent tree a wild rose blooms. (14)

E.Q. Tznpoet (appeared in the last College Magazine of February 1986.)

REFERENCES

1. College Magazine December 1977
2. HCL D863
3. College Magazine December 1977
4. HCL D 863
5. HCL D 863
6. College Magazine December 1978
7. College Magazine December 1978
8. College Magazine January 1981
9. The Countryman Magazine 1980
10. College Magazine October 1981
11. College Magazine February 1986
12. College Magazine February 1986
13. Final Chorus in Stainer's *Crucifixion*
14. College Magazine February 1986

CHAPTER SIXTEEN
CLOSURE AND AFTERWARDS

THE CLOSURE

Over the first sixty years of its existence, it would be true to say that St Michael's had relied heavily on two sources for most of its income. Firstly, as already mentioned, Ouseley kept the College going throughout his lifetime, often under great personal hardship. He was helped and often 'bailed out' at various times during the first thirty years of the College's existence by the generous financial help of Miss Georgina Rushout, and who had also provided the Church and College with many extra things such as altar frontals and books for the Library.

After Ouseley's death, there were fears for the future of the College, but three years after the appointment of John Hampton as Warden, the College was 'saved' by the death of Georgina Rushout and her generous bequest to the College of £ 20,000, a large sum of money in 1892. From then onwards, the College continued to survive in its original form until Hampton's retirement as Warden. Indeed, his brief on appointment was to run the College as the Founder would have wished. Owing to the very small number of extra non-singing boys (known as Commoners), who provided much of the extra income of the College, it is very doubtful if the College would have survived much longer in its original form.

> The essence of the problem was that Ouseley's original conception was not really practicable. He very admirably chose to use his father's considerable wealth in this way, but it was a very romantic conception, not fully grounded in commercial reality. (1)

In 1917, Ernest Swann was appointed as Warden and he was able to lay the foundations to develop the College into a small, but thriving preparatory school and did much to stabilise its previously precarious existence. He realised immediately that it could not survive without the recruitment of more boys paying the full fees as non-choristers. (As well as choristers and probationers, sons of clergy were allowed reduced fees too.) Chapter Eleven recorded in detail the changes and developments made by Swann in his successful efforts to increase numbers. During his Wardenship, from 1917 to 1936, the numbers grew steadily as facilities improved and perhaps this can be regarded as the most successful period in the history of the College. It was even possible to establish a Reserve

Favourite views of the college
1. Sketch by John Gray
2..Photograph, c. 1980

Entrance to St. Michael's College, 1980's

Fund, in which was deposited any surplus income left after the end of each financial year, and which was to prove a godsend in the last years of the College's life.

Each Warden of St Michael's faced similar problems to those encountered by other small preparatory schools. In order to increase numbers, you needed to offer better facilities, and in order to provide improved facilities, you needed to least a stable, but preferably, increasing pupil base. In order to attract more pupils, each school had to offer something 'special' and St Michael's had its Choral Foundation, which it was hoped would be an attraction to boys and their parents. At the same time, mainly small numbers of boys learnt musical instruments, usually the piano, although in its later years, with the availability of a greater range of musical instruments and generally more affluent parents, the school was able to have a small orchestra with between 12 and 20 young players, often augmented by staff and one or two local people. As school numbers changed, the orchestra, disappeared for a time and then reappeared a few years later. At times, up to half the total school numbers were learning at least one musical instrument.

Another problem that was present throughout the life of the College was that of Staffing. As Watkins Shaw explains,

> The problem of staffing was no light burden to the Wardens. In times past, there were always young men to be found who, for board and lodging and a few pounds a week would spend two or

279

three years in 'prep' schoolmastering without thoughts of making it a career. With increasing professionalism, those days were over; and St Michael's could in no way match the Burnham Scale of salaries. Moreover, there was the question of men's voices in the choir. The neighbourhood offered little or no additional employment to attract lay-clerks of the standard of cultivated musicianship now required. In post-war years, there were rarely more than five lay-clerks, some being local residents who sang more for the satisfaction than as a means of remuneration........Other singers had to be supplied within a tiny teaching staff, which must also provide supervisory duties while the choir was at work. On losing a tenor singer who taught French and coached cricket (say), a Warden might be faced with one who could teach not French, but Mathematics and was no good at cricket. Or he might find an excellent French master whose voice and musical skill was unacceptable to the Organist. Not only did this impose restraints on the recruitment of the ideal teacher or the ideal singer and involved some thin patches, but it called for continuous resource and elasticity in the planning of duties. (2)

It was also noted that on occasion, 'duff' teachers were appointed, or those who had unsatisfactory qualifications but a good singing voice, and this sometimes led to a poor teaching and unsatisfactory results. One year, the school gained seven scholarship awards, but only one boy was able to take his up his award as the others had failed the Common Entrance Examination.

Over the years, efforts to increase the numbers continued, with various appeals (only moderately successful), which were intend to re-endow the College and to provide more and better facilities.

During the time of Warden Paxman in the 1970's, a small number of girls were admitted, often sisters of boys already at the College, and this helped to provide more income. This was followed by the opening of a pre-preparatory department, which flourished over the years leading to closure. Also during this time, there was the Houghton Award for teachers, which attempted to bring teachers' salaries up to a more realistic level. 'It imposed a heavy strain on St Michael's in the effort to keep up with it, though not completely to match it.'(3)

It was around this time that the Governing Body were beginning to be concerned about the future of the College. At the end of some years, the College had been left with a small deficit, which had been covered by the Reserve Fund. On other occasions, any projected deficit had been covered by the raising of the school fees. Acting against advice that they had been given, it was a mistake to decide to raise the fees by 15 % in both of two consecutive terms. The results were obvious in that numbers fell as parents took their children elsewhere.

Other steps were taken to cut costs and considerable savings were made when Warden Walters was able to employ and pay part-time staff on an hourly basis rather than on the usual termly or yearly contract. Despite its difficulties, the school could not reveal its problems as this would jeopardise future recruitment and ultimately, hasten its closure.

> At this point, a possible solution presented itself which seemed to have much to commend it. A proposal was received that the College should move and become a junior choir house to an established independent school. After prolonged and hopeful negotiations, it became apparent at the last that an important legal point would preclude the Charity Commissioners from giving the required consent, and the idea had to be abandoned. Thus a year went by during which, by the desire of the other party, (besides obvious other objections), nothing could be said, and matters were now very serious indeed. That was in the summer of 1983, when there was just enough reserve to meet one more year's deficit, after which it would be unsecured. (5)

The public face of the College continued to appear a confident and outgoing one, but when boys returned to College after half-term in February 1984, the Chairman of the Governors, Harry Pitt, and the Warden held a meeting with parents. Mr Pitt told parents that the College was approaching a severe financial crisis and that the school could not guarantee continuing in existence beyond July 1985.

The Winter 1984 edition of the magazine *This England,* started a new series, looking at English Independent Schools, and St Michael's was chosen as their first feature. 'Today, St Michael's is a flourishing preparatory school, carrying on its Founder's principles, adapted to modern conditions.'(6) This was a rather inaccurate statement, bearing in mind that the closure of the College had already been contemplated for at least a year.

> Maybe it would have been well to have brought the College to a close in the summer of 1984, but the Warden refused to give up hope; and however bleak the outlook, those concerned felt that they could not but make possible one more year's effort. If only five pupils paying full fees could be recruited! Surely there was a duty not to give in just yet! But to make possible that further year's effort, some exceedingly painful economies had to be inflicted.(7)

After the Michaelmas and Winter Terms of the academic year 1984 – 85, it became clear that the College would have to close. The announcement of this took place at the end of the Winter Term 1985, just before Easter. Having made public their decision to close the School, the Trustees now had to make formal arrangements to close the school. On hearing the news, a Committee of Parents, Old Boys and friends of the College was formed to co-ordinate individual efforts to keep the College open. Letters were written to the *Church Times* and other newspapers, and Peter Woolnough, a former choral scholar and now choirmaster of St Chad's, Headingley, contacted all the major schools to enlist their support in an attempt to save the College. The results were not what he expected. Although having great sympathy with his request, other schools could offer little support as in truth, many of them were also struggling financially in those inflationary times of the early 1980's. The College was featured on the BBC *Newsnight* programme and support began to grow. A business plan to support a newly-established school was drawn up by a London firm of accountants who specialised in dealing with independent schools, and who also gave much helpful advice. As an Associate Member of the Woodard Corporation, St Michael's was also offered advice and moral support from that organisation. Many prominent musicians, including Christopher Robinson, Sir Charles Mackerras, Sir Charles Groves, the Friends of Cathedral Music and the Royal School of Church Music all gave their support to the efforts of everyone in their endeavour to save the College.

The Warden, Andrew Walters, devoted many hours to marketing the school, trying to increase the numbers with full fee-paying pupils. It is clear that, despite the decision of the Trustees, he was determined to keep the school open if at all possible.

In the four years prior to closure, the total numbers of pupils were the largest they had been, but on closer examination, these figures would reveal that up to a third of the school were pre-prep pupils, paying only a small day fee. There were also the Choristers, Probationers and sons of Clergy, all paying reduced fees. In reality, the number of pupils paying full boarding fees had been gradually declining over a number of years and over the two years from 1982 to 1984, the number of pre-prep numbers had also dropped considerably, down from 30 in 1982 to 18 in 1984.

The perceived emphasis on music had often been deemed to be a hindrance in recruitment in that boys had to be musical in order to be accepted for St Michael's, which was not the case. Indeed, one Old Boy was heard to remark that he would not be sending his son to St Michael's as he wasn't musical. One member of staff looked into the possibility of setting up a Specialist Music College at St Michael's on the lines of Chethams' School in Manchester and to many staff and parents, this seemed to be an excellent idea and something which could ensure the survival of the College, but again, this idea did not develop any further.

Since the College closed, much has been said about the Trustees, Governors and Fellows and it may be useful to explain their different roles.

The <u>Fellows</u> met once a year and were kept informed of developments in the running of the College. Their role was to advise the Governing Body. They included many famous leading figures in church music such as Sir David Willcocks, Christopher Robinson and Roy Massey. While they very much regretted the closure of the College, they understood the impossibility of carrying on.

The Governors were in charge of the business of running the school, including the appointment of staff, purchase of equipment, general repairs and maintenance and looking after the College grounds, as well as fixing the level of fees and scholarships. One of them was a Parent Governor, and as a successful businessman, lent his expertise in the areas of appeals and marketing. Another, David Annett, was a former Headmaster of King's School, Worcester, who agreed to run the College for almost a year when the Warden was ill, and two more were experienced teachers. The decision to close the College was taken by the Governors in the light of the Trustees' inability to bail the Governors out with further funding.

The Trustees were not necessarily Governors. Their duties were to safeguard the permanent endowment of the College by investing appropriately the relevant funds and passing on the proceeds to the Governors. The Trustees had a residual responsibility for the College and direct responsibility for the Library, all of which they owned in law. When the school ceased to function, the Governors went out of business and the Trustees had to see to the winding up of the College and its assets.

The roles of Fellows, Governors and Trustees were quite distinct, though some confusion was caused by some people acting both as Trustees and Governors, although their responsibilities were kept quite separate. Fellows and Trustees carried on in office much longer than most members of the Governing Body, where there was a reasonable turnover.

However, some parents felt that the Trustees, after the closure of another local boarding school, were afraid of being responsible for any debts which may occur and acted too hastily as a result. Beth Wili, mother of Graham and Alistair, two former St. Michael's boys, became Chairman of the Action Committee and worked tirelessly to further the St. Michael's cause. The Trustees made an offer to the group of parents for them to take over the management of the College, offering them the buildings on a repairing basis at a nominal rent, and thus continue the school on its present site. For those parents involved, this was not an option or responsibility that they could take on and so the offer was turned down. The parents felt that the only viable option was to re-start the school on another site, closer to large centres of population.

Many boarding schools faced periods of financial hardship and uncertain viability as economic factors came into consideration in the late 1970's and early 1980's. Numbers had begun to fall and governing bodies began to get worried. The effects of these periods of 'recession' occur and re-occur and it was felt by some St. Michael's parents that if the school had carried on another two years or so, economic factors would have improved and the school numbers would have started to rise again with the consequent improvement in finances. However the Trustees had no powers to raise loans to cover temporary trading losses. In law, they had to operate as a strict trust rather than as a limited company, and this important point was not clear to many people.

Even today, over fourteen years after the school's closure, there is considerable anger felt by many parents and former pupils, staff and officers employed by the College, at the closure, and while some prominent musicians continue to express their dismay and sadness at its closure, others saw that the Trustees had no option, a decision supported by a BBC broadcast at the time.

By the summer of 1985, the Action Committee felt that the school should be re-housed elsewhere, with the possibility of establishing a new charitable trust and re-opening the College in a more accessible location, nearer to large centres of population, and thus continue the musical ideals which Ouseley had founded at St Michael's. In the summer of 1985, someone involved in education, and with a great interest in church music, offered to re-house the College in alternative accommodation in a more accessible area, but eventually after examination, this proved unworkable. Although things seemed to be going well with the campaign to save St Michael's, even ten months after its closure, the hard work and well-meant intentions of parents, Old Boys and friends eventually came to naught and it proved impossible to save the College.

AFTERWARDS (1985 – 1990)

After the end of July 1985, when the last boys and girls had left St Michael's, it would seem hard to believe that the buildings would remain empty for almost five years. Throughout this time, the Trustees were responsible for maintaining the condition of the buildings as good as possible, by keeping a small skeleton staff to keep things ticking over. Major Downes, the College Bursar, undertook any administrative work and saw that the buildings were kept clean and that the heating was on as and when necessary. Derek Lanman had joined the College as an assistant to the Gardener in 1951 as a young teenager and was later to become Gardener himself. He was also kept on to maintain the lawns and flower beds, etc. and to operate the heating system and to help the Bursar with any other necessary jobs. (A job he still does today, almost fifty years later.)

Eventually, the College was put up for sale, and with a number of false starts, took a long time to sell. One prospective buyer wanted to knock most of the buildings down and build a residential home and this prompted an application for listed building status for the College and Church, which was soon granted.

Negotiations now carried on with the Bodleian Library under the terms of Ouseley's Will for the disposal of the College Music Library. It was agreed that all the manuscripts should be presented as a donation to the Bodleian, including the priceless copy of Handel's *Messiah*. However, the

Music Library also had a large collection of scores and printed books and the Bodleian had a first option on these at an agreed professional valuation. This enabled the Bodleian to fill gaps in their own collections, the remainder being sold by Sotheby's. Tenders, subject to a time limit, were then invited for the sale of the books in the main College Library. Eventually, most of the books in the College Library were sold for approximately £100,000, considerably more than Sotheby's valuation of £74,000. They were already familiar with the contents of the College Library, as some items had been sold at the same time as the Toulouse-Philidor Collection in 1978.

Looking through the Internet, the 'surfer' will learn that in June 1991, 297 books and scores were purchased by the Mrs J W Jennings Music Collection in the Crouch Library at Baylor University, Waco in Texas and there are certainly other Libraries and institutions across America with books from St Michael's.

Also on the Net, the following Bodleian Library Report (1985 – 1993) features their acquisition of the Music Library from St Michael's.

> The outstanding event has been the acquisition of the magnificent music manuscripts, printed music and treatises of St Michael's College, Tenbury. Its musical library was assembled almost entirely by the College's Founder, Sir Frederick Arthur Gore Ouseley, who was also Professor of Music in this University. It was his wish, as expressed in his will, the collection should come to the Bodleian should the College ever close. In the event, legal complications were to prevent the entire collection being a gift to the Library, but an amicable deed of compromise was agreed with the Trustees of St Michael's, by which the manuscripts would be donated and the Library would purchase such of the printed material as it required. A successful fundraising venture raised £185,000 which enabled us to acquire copies of everything that was not already in the Bodleian, some 5,000 printed items, ranging from the treatises of 1480 by Gaffurius to First Editions of Beethoven, Schubert and Schumann. The money raised also allowed for their cataloguing. The manuscripts number of 1,000 and have increased the stock of Bodleian music manuscripts by almost 50 %. They range from 16th Century partbooks to autographs of Ouseley's own compositions. (8)

THE OUSELEY TRUST

After much careful consideration with the Charity Commissioners, the Ouseley Trust was constituted as a registered charity by a scheme made by the Charity Commissioners for England and Wales on 6 December 1989. The Scheme provided for 12 trustees – six nominative and six co-optative (ie. elected by the Trustee body).

The Trust's objective is to 'promote and maintain to a high standard the choral services of the Church of England, the Church in Wales or the Church of Ireland (whether simple or elaborate) in such ways as the trustees think fit…, including the promotion of the religious, musical and secular education of pupils attending any school in which instruction in the doctrines of any of the said churches is given and performance of their choral liturgy is observed.'

The trustees' current policy is to concentrate their resources on: courses of instruction; endowment grants; choir school fees; the purchase of music; and the repair of organs. In addition, careful consideration is given to other applications that involve unique and imaginative ways of fulfilling the Trust's objectives. Awards are made by the trustees at their biennial meetings after all applications have been considered.

The Trust has maintained its close relationship with a number of other charities and organisations, notably the Choir Schools Association Bursary Trust, the Corporation of the Sons of the Clergy and the Royal School of Church Music.

The Trustees' policy is to continue their pursuit of the objects of the charity by making grants to cathedrals, choral foundations and parish churches throughout England, Wales and Ireland.

In the year ended 31 December 1998, grants have been given under a number of headings, including two awards for the repair of organs and awards for the provision of music to three churches. The majority of the awards were given in two categories, the first being made towards chorister fees at the following schools;

Wells Cathedral School and Junior School	King's School, Rochester
Hereford Cathedral School	Salisbury Cathedral School
Llandaff Cathedral School	Exeter Cathedral School

Secondly, a number of endowments for choristerships have been established, including St David's Cathedral, King's College, Cambridge, Ely Cathedral, St Mary's, Portsea, St Fin Barre's Cathedral, Cork and Clare College, Cambridge.

At Exeter University, the Ouseley Choral, Senior Choral and Senior Organ Scholarships have been established.

As part of these endowments, the Trust has provided an Ouseley medal, which is presented to choral foundations which have instituted an Ouseley choristership.

A number of other awards are also made, including a yearly contribution to maintaining the tradition of choral music at St Michael's Church, Tenbury (see Chapter 17), something which is greatly appreciated by all who attend the Church, whether it be for services, organ recitals or other concerts.

The Ouseley Trust continues its important work and by the year 1999, it has given over £1,000,000 in support of its aims. A splendid achievement, appreciated by all who have received its help.

THE ST MICHAEL'S COLLEGE SOCIETY

At the Commemoration to celebrate the Fiftieth Anniversary of the founding of the College in September 1906, a meeting of Old Tenburians decided to form an Association, consisting of the Warden, Fellows and Old Boys of the Society, to be called the *St Michael's College Society*. The Society has continued to play an active part in the life of the College for the last eighty years of its life and also to the present day. Reunions are held every August and in recent years, thanks to the generosity of the present owners of the College, the reunion now takes place at the College over a weekend. A cricket match is usually played on a Saturday morning against a local village team, with a break for lunch at *The Fountain*. Later in the afternoon, a rehearsal takes place in the Church, with old Boys and friends forming a choir for Evensong, followed by the Annual General meeting of the Society held in the College Library. In the evening, many Old Boys attend a reunion dinner, held in the College Dining Hall, with invited guest speakers. On the Sunday, some members take part in the annual golf challenge, held at a local golf course.

In 1998, the membership rules of the Society were amended to include friends and others who have the interests of St Michael's College and Church at heart, such as local parishioners, who organise the yearly music programme of visiting choirs, organ and other recitals and help to keep St Michael's alive in the world of church music.

Membership of the Society is growing steadily and information can be found on the Internet at the following Website.

www.smsociety.co.uk

REFERENCES

1. Letter from Professor Brian Harvey to author, October 10th 1999
2. Watkins Shaw p. 74 – 75
3. Watkins Shaw p. 77
4. *The Countryman* magazine 1980, p. 78
5. Watkins Shaw, p. 81
6. *This England* Magazine Winter 1984, p. 40 – 41
7. Watkins Shaw, p. 81
8. Bodleian Library Internet Report (1985 – 1993)

Knight Frank & Rutley

HEREFORD
14 Broad Street,
Hereford HR4 9AL.

0432 273087

Viewing By Appointment Only

TPGJ/002840

ST MICHAELS COLLEGE
TENBURY WELLS
WORCESTERSHIRE

Kidderminster 19 miles Hereford 24 miles Worcester 24 miles Birmingham 42 miles

A SUBSTANTIAL PERIOD BUILDING BUILT IN THE GOTHIC STYLE WITH FULL RANGE OF
ANCILLARY BUILDINGS, SURROUNDED BY BEAUTIFUL COUNTRYSIDE AND IDEALLY SUITED
FOR INSTITUTIONAL OR EDUCATIONAL USE

MAIN HALL DESIGNED BY HENRY WOODYER, HOUSE WITH CLASSROOMS & STAFF ACCOMMODATION,
SEPARATE THEATRE, MUSIC BLOCK WITH THEATRE & PRACTICE ROOMS, CLASSROOM BLOCK,
2 SEMI DETACHED COTTAGES, DETACHED HOUSE,
OUTBUILDINGS, TENNIS COURTS, GARDEN, SPORTS FIELD, WOODLAND & PADDOCKS

EXTENDING IN ALL TO NEARLY 24 ACRES
FOR SALE FREEHOLD AS ONE LOT

These particulars are given subject to the notice overleaf, to which your attention is drawn

May 1990 – the college is sold

288

CHAPTER SEVENTEEN

(a) St. Michael's College today
(b) St. Michael's Church today

ST MICHAEL'S COLLEGE TODAY

In May 1990, after lying empty for almost five years, St Michael's College was sold by the Trustees to Cloisters International College Ltd, who planned to open what the *Tenbury Advertiser* called 'A School for Europe.' Paul Bailey, Chairman and Managing Director, spoke of the three main elements which he believed to be important in private education. These were teaching and the curriculum, the accommodation offered and the relationship between the school and the parents. It was planned to have the buildings refurbished and redecorated in time for the first students to arrive in June of that year. The school would be a co-educational one for up to 130 students, catering for those aged between 14 and 20, and as most of them would be foreign, the teaching of English would be the most important aspect of the curriculum, together with International Studies and other courses aimed at preparing students for higher education or a profession. It was envisaged that students could be at the College for short courses of three or four weeks, or could stay for up to three years, studying for external examinations such as international GCSEs and linking with education in their own countries. It was also hoped to offer appropriate courses to British students, such as office skills, computer studies and accountancy. Other aspects of the school included the teaching of ballet with a specialist teacher, and the development of social and sporting skills. Starting with very small numbers, and helped by intensive marketing around the world, the school gradually built up its student population. It was also possible for other agencies to become involved and King's College Madrid began sending students to study through the academic year. This also increased the numbers and helped the College to become established.

Running an international school relies on a number of factors to ensure its success, with continuous and intensive marketing being a high priority, to ensure that the school becomes well known in as many countries as possible. As a result of the international aspect, another factor which can affect a school is the fluctuation of currencies, which can often reduce the income of many parents and thus affect their children's education. A third factor can also be the effect of international events

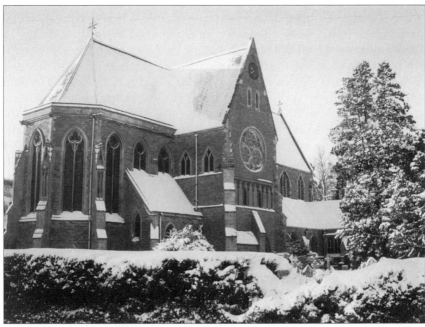

St. Michael's Church and College, winter 1996

which are beyond the schools' control. In the case of Cloisters, outside influences which caused problems were the Gulf War, resulting in a considerable drop in student numbers, and the financial problems caused by 'Black Wednesday', which saw interest rates spiral out of control to 23 %.

As a result of these problems, in 1994, St Michael's became part of the King's Educational Group, which is based in Madrid. King's College Madrid was established by Roger Fry in 1969 as a British Day and Boarding School and is a member of the Headmasters' Conference (HMC–Overseas List.) As the organisation developed, English Summer Schools and overseas Language Courses were started in various centres in Spain and abroad. Later developments took the organisation into the world of adult education, through the provision of Business English Programmes, which are taught in two permanent Language Centres.

In 1994, the Group purchased St Michael's College from Cloisters International as an international independent boarding school. The school is uniquely organised in two parts. Firstly, considerable numbers of Spanish students come to England for a year as part of their secondary education, or to take the whole of their secondary education in England. The tuition is undertaken by Spanish teachers in most academic subjects, following the Spanish educational system and students undertake the normal Spanish curriculum examinations in ESO and Bachillerato, which are the Spanish equivalent of GCSE's and A levels. Alongside this, the school caters for international students, who can come for a year to learn basic English through an intensive course, or study for the International certificate in Secondary Education in a number of subjects (IGCSE) over two years, followed by a further two year course to study Advanced level GCEs. Students in recent years have come from Brazil, Russia, Poland, Latvia, Hongkong, Taiwan and Japan. Maria Fry, the Managing Director of the College, travels all over the world to educational workshops and conferences in order to attract students to St Michael's.

The school offers a variety of recreational opportunities, with a new outside games court, which is floodlit and can be used for tennis, basketball, netball or football. Other types of leisure activities include arts and crafts and music, as well as regular weekend excursions and midweek educational visits to places of interest.

In addition to academic students, the College becomes a scene of frenetic activity every summer, when from June to August, the College runs a Summer School. Again, students come from all over the world to enjoy a hectic programme of English lessons and activities, sports and visits to such places as Alton Towers, Oxford and London, as well as more local excursions. The age range of these students is usually wider, from the age of 9, through to 16 or 17, and as well as the countries already mentioned, students have come from Italy, Portugal, Mexico and Spain.

The great variety of nationalities at the school provides a stimulating environment for both teachers and students alike. With its links to schools and organisations throughout the world, this enables the 're-born' St Michael's to play an important role in international education.

ST MICHAEL'S CHURCH TODAY

The Reverend Graham Atkins had been Chaplain of St Michael's and responsible for the parish church since the appointment of Warden Walters in 1977, who was not ordained at the time of his appointment. In common with Brian Demaus and John Gray, these three teachers left St Michael's in the summer of 1984, as a result of a severe cost-cutting exercise by the Governing Body. From that point, the parish church of St Michael was in a state of interregnum. In September 1984, a year before the College closed, the Venerable Ian Griggs, Archdeacon of Ludlow and later Bishop of Ludlow, became priest-in-charge of the parish.

Over recent years, the needs of the parishioners had often been subservient to the needs of the College and with the proposed closure of the College, it was be reasonable to assume that St Michael's may not have been able to continue as a parish church, had not Ian Griggs not stepped in to rejuvenate the struggling church and its members.

In December 1985, John Gray became a lay reader attached to the parish of St Michael's and at the same time, commenced evening class studies with a view to ordination in the future. In May 1987, the Parochial Church Council asked for the parish of St Michael's to be included in a Tenbury Team Ministry. In September 1987, there were now three clergy instead of two in the Tenbury team and on 1 October 1987, the appointment of Ian Griggs as Bishop of Ludlow was announced. It was then planned for the Rector of Tenbury to be in charge of St Michael's church. Ian Griggs still continued as priest-in-charge until the end of April 1988, while the procedures for the formation of the Team Ministry were begun. (Ian Griggs had already arranged all the services up to the end of 1988.) On 28 April 1988, the Reverend Duncan Dormor was instituted as Rector of Tenbury, although officially, the interregnum at St Michael's continued through 1988 until the Order-in-Council promulgating the Tenbury Team Ministry came into being towards the end of the year.

At Petertide 1989, John Gray was made deacon and after his ordination as a priest at Michaelmas 1990, he became a non-stipendiary (honorary) assistant curate in the Tenbury Team Ministry, with responsibility for the parish of St Michael's. His duties were to included the pastoral care of the people of the parish and officiating at Sunday and other services. Now the parish had the services of a priest available, it began to take on a new lease of life, freed from the overriding demands of the College.

As a schoolmaster for 28 years, John related well to young people and he soon established a monthly Family Service, encouraging active participation by the children and young people who attended. Older boys

THE CHURCH OF ST. MICHAEL & ALL ANGELS
TENBURY WELLS

ORGAN APPEAL 1989

Patron: Roy Massey Esq., Organist of Hereford Cathedral

and girls read lessons and took prayers, while the younger children had a very responsible job in lighting a large number of candles at the beginning of a service and extinguishing them all at the end. Activity sheets were given out during the service, based on relevant Christian themes, together with a children's competition page in the monthly Parish Magazine, with prizes being awarded at the next Family Service. This service has been a great success over recent years, with more and more young families moving into the village or the local area, helped by the building of new housing.

John Gray, helped by an active and imaginative Music Committee, was keen on maintaining the choral tradition in the church and a programme of recitals and concerts is arranged on a yearly basis. There are also an ever increasing number of choirs wanting to come and sing the services at St Michael's. The church is greatly helped by the yearly award of a grant from the Ouseley Trust, which enables the choral music tradition to be maintained. There are usually some four organ recitals each year and organists who have played at St Michael's include Simon Holt, Adrian Lucas, Francis Jackson, John Sanders, David Briggs, Roger Judd, Andrew

```
                    ST. MICHAEL'S CHURCH, TENBURY

                    Saturday, 28th October,1995

                              7p.m.


                    O R G A N    R E C I T A L

                               by

              DR. FRANCIS JACKSON, O.B.E.   Francis Jackson

                 Organist Emeritus, York Minster

                       * * * * * *


                       P R O G R A M M E


    Fugue in G, BWV 577 (alla Gigue)            Bach

    Chorale Prelude 'Ach bleib bei uns' BWV 649  Bach

    Sonata 4, opus 65                           Mendelssohn

         i    Allegro con brio
         ii   Andante religioso
         iii  Allegretto
         iv   Allegro maestoso e vivace

                       I N T E R V A L

    Modal Suite                                 Flor Peeters

         i    Koraal
         ii   Scherzo
         iii  Adagio
         iv   Toccata

    Three pieces                                Francis Jackson

         Prelude for a solemn occasion
         Exultet, opus 96
         Scherzo Amabile opus 92

    Postlude in D                               Smart


                 * * * * * * * * * * * * * * * * * *



    Refreshments will be served in the interval.


    Programme £4 single (concessions £2.50p)  £6.50 double
```

Lumsden and Mark Lee. Visiting choirs singing the Sunday services have included the Orrishmere Singers, the Hereford Wye Singers, the Hereford Church Singers, the Malvern Girls' College choir, Ruthin parish church and Halesowen parish church. In August 1998, the Coventry Cathedral choir, under the direction of Rupert Jeffcoat, spent a week living in the College and singing Evensong in the Church at each day. Every

---

St MICHAEL & ALL ANGELS CHURCH, TENBURY WELLS

ORGAN RECITAL by DAVID BRIGGS
Organist - Gloucester Cathedral

SATURDAY 5th JULY 1997 at 7 pm

PROGRAMME

Toccata and Fugue in FBWV 540 - J.S. BACH
*

Variations on "Mein Junges Leben hat ein end" - J.P. SWEELINCK
*

Fantasia and Fugue in G - Sir Hubert PARRY
*

Scherzo (Symphonie 2) - Louis VIERNE
*

Andante sostenuto (Symphonie Gothique) - Charles-Marie WIDOR
*

Flight of the Bumble-bee - N. RIMSKY - KORSAKOFF
*

Toccata (Suite Op 5) - Maurice DURUFLE
*

IMPROVISATION
*

DAVID BRIGGS became Director of Music at Gloucester Cathedral in 1994 following appointments at Truro and Hereford Cathedrals and King's College, Cambridge. In August 1995 he conducted his first Three Choirs Festival to much critical acclaim.

As one of the most notable organists of his generation, he circumnavigates the globe three times this year. During his U.S.A. tour in February he opened the prestigious Los Angeles Bach Festival, where he was compared to Dupre and Horowitz and nominated successor to Virgil Fox and Pierre Cochereau. In April he led a highly successful tour of Australia and New Zealand with the Gloucester Cathedral Choir. Other highlights of 1997 include a summer recital at the Hallgrimskirkja, Reykjavik, and a solo tour of Australia and New Zealand in October, including a recital on the largest organ in the southern hemisphere, at Sydney Town Hall. He has made numerous commercial recordings and his recent recording from Gloucester won a 'Soundings' Award in *Gramophone* and a coveted place on the cover CD. A leading exponent in the art of improvisation, he is the only Englishman ever to have won the Tournemire Prize at the St. Alban's International Improvisation Competition and last year his CD of organ improvisations broke new ground in this country. He is Visiting Tutor in Improvisation at the Royal Northern College of Music.

Admission and Programme: £4 (concessions £2.50)

St. Michael's College Society's support for this Recital is gratefully acknowledged

---

Christmas, the church is fortunate to have the Birmingham University Singers, led by John Wenham, who stay in the College and in local homes for one night, after a Carol Service on the Saturday evening and before a Sung Eucharist and Crib Service, usually on the Sunday before Christmas. Other recent concerts have included the Ex Cathedra group of singers, who gave a concert covering 1000 years of music on 16 October 1999 to a packed church of over 200 people. Another interesting development in the past year has been the formation of a small group of local singers, the St Michael's Singers, led by Bryan Fisher, who sing for some of the

MUSIC AT ST. MICHAEL'S CHURCH TENBURY WELLS

A SERVICE OF MEDITATION

CRUCIFIXION

by

John Stainer

sung by
THE HEREFORD CHURCH SINGERS
(Director: Peter Percival)
on
Good Friday
10th April 1998
at 7.00 p.m.

Admission Free
Retiring Collection in Aid of St. Michael's Church Fabric Fund

MUSIC AT ST. MICHAEL'S CHURCH TENBURY WELLS

CHAMBER CHOIR
presents

A NEW HEAVEN

A Millennium of Music

Directed by Jeffrey Skidmore
Organist - Ian Ledsham

Saturday 16th October
7 p.m.

Admission by Programme £8.00
Proceeds in Aid of St. Michael's Church Fabric Fund
Supported by St. Michael's College Society

services when there are no visiting choirs, so once again, St Michael's church has its own choir.

The village has become an even more lively and thriving community over the last few years, helped by the building of a splendid new village hall, and this acts as a focus for many village and church activities including art exhibitions, Local History Society, Youth Club, Pantomimes, dances, Summer Fetes and other community activities.

On New Year's Day 1999 the church and village was stunned to hear of the sudden death of John Gray, after an association with the College and church lasting over forty years. His funeral took place in a very full St Michael's church on 12 January 1999, attended by many Old Boys of the College and parishioners and a choir of Old Boys and friends sang during the service. It was entirely appropriate that John Gray's mortal remains should be buried at the end of the churchyard below the great East Window, alongside the graves of Ouseley, Hampton and Swann. Parishioners soon launched an Appeal Fund to provide a suitable headstone for John's grave and by the end of 1999, the required amount had been raised. Now John has gone, other people in the parish have taken up the challenge to keep the church going and as well as help from Duncan Dormor, the Rural Dean and Rector of Tenbury, two local retired priests, the Reverend Michael Staines and the Reverend Denis Boyling, take services on a regular basis, with the organisation of the monthly Family Service in the hands of Gwen Arnold, wife of one of the St Michael's churchwardens.

Despite the closure of the College, Ouseley's vision and the heritage of St Michael's remains alive, though perhaps not in a way he expected. Church and College are now separate entities, but co-existing happily alongside each other. The College now embodies a vision of international education, while the church remains at the centre of parish and community life. Both can face the future with confidence.

The Swann building, 1997

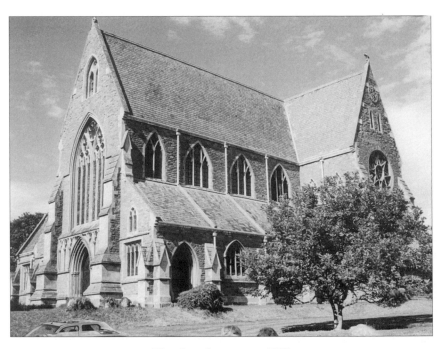

The church, summer 1999

APPENDIX ONE – THE BUILDINGS

(Described by the Architect Charles Nicholson)

The Architect of St Michael's College was Henry Woodyer, a pupil of Butterfield, and the buildings have undergone no material alteration since they were completed in 1856, a fact which testifies to the excellence of their general arrangement and construction. The general layout of the College is good and the buildings look well from all sides; the architectural details are consistent and of considerable refinement.

Woodyer never experimented in audacious colour schemes, but in many respects his work was obviously inspired by that of his master, Butterfield.

A great deal of Woodyer's work was done in Surrey and Hampshire, the parish church at Dorking being a very noteworthy building. In the course of his career he did a good deal of domestic work which it is interesting to compare with that done by Butterfield. Both master and pupil obviously paid close personal attention to detail, but the master's outlook was far more modern and progressive than that of the pupil.

The buildings at Tenbury are contemporary with Street's theological college at Cuddesdon, and the two buildings are very much alike in detail, but Street's college is not so well planned as Woodyer's, nor are its architectural merits greater.

Evidently at Tenbury there was no stint of money; dignity was demanded, luxury was despised. So the architect's opportunity must have been an ideal one and Woodyer rose to the occasion.

The general disposition of the buildings is quite simple. The church stands on the north side of the site next to the high road; the college buildings are concentrated in a single block to the south of the church, and the Warden's lodging, backed with a timber cloister connecting the college buildings with the church, forms the east side of a three-sided quadrangle open to the west.

The site falls steeply from north-east to south-west ands full advantage has been taken of this. The buildings are undeniably pictorial, although they are pronounced examples of a school of architecture with which present-day critics are not in sympathy. The details are on the whole good and carefully thought out, but give the impression that the architect aimed at producing a collection of reproductions of thirteenth and

Cloisters and main building looking south-east, 1970's
Photo courtesy of English Heritage, National Monuments Record

fourteenth century ornament; a genuine medieval building would have been much simpler.

It was never, of course, intended that the College should be mistaken for anything other than a nineteenth-century building: the gothic revival architects did not attempt such follies, though their enemies accused them of doing so. But they did hope to recapture some of the spirit of the medieval builders, and in this, it must be confessed, that Woodyer was only successful to a very limited extent, though he took great pains to do his work in a consistent manner, reviving traditional methods of construction as well as medieval principles of design and ornament. Probably, however, he as nearly hit the mark as any of his contemporaries.

He must have been in complete sympathy with his employer; his architecture seems the exact counterpart of the Founder's ideas concerning church music and ceremonial.

The church, which is the dominant feature of the College, though not on a large scale, is very successful in expressing the fact that it is something more than a mere parish church. Moreover, it looks a good deal larger than it is and does not look like a small copy of a large church. In attaining these results, Woodyer succeeded where others failed.

The building is cruciform and the chancel has an apse. Nave, chancel and transepts are of equal height and have very steep roofs with a timber vaulted ceiling, which is unbroken from east to west, the transept vaultings being treated independently, a very clever device for obtaining an effect of considerable internal length. The architectural detail is based upon English fourteenth-century work of a somewhat florid type, but quite refined and shapely. Both the masonry and the structural woodwork are very good and solid, but the arches between the nave and aisles, which are carried on thin columns of blue Penmant stone with heavy capitals carved with decadent foliage, detract from the effect of an otherwise very dignified interior.

Externally, the church looks exotic and rather pretentious, but it is not fair to criticise it as an isolated building; it should be regarded as a part of a group of buildings designed to fulfil very exceptional requirements.

The arrangements and fittings of the church are quite interesting. Some of the carving is quite good. The glass in the apse is exceptionally fine: it is by Hardman, and recalls that in the apse at St Chad's Cathedral in Birmingham, presumably designed by Pugin. (1) The rest of the glass is tolerably good and there are some scraps of old glass in the windows of a small passage round the south transept. (2) This transept is filled up with the organ and the north transept forms a baptistry, with the font in the centre under a very tall cover. There is a well in the corner of the baptistery and the chapel to the east of this transept has been furnished in recent years.

The arrangements of the sanctuary are of quite unusual dignity and are more generous than those considered adequate in many of our cathedrals.

There are no seats in the transepts; the steps are extremely well arranged and there are not too many of them. There are canopied sedilia on the south side with a credence table, strange to say, is on the north side of the altar. This is of good proportions, and stands forward in the apse under a not very successful canopied reredos.

The sanctuary is paved with mosaics and the chancel with encaustic tiles, simpler tile paving being used in the nave.

The choir seats are in line with the transepts. There are fourteen stalls with carved misericords. Front desks for the boys have been added in recent years. There are no return stalls, but the chancel is enclosed with very good and simple iron screens; the western one was originally adorned with a row of seven candlesticks (now electric ones.) The pulpit is a commonplace stone one. The nave is seated with very unworthy pews of pitch pine and the heating and lighting arrangements are modern. The chancel was originally lighted with candles fixed on the choir desks and there were hanging coronas of lamps and candles elsewhere.

In some practical details Woodyer's work is open to criticism. Here, for instance, there is no convenient access to the greater part of the roofs for

The nave of St. Michael's Church looking west, 1970's
Photo courtesy of English Heritage, National Monuments Record

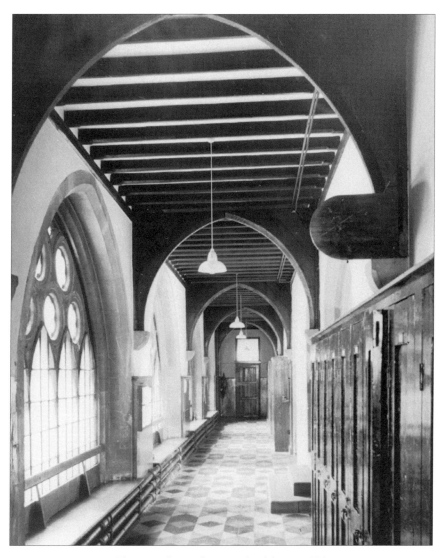

The corridor in the main building, 1970's
Photo courtesy of English Heritage, National Monuments Record

The dining hall looking east, 1970's
Photo courtesy of English Heritage, National Monuments Record

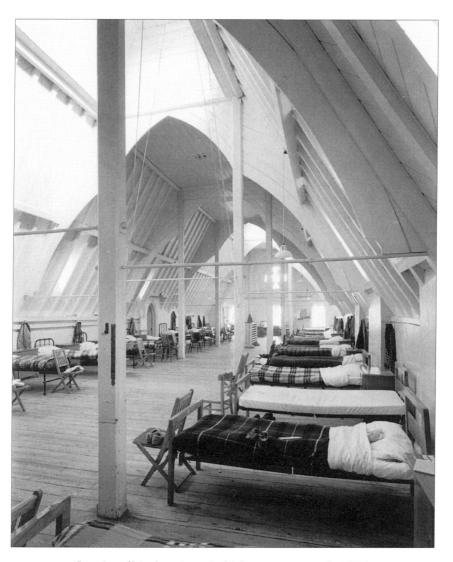

Interior of big dormitory (cubicles now removed), 1970's
Photo courtesy of English Heritage, National Monuments Record

purpose of repair. Such an omission was seldom made by Woodyer's master, Butterfield. The only piece of roof at Tenbury which possesses a parapet is that of the apse; elsewhere, very long and heavy ladders must be required for all repair work.

Again, the access originally provided to the great dormitory was very inadequate. But if Woodyer was sometimes forgetful he was upon the whole a sound constructor and his buildings have stood the test of time very well.

From a purely architectural point of view the secular portions of the College buildings are more successful than the church. Although they can obviously be criticised as foreign-looking and over-ornate it cannot fairly be denied that the work is finely proportioned and consistently carried out. The main block has a long cloister facing north, with a series of rooms opening from it facing south; the library at the east end and the hall at the west with smaller rooms and a mezzanine between them. Near the hall is a wing, projecting northward containing offices, and at the end of the building the fall of the ground enabled the architect to plan a roomy and airy basement storey.

The great dormitory is formed in the roof of the main block and there is a smaller dormitory, known as the 'chapel dormitory' in the roof above the north-west wing. The Founder is said to have provided this room to serve as a domestic chapel in the event of any trouble with the ecclesiastical authorities, but happily he was left in peace at Tenbury to do his work in his own way.

The Warden's House on the east side of the three-sided courtyard is sensible designed with well lighted, comfortable rooms, and the timber cloister against the west side of the Warden's house is quite an attractive piece of craftsmanship. (3)

All the interior of the domestic buildings is treated consistently, not, as one often sees in domestic gothic buildings of the period with conventional jerry-builders' internal finishings. Here the ceiling joints are exposed, the doors and fireplaces simply and naturally treated, such details as the door hinges being carefully and well designed.

The library is a fine room, though rather dark, and so lofty that the upper bookshelves are difficult of access; there is no gallery. The dining room is a beautiful room, not very large but lofty in proportion, well lighted and panelled and furnished in oak. There is a picturesque minstrels' gallery over the screened entrance lobby and there used to be a large canopied fireplace before the present heating was put in.

In the hall there is a good portrait head of Dr. Blow by Sir Peter Lely: other paintings of interest include a portrait of Dean Aldrich by an anonymous artist, and one by John Lucas, R A, which was exhibited at the Royal Academy in 1835 and which portrays the Founder at the age of nine. (5)

But the foregoing notes are concerned with the buildings rather than with what they contain. And these buildings are of very considerable interest, both as fine architecture and as a favourable impression of the artistic ideas of a bygone generation of great men.

NOTES

1. Hardman also made the glass in the Ante-Chapel of Eton College in 1859, with one window being re-made with undamaged pieces after bomb damage during the Second World War.
2. The South Transept Passage linked directly with the Cloisters and the rest of the College buildings through the South Door and choristers processed into church through this passage for every service.
3. In the Founder's appeal to endow the College shortly after it opened, funds were required to complete the enclosing of the Cloisters and also build a tower at the west end of the church. Due to the financial constraints which surrounded the College throughout its existence, this scheme was never completed.
4. This painting is now deposited with the Royal College of Organists.

One of Woodyer's ornate door hinges
Photo courtesy of English Heritage, National Monuments Record

APPENDIX TWO

WARDEN

1856	Frederick Arthur Gore Ouseley

FELLOWS

1856	James Wayland Joyce
	Hubert McLaughlin
	Henry Fyffe
	John Rich
	John Jebb
	Edward John Ottley
	Alfred Trevor Crispin
	Edwin George Monk
1857	Anthony Latouche Kirwan
	William Sewell
1858	Richard Whitmore Norman
	Thomas Thorpe
1859	John Joseph Miller
	Thomas Ascough Smith
1860	William Morgan Campion
1861	Thomas Littleton Wheeler
1862	John Capel Hanbury
	William James Earley Bennett
	Henry Williams Baker
	James Elwin Millard
1864	Henry Aldrich Cotton
	Henry John Burfield
1868	Robert Corbert Singleton
1872	Frederick Maude Millard
1877	Marmaduke Charles Frederick Morris
	Vincent King Cooper
1881	John Samuel Sidebotham
1883	Henry Chittenden Rogers
1884	Edward Charles Corfe
1886	John Henry Mee
	William Rayson
1888	Charles John Corfe

WARDEN

1889   John Hampton

FELLOWS

1893   Arthur Henry Saint Pattrick
1894   James Leigh
        William Claxton
        Frederick Wayland Joyce
1894   John Stainer
        Arthur Hew Dalrymple Prendergast
        Walter James Francis Erskine, Earl of Mar and Kellie
        Charles Plummer
        James Barclay Joyce
1902   Walter Parratt
        George Robertson Sinclair
        Alexander Frederick De Gex
1911   Frederick Bennett
1916   Geoffrey Charles Edward Ryley

WARDEN

1916   Geoffrey Charles Edward Ryley

FELLOWS

1916   John Hampton
        Ernest Breffit

WARDEN

1917   Ernest Henry Swann

FELLOWS

1918   Walter Howard Frere
        Percy Carter Buck
1920   Edmund Horace Fellowes
1921   Arthur Stuart Miles
        Reginald Waterfield
        Ivor Algernon Atkins
        Sydney Hugh Nicholson
1922   Montague Frederick Alderson
        Arthur Hubert Barnes
        George Lawrence Harper Gardner
1923   Arthur Maitland Sugden
        Hugh Hippsley Ayscough Ayscough

1924	Paul John Henry Butler
1927	Percy Clarke Hul.l
1931	Henry Cope Colles
1932	Archibald Slater
1934	William Bourne Glennie
	William Ralph Prescott
	John Cavendish Lyttelton, Viscount Cobham
1935	Hubert Ingleby
1936	Edward Richard Trevor Corbett

WARDEN

1936	Cuthbert Harold Septimus Buckmaster

FELLOWS

1936	Ernest Henry Swann
	Ernest Bullock
	John Francis Clayton
1940	William Neil McKie

ACTING WARDEN

1941	Albert Victor Billen

FELLOWS

1943	Cyril Vincent Taylor
	Geoffrey Michael Joyce
1945	Albert Victor Billen
	Frederick Stuart Miles

WARDEN

1947	Noel Henry Kemp-Welch

FELLOWS

1947	Harold Watkins Shaw
	George Hewitt Frost
	Henry Bentham
1949	Heathcote Dicken Statham
	Henry MacLeod Havergal
	Herbert Kennedy Andrews
	Laurence William Grensted
1953	David Colin Dunlop
	David Valentine Willcocks
	Edgar Broadhurst
	Gerald Hocken Knight

1954	David John Walters
	Albert Meredith Davies
1956	Harry Griffiths Pitt

WARDEN

1957	Desmond William Griffiths Stride

FELLOWS

1958	Herbert Whitton Sumsion
	John Henry Huby Oliver
	Seiriol John Arthur Evans
1960	Christopher Hassall
1961	Irven David Edwards
1963	Kenneth Henry Lowry Lamb
	William Francis Martin Madden
1964	John Willis Hampton
	Christopher John Robinson

WARDEN

1965	Denis James Paxman

FELLOWS

1965	Reginald Stanley Thompson
	Andrew Hunter Dunn
1967	Thomas Berkeley Randolph
1968	George Herbert Balmer Cole
	Thomas Freeman Higginson
1969	Wilfred Reginald Derry
1973	Ivor Christopher Banfield Keys
	Lionel Frederick Dakers
1974	Esmond James Bulmer
1975	Brian Wilberforce Harvey
	Roy Cyril Massey

WARDEN

1977	Andrew Farrar Walters

FELLOWS

1977	Richard Good Smethurst
1980	David Maurice Annett
	Graham Charles Phipps
	Keith Reid Wilkes
1982	Nicholas Edward Walker

ORGANISTS

1856 – 57	John Capel Hanbury
1857 – 59	John Stainer
1874 – 77	Langdon Colbourne
1877 – 86	William Claxton
1886 – 89	Walter James Lancaster
1889 – 93	Allan Paterson
1894	Charles Harry Moody
1894 – 96	James Lyon
1896 – 1907	Edgar C. Broadhurst
1908 – 09	Maurice Gordon Burgess
1910	Percy C. Davis
1911 – 12	Normal Charles Wood
1913 – 18	Arthur John Baynon
1919	Ernest Bullock
1920 – 25	Heathcote Dicken Statham
1925 – 31	Stanley Thorne
1931 – 35	Laurence Crossthwaite (from 1934, Organists were also Choirmasters)
1935 – 52	Maxwell Graham Menzies
1952 – 59	Kenneth Graham Beard
1959 – 72	Lucian Nethsingha
1973 – 85	Roger Lewin Judd (now designated as Master of the Music)

APPENDIX THREE (A)

CATALOGUE OF THE COMPOSITIONS OF THE REVEREND SIR FREDERICK ARTHUR GORE OUSELEY, Bart., Mus.D. Oxon., Compiled by Mr. John S. Bumpus in 1892 and revised in 1896.

In his original prefatory note, Mr. Bumpus says

> I have used my best endeavours to make the list as complete as possible up to the time of going to press; but there are, doubtless, very many compositions existing only in manuscript in various private hands, besides those I have mentioned. For Sir Frederick Ouseley had such a facility in writing, than anybody who asked him for a particular composition was sure to receive it, and scarcely ever was a copy of it made. The first copy in his own handwriting – and a beautiful handwriting it was – was always fair, and ready for the printer.

> I beg to acknowledge, with feelings of deepest gratitude, the very courteous and ready assistance of the Reverend John Hampton (Sir Frederick's successor at Tenbury), in response to several of my enquiries.

NB. Compositions in this section have all been published by Novello, unless otherwise stated.

SERVICES (USUALLY FOR FOUR VOICES)

A　　　Te Deum, Jubilate, Kyrie, Credo, Sanctus, Gloria, Cantate and Deus Misereatur (written for Christ Church, Oxford)

B flat　Magnificat and Nunc Dimittis

B minor Te Deum, Benedictus, Kyrie, Credo, Sanctus, Gloria, Magnificat And Nunc Dimittis

C (for double choir)

　　　　Venite, Te Deum, Benedictus, Kyrie, Credo, Sanctus, Gloria, Magnificat, Nunc Dimittis, Cantate and Deus Misereatur. (written for the re-opening of Hereford Cathedral after restoration June 30th. 1863)

C　　　Kyrie, Credo, Sanctus, Gloria

D　　　Chant Service for the Te Deum

D	Gloria to match and complete Rogers in D
E	Te Deum, Jubilate, Kyrie, Credo, Sanctus, Gloria, Magnificat, and Nunc Dimittis
E flat	Te Deum, Jubilate, Kyrie, Credo, Sanctus, Gloria, Magnificat, and Nunc Dimittis
E flat	Magnificat and Nunc Dimittis (men's voices for St. Paul's)
F	Te Deum, Benedictus, Kyrie, Credo, Sanctus, Gloria, Magnificat And Nunc Dimittis
F	Te Deum (composed for Ely Diocesan Church Music Society)
G	Te Deum, Jubilate, Sanctus, Kyrie, Credo, Magnificat and Nunc Dimittis

ANTHEMS IN SHORT FULL STYLE

Blessed be the Lord God of Israel
Except the Lord build the house
From the rising of the sun
Happy is the man
Hear my cry, O God
I will love Thee, O Lord
Is it nothing to you?
Judge me, O God
Lord, be merciful to us sinners
Lord, I call upon thee
Love not the world
My song shall be always
O Lord Thou art my God
O Saviour of the world
Rend your hearts
Righteous art thou, O Lord
Haste Thee, O God
How goodly are Thy tents
I will give thanks
O God, wherefore art Thou absent
O praise the Lord all ye heathen
How long wilt Thou forget me
I know that the Lord is great
O Almighty and Most Merciful God
O how plentiful
O love the Lord
Thy mercy, O Lord
Blessed is the man
Be merciful unto me

O Lord, we beseech Thee
Save me, O God
To the Lord our God
Unto Thee, O Lord
All the kings of the earth
Behold, how good and joyful
Blessed is he whose unrighteousness
In God's word will I rejoice
Like as the hart
O praise our God, ye people
The salvation of the righteous
Whom have I heaven but Thee?

LONGER ANTHEMS

And there was a pure river of Water of life
And there was war in Heaven (composed for the Feast of St. Michael and All Angels)
Ascribe ye greatness
Awake, thou that sleepest
Behold now, praise the Lord (composed for the great Choral Festival in Peterborough Cathedral (June 1863)
Blessed be Thou (composed for the re-opening of Hereford Cathedral on June 30th. 1863)
Christ is risen from the dead
Give thanks, O Israel
Great is the Lord
Hear O Lord, and have mercy
Help us, O God
I waited patiently
I will give thanks
I will magnify Thee
I saw the souls of them that were beheaded
In Jewry is God known
In the sight of the unwise (From St. Polycarp)
It came even unto pass (written for the re-opening of Lichfield Cathedral on October 22nd, 1861 and sung by 980 voices)
It is a good thing to give thanks (composed for a great Choral Festival at Salisbury Cathedral June 6th. 1889)
Let all the world in every corner sing
O praise the Lord with me
O send out Thy light
O ye that love the Lord

O sing unto God
One thing have I desired of the Lord (composed for the Choral Festival at
Tewkesbury Abbey in September 1884)
Plead Thou my cause
Rejoice with Jerusalem
Sing, O Daughter of Sion
Sing unto the Lord (composed for Norfolk and Suffolk Annual Church
Festival 1865)
The Lord is King
The Lord is my Shepherd
The Lord shall roar out of Sion
They that wait upon the Lord
Thou art my portion
Thus saith the Lord
Unto Thee will I cry
Who shall ascend
Why standest thou so far off

NB. A number of these anthems were elaborately scored for full band and
organ by Ouseley himself

CHANTS

Twenty-nine single and six double chants as printed in ANGLICAN
PSALTER CHANTS (EDITED BY E.G. Monk and F.A.G. Ouseley and
published in 1876)
Thirteen single and six double chants, as sung at St. Michael's.
Two double chants in G and B flat and seven single chants for the London
Chant Book (1886)
Double Chant in B flat for the Choir Chant Book

HYMN TUNES

In the enlarged edition of *Hymns Ancient and Modern,* ed. W.H. Monk (1889)
The radiant morn hath passed away (St. Gabriel)
Sweet Saviour, bless us ere we go (Christ Church)
Once more the solemn season (Hereford)
Throned upon the awful tree (Grethsamane)
They come, god's messengers of love (Woolmers)
For man the Saviour shed (Aberystwyth)
Behold the Sun (Brightness)
Be near us, holy Saviour (Sharon)
When all Thy mercies (Contemplation)
Praise the Lord, His glories show (St. Ethelbert)

Children of the Heavenly King (Bewdley)
Jesu! Name all name above (Theoktistus)
In *The Hymnary,* ed. By J. Barnby (1872)
Go to dark Gethsemane
Father, by Thy love and power
O Lord, the heaven Thy power displays
O love, how deep
O Lord of health and life (Langley)
Be present, Holy Trinity

In *Church Hymns (SPCK)* ed. By Arthur Sullivan (1874)
The radiant morn (St. Gabriel)
O God the Son Eternal (Tenbury)

In *The Dublin Church Hymnal* ed. Stewart (1883)
Go to dark Gethsemane
Glory to God on High (St. Augustine)

In Maurice's *Choral Harmony* 1854
Weep no more, Zion (Langley)
The God of harvest praise
To God Hosannas sing (Peterstowe)
Hosanna be our cheerful song (Tenbury)

In *The National Book of Hymn Tunes, Kyries and Chants* (1884)
The tunes Exultation and Faith

In *The Anglican Hymn Book* ed. E.G. Monk (1871)
Saviour, breathe an evening blessing
O Death, thou art no more
Far from the world, O Lord (Lovehill)
Ye servants of the Lord
If thou wouldest life attain
The God of harvest praise (St. Augustine)
Walking on the winged wind

In *The Children's Hymn Book* (Rivington's)
All things bright and beautiful
Easter flowers are blooming (In Excelsis Gloria)
Shepherd, good and gracious (Star of the East)

In *The Holy Year* ed. W. H. Monk 1868)
When the Architect Almighty (Shekinah)
O Lord Who in Thy love divine (Ordination)

In *The Home Hymn Book* (1887)
When sinks the sun (Thornton)

In *The Hymnal of the Episcopal Church of America*
Pain and toil are over now (Pruen)

In *Hymn and Tune Book* ed. Chope (1863)
Great mover of all hearts (St. Cyril)

In Dean Alford's *Year of Praise* (1867)
Ten thousand times ten thousand (Eastham)

In *The Song of Praise*
Angels Holy (St. Winifred)

In Steggall's *Hymns for the Church of England* (1868)
You, that like heedless strangers
O God, the Son Eternal

In the Appendix to *Hymns Ancient and Modern (1868)*
Hail, gladdening light

Now brothers to the holy ground (Funeral hymn)
Arrangement of the tune *Hanover* for chorus, orchestra and organ
Royalty – a hymn for Coronation Day (June 28th)
Holy Lord, Thy tender mercies (Home Mission Hymn)

CHRISTMAS CAROLS

Angels singing, church bells ringing
Come, tune your heart
In Bethlehem, that noble place
Listen, lordlings, unto me

CANTATA

The Lord is the true god (Exercise for his degree of Bachelor of Music)
Oxford 1850 – unpublished)

ORATORIOS

The Martyrdom of St. Polycarp (Exercise for his degree of Doctor of Music
1855
Published by Novello)
Hagar (produced for the Three Choirs Festival at Hereford, 1873)

ORGAN MUSIC

Set of six Preludes and Fugues
Set of Seven Preludes and Fugues
Set of Eighteen Preludes and Fugues
Set of Six Short Preludes
Set of Three Andantes
Two Preludes and Fugues
Two Sonatas
Voluntary for Christmastide
Voluntary in F
Overture to the Oratorio *HAGAR*
March from the Oratorio *ST. POLYCARP*
Andante Espressivo

WORKS EDITED BY OUSELEY FOR CHURCH USE

A Collection of Cathedral services by English Masters of the 17th. And 18th. Centuries. (Novello 1853)
Included services by Aldrich, Childe, Church, Creyghton, Farrant, Foster, Kelway, Kempton, Ouseley, Rogers and Tomkins.

The Sacred Compositions of Orlando Gibbons (Novello 1873)

A Collection of Anthems for Certain Seasons and Festivals
(2 vols. Novello 1861 – 66)

Anglican Psalter Chants – Single and Double – *ed. With E.G. Monk 1876*

The Psalter Pointed for Chanting ed. With E.G. Monk

Tallis Preces and Responses

Final Amen (Composed for use in Winchester Cathedral at the end of Evensong on Sundays)

SECULAR

INSTRUMENTAL MUSIC

Overture in D for full orchestra
Overture in D minor   ditto
Overture in F   ditto
Concert March in G   ditto
Concert March in D   ditto
Minuet and Trio   ditto
String Quartet in C

String Quartet in D minor
String Quartet in A
Fugue in 4 parts for Strings
Minuet and Trio for a very large orchestra
A set of unpublished *Songs without Words* written between 1839 and 1849

VOCAL MUSIC

GLEES

Ah, who should nature
Gem of the crimson-coloured even
Go, lovely rose
Go, tuneful bird
O Memory
Sweet Echo
The Water Sprites
The Spirits of the Wood
Though I may never more behold
When o'er the silent sea

MADRIGAL

Your shining eyes

PART SONGS

Place the helm on my brow
War, wine and harmony
Life

SONGS

A Set of Six
1. Oh, where
2. Under the snow
3. Home
4. The Sparrow
5. Apple Blossoms
6. The resting-place

How beautiful is day
The Skylark
The ploughshare of Old England
Zephyr, Shoud'st thou chance
Old Bells

THEORETICAL AND OTHER WORKS

A Treatise on Harmony (Oxford 1868)

A Treatise on Counterpoint, Canon and Fugue, based on Cherubini (Oxford 1869)

A Treatise on Musical Form (Oxford 1875)

History of Music (by Naumann), edited and translated by Ouseley (2 vols. Cassell, 1882)

The Choral Worship of the Church (Sermon preached at Derby 1861)

Jerusalem at Unity – a Sermon (1863)

Secular Education – a Sermon (1869)

Essay on *The Education of Choristers in Cathedrals*, No. 9 in *Essays on Cathedrals*, edited by Dean Howson of Chester –(Murray 1872)

Papers read before The Musical Association by Sir Frederick Ouseley, president from its formation in 1874

1. Contributions on the History of Ecclesiastical Music of Western Music 1876
2. On the Early Italian and Spanish Treatises of Counterpoint and Harmony 1879
3. On some Italian and Spanish Treatises of Music of the Eighteenth Century 1882
4. On the Position of Organs in Churches 1886

Paper on *Organs*, read at the Musical Institution 1852

Papers on *Church Music*, read at the Church Congresses at Manchester (1863),

Wolverhampton (1867), Leeds (1872) and Brighton (1874)

Manuscript works (now in the Bodleian Library)

Let tears fall down (Ode on the death of the Duke of Wellington), scored for full Orchestra (1852)

Now let us praise famous men (Ode on the Installation of the Chancellor of the University of Oxford), scored for solo, five-part chorus and full orchestra (1855)

Peace Ode (after the Crimean War) – scored for solo, five-art chorus and full orchestra (1855)

There are a number of his childhood compositions in a small volume (containing some 243 compositions) and other examples of early composition now deposited at the Bodleian Library, Oxford

APPENDIX THREE (B)

OUSELEY'S MUSIC STILL PERFORMED TODAY

Most of Ouseley's compositions have been consigned to obscurity, being part of that large corpus of middle to late Victorian church music which tends to gather dust in church and cathedral music libraries, before finally being discarded in order to create space for the music of more modern composers.

In order to find out more about the use or non-use of Ouseley's music, a survey was carried out of almost fifty Cathedral and College Organists, of whom only five failed to reply. This endeavoured to find out what music of Ouseley's was in their library and if any was used.

A summary of the results is given below.

ANTHEMS	No. of Cathedrals and Colleges
From the rising of the sun	27
O Saviour of the World	17

(These first two anthems were occasionally performed as part of the repertoire)

How goodly are Thy tents	11
It came even unto pass	9

(These two anthems and those listed below were rarely performed)

Jerusalem on High)
Is it nothing to you)
O Praise the Lord) These anthems were listed by up only three
    cathedrals
Great is the Lord) but not as being currently performed
Save me O God)
In the sight of the unwise)

NB. Both St. Paul's Cathedral and Magdalen College, Oxford have an extensive library of Ouseley's anthems.

CANTICLES

For the occasional special event, Hereford Cathedral have used their former Precentor's *Magnificat and Nunc Dimittis in F*, but generally, usage of Ouseley's other Canticle settings occur very rarely elsewhere, if at all.

CHANTS

In many cathedrals and College Chapels, a variety of Ouseley's single and double chants are in regular use.

HYMNS

Looking at the development of hymnbooks, from the middle of the 19th Century up to the present day, Ouseley's name as a composer has all but disappeared, apart from the well-known hymn *When all Thy mercies O my God*, sung to the lovely tune, *Contemplation.* There are one or two more which are occasionally sung, including *The radiant morn hath passed away*, sung to the tune *St. Gabriel*

At the annual Commemoration Festival on the Feast of St. Michael and All Angels, the following hymns are regularly sung at St. Michael's Church, with the help of a visiting choir.

They come God's messengers of love (Woolmers)

Jesu! Name all names above (Theoktistus) (This hymn is a splendid one and should be more widely sung.)

ORGAN MUSIC

There are few examples of Ouseley's organ music still in print. (*Two Preludes* are published by Novello), but thanks are due to the enterprising and imaginative organ music publishers OECUMUSE, who are regularly re-publishing organ music by Ouseley and other Victorian composers such as Smart, Stainer and Stanford, as well as more modern composers.

It should also be noted that such an eminent Organist as John Scott of St. Paul's Cathedral has been playing one of Ouseley's *Preludes and Fugues* during his 1999 season of Organ Recitals.

APPENDIX FOUR

SPECIFICATION OF THE ST. MICHAEL'S ORGAN

by Roger Judd

In April 1873, Ouseley engaged a competent organ builder, 'Father' Henry Willis, to put the organ in good order. He undertook to dismantle the entire instrument, take it back to his London factory, and bring it back in playing order within five months. Willis agreed to use only the best parts of the old instrument. He re-voiced the pipework, so that, although the pipes were not made by Willis, they sound like Willis pipes. it is this organ, with a few small differences, the listener will hear today. Originally, the organ's action was by Barker lever, but in 1895 and 1916, this was changed to tubular pneumatic action. Also in 1895, the Solo organ was enclosed in a box, giving what is thought to be the earliest enclosed Tuba in the country. In 1916, the console was modernised with new stop-knobs and installation of fully adjustable combination pistons – these work splendidly to this day (1999). In 1953, some work was necessary to the action, and the original sharp pitch was lowered. More repair work was done in 1975 when a small number of tonal changes were made and in 1995. These were done by Harrison and Harrison, who now look after the organ in rather different circumstances from 1867. Basically, however, the organ sounds unchanged since 1873, unmistakably a Willis, but of unusual pedigree.

Here is the present specification of the instrument:

GREAT ORGAN

Bourdon	16	ft
Double Diapason	16	ft
Open Diapason I	8	ft
Open Diapason II	8	ft
Stopped Diapason	8	ft
Claribel Flute	8	ft
Flauto Traverso	4	ft
Principal I	4	ft
Principal II (1953)	4	ft
Twelfth	2 2/3	ft
Fifteenth	2	ft
Fourniture	3	ranks
Mixture	2	ranks
Tromba	8	ft
Clarion	4	ft

SWELL ORGAN

Bourdon	16	ft
Open Diapason	8	ft
Lieblich Gedackt	8	ft
Salicional	8	ft
Voix Celeste	8	ft
Lieblich Flute (1953)	4	ft
Geigen Principal	4	ft
Flageolet	2	ft
Mixture	5	ranks
Contra Fagotto	16	ft
Hautboy	8	ft
Cornopean	8	ft
Clarion	4	ft

CHOIR ORGAN

Lieblich Gedackt	8	ft
Dulciana	8	ft
Lieblich Flote	4	ft
Gemshorn	4	ft
Nazard (1975)	2 2/3	ft
Piccolo	2	ft
Tierce (1975)	1 3/5	ft
Mixture (1975)	3	ranks
Corno di Bassetto	8	ft

SOLO ORGAN

Viola da Gamba	8	ft
Flute Harmonique	8	ft
Concert Flute	4	ft
Orchestral Oboe	8	ft
Clarinet	8	ft
Tuba	8	ft

PEDAL ORGAN

Contra Bourdon		
(from Bourdon)	32	ft
Open Wood	16	ft
Open Metal	16	ft
Violone	16	ft
Bourdon	16	ft
Quint	10 2/3	ft
Violoncello	8	ft
Principal		
(from Open Wood)	8	ft
Fifteenth	4	ft
Mixture	5	ranks
Ophicleide	16	ft
Clarion	8	ft

BIBLIOGRAPHY

BOOKS

Barrett, P   *Barchester – English Cathedral Life in the Nineteenth Century*   SPCK 1993

Bennett, W J E   *Pastoral Letter to his Parishioners*   Cleaver 1846

Farewell Letter to his Parishioners   Cleaver 1851

Boden, A   *Three Choirs – A History of the Festival*   Sutton 1992

Bumpus, J S   *English Cathedral Music*   Laurie 1908

Charlton, P   *John Stainer and the Musical Life of Victorian Britain*   David and Charles 1984

Clutton, C and Niland, A   *The British Organ (2nd. Edition)*   London 1982

Colles, H C and Alderson, M   *History of St. Michael's College, Tenbury*   SPCK 1943

Dibble, J   *C. Hubert Parry – His Life in Music*   Oxford 1992

Fowler, J T   *Life and Letters of J.B. Dykes*   Murray 1899

Havergal, F T   *Memorials of F.A. G. Ouseley*   Ellis 1886

Helmore, F   *Memoir of the Reverend T. Helmore*   Masters 1891

Hereford Cathedral: A History   (published in 2000)

Pearce, C W   *The Life and Work of Edward John Hopkins* Musical Opinion 1900

Joyce, F W   *Life of Sir F.A. Gore Ouseley*   Methuen 1896

Oakeley, E M   *The Life of Sir Herbert Oakeley*   George Allen 1904

Otter, J   *Nathaniel Woodard: A Memoir*   Bodley Head 1925

Rainbow, B   *The Choral revival in the Anglican Church*   Oxford 1970

Routley, E   *A Short History of English Church Music*   Mowbrays 1977

Watkins Shaw, H *Sir Frederick Ouseley and St. Michael's College, Tenbury,*   The Ouseley Trustees 1986

Young, P   *Letters to Nimrod*   Dobson 1965

OTHER PRINTED SOURCES

	A Short History and Guide to the Church of St. Michael's and All Angels	Tenbury Wells 1993
	The Architect 1903	
	The Cathedral Quarterly 1913	
Barrett, P	*The College of Vicars Choral of Hereford Cathedral*	Friends of Hereford Cathedral 1980
	The Countryman Magazine 1980	
	The Freeman's Journal, Dublin – 2 March 1848	
	The Harmonicon – May 1833	
Morgan, F C	*Hereford Cathedral Church Glass*	Friends of Hereford Cathedral 1979
	Memorabilia – The 50th Anniversary of St. Michael's College	1906
	The Musical Times 1901	
	The Old Chorister 1986	
	The Organ – Vol V, January 1926	
	The Organ – Vol XXIII, January 1944	
	The Organ – Vol XXVII, January 1948	
	Organists' Review – November 1999	
Ouseley, F A G	*On the position of Organs in Churches*	(Paper to The Musical Association) February 1886
	The Parish Choir – Vol III	
	Diary of Warden Singleton – Radley College 1848	
	The Royal College of Organists Calendar 1889	
Stainer, J	*The Character and Influence of Sir Frederick A.G. Ouseley*	(Paper to the Musical Association) – 1889
	The Tenbury Advertiser 1936	
	This England Magazine Winter 1984	
	Three Choirs Festival Brochure – Hereford 1970	
	Three Choirs Festival Brochure – Hereford 1979	
	Three Choirs Festival Brochure – Hereford 1982	
	The Three Pears Magazine, Worcester 1931	
	The Times, November 5th 1874	
	The Organs and Organists of Wells Cathedral	Wells Cathedral Publications 1998

MANUSCRIPT AND OTHER SOURCES

HCL D 863

This is the reference number for the Ouseley / St Michael's Archive which is held in the Hereford Cathedral Library. The material includes both manuscript and printed sources and an almost complete collection of the College Magazine (1918 – 1985). A catalogue is available from the Library.

Canon Alderson's Journal 1958 (in possession of Prebendary Derrik Jenkyns)

Colonel John Blashford-Snell Personal reminiscences given to author

Department of Western Manuscripts, the Bodleian Library, Oxford

Ref. B250 *The Diary of Sir Gore Ouseley*

BUISSC – Birmingham University Information Services – Special Collections
Ref. Ladd 5188, Ladd 5206 – 5214

Maria Hackett Letters in the Royal College of Music Library

MFCMCMLNY – The Mary Flagler Cary Music Collection,
the Morgan Library, New York

The National Society for Religious Education Archive, London

Copy of Ouseley letter to Harrison's (Organ Builders) – September 7th 1868
(in private collection)

The Reverend Harry Rooke – Personal reminiscences sent to author

The Royal Archives, Windsor Castle

St Helens's Records Office, Worcester

INDEX